FAMILIES BEFORE AND AFTER
PERESTROIKA

PERSPECTIVES ON MARRIAGE AND THE FAMILY
Bert N. Adams and David M. Klein, *Editors*

COMMUTER MARRIAGE: A STUDY OF WORK AND FAMILY
Naomi Gerstel and Harriet Gross

HELPING THE ELDERLY: THE COMPLEMENTARY ROLES
OF INFORMAL NETWORKS AND FORMAL SYSTEMS
Eugene Litwak

REMARRIAGE AND STEPPARENTING:
CURRENT RESEARCH AND THEORY
Kay Palsey and Marilyn Ihinger-Tallman (Eds.)

FEMINISM, CHILDREN, AND THE NEW FAMILIES
Sanford M. Dornbusch and Myta F. Strober (Eds.)

DYNAMICS OF FAMILY DEVELOPMENT:
A THEORETICAL PERSPECTIVE
James M. White

PORTRAIT OF DIVORCE:
ADJUSTMENT TO MARITAL BREAKDOWN
Gay C. Kitson with William M. Holmes

WOMEN AND FAMILIES: FEMINIST RECONSTRUCTIONS
Kristine M. Baber and Katherine R. Allen

CHILDREN'S STRESS AND COPING:
A FAMILY PERSPECTIVE
Elaine Shaw Sorensen

WHEN LOVE DIES: THE PROCESS OF
MARITAL DISAFFECTION
Karen Kayser

FAMILIES BEFORE AND AFTER *PERESTROIKA*:
RUSSIAN AND U.S. PERSPECTIVES
*James W. Maddock, M. Janice Hogan
Anatolyi I. Antonov, and Mikhail S. Matskovsky (Eds.)*

FAMILIES BEFORE AND AFTER
PERESTROIKA
RUSSIAN AND U.S. PERSPECTIVES

EDITED BY
James W. Maddock
M. Janice Hogan
Anatolyi I. Antonov
Mikhail S. Matskovsky

THE GUILFORD PRESS
New York   London

© 1994 The Guilford Press
A Division of Guilford Publications, Inc.
72 Spring Street, New York, NY 10012

Printed in the United States of America

This book is printed on acid-free paper.

Last digit is print number: 9 8 7 6 5 4 3 2 1

Library of Congress Cataloging-in-Publication Data

Families before and after perestroika : Russian and U.S. perspectives
 / edited by James W. Maddock . . . [et al.].
      p.   cm. — (Perspectives on marriage and the family)
    Includes bibliographical references and index.
    ISBN 0-89862-085-6
    1. Family—Soviet Union. 2. Family—United States. 3. Family—
Former Soviet republics. I. Maddock, James W. II. Series.
HQ637.F34   1993   93-23409
                                                              CIP

Dedicated to the memory of
Reuben Hill, Ph.D., and Anatolyi Kharchev, Ph.D.

Contributors

Anatolyi I. Antonov, Ph.D., is a professor and Chair of the Board on Family Sociology in the Sociology Department at Moscow State University. He is interested in the problems of contemporary urban families, and particularly in the impact of social change on demographic trends and fertility-related behavior.

Pauline G. Boss, Ph.D., is a professor in the Department of Family Social Science at the University of Minnesota. Her research interests are in stress and coping in families, with particular emphasis on boundary ambiguity as a factor creating stress.

Vladimir A. Borisov, Ph.D., is an associate professor of the Board on Family Sociology in the Sociology Department at Moscow State University. He is interested in the impact of demographic factors on social policy.

Sharon M. Danes, Ph.D., is an associate professor and extension specialist in the Department of Family Social Science at the University of Minnesota. She conducts research on farm families, with a particular focus on the role of women in the interface of work and family.

Daniel F. Detzner, Ph.D., is an associate professor in the Department of Family Social Science at the University of Minnesota. His research interests focus on aging families, with particular emphasis on cross-cultural comparison of family development.

William J. Doherty, Ph.D., is a professor in the Department of Family Social Science at the University of Minnesota. His research interests include the emotional consequences of divorce and the study of families with chronic illness and health behavior problems.

Olga N. Doudchenko, Ph.D., is a researcher at the Institute of Sociology of the Russian Academy of Sciences. She is interested in the study of socioeconomic influences on contemporary urban families and on the relationship between women's work and childbearing patterns.

Ekaterina V. Foteeva, Ph.D., is a researcher in the Center for Family Studies at the Institute of Sociology, Russian Academy of Sciences. She is interested in the impact of demographic and socioeconomic influences on family relationships.

Tatyana A. Gurko, Ph.D., is a researcher in the Center for Family Studies at the Institute of Sociology, Russian Academy of Sciences. She is interested in marital relationships and in factors related to childbearing.

Susan Hartman, M.A., is executive director of CONNECT US–RUSSIA in Minneapolis, Minnesota, with a particular interest in cross-cultural perspectives on family life. She also has a part-time private practice in individual, marriage, and family therapy.

M. Janice Hogan, Ph.D., is a professor in the Department of Family Social Science at the University of Minnesota. Her research interests focus on decision making and financial management in families, with particular emphasis on gender role relationships.

Marlene Johnson, J.D., is the former lieutenant governor of Minnesota. Currently, she is a senior fellow on universal family policy at the Center for Policy Alternatives in Washington, D.C. Her interests are in child advocacy and public policy support of families.

Igor S. Kon, Ph.D., is a professor and research fellow at the Institute of Ethnography, Russian Academy of Sciences. His research interests include child and adolescent development, human sexuality, and friendship patterns of children and youths.

James W. Maddock, Ph.D., is an associate professor in the Department of Family Social Science at the University of Minnesota. His interests are in the impact of gender and sexuality on interpersonal relationships in the family, with particular emphasis on characteristics of healthy family sexuality.

Mikhail S. Matskovsky, Ph.D., is professor and head of the Center for Family Studies at the Institute of Sociology, Russian Academy of Sciences. He is also director general of the International Center for Human Values in Moscow. He is interested in theory and methods of family research.

David H. Olson, Ph.D., is a professor in the Department of Family Social Science at the University of Minnesota. He is interested in conceptual and methodological issues in family research and in the application of theory and research to practical problems of family life.

Alexander B. Sinelnikov, Ph.D., is a researcher in the Center for Family Studies at the Institute of Sociology, Russian Academy of Sciences. He has a particular interest in gerontology from the standpoint of the family and broader social policy.

Ludmilla V. Yasnaya, M.A., is a researcher in the Center for Family Studies at the Institute of Sociology, Russian Academy of Sciences, and is also on the staff of the International Center for Human Values in Moscow. Her research interests focus on family problems of working women.

Galina A. Zaikina, Ph.D., is a researcher in the Center for Family Studies at the Institute of Sociology, Russian Academy of Sciences. Her research interests focus upon marriage and family relationships.

Shirley L. Zimmerman, Ph.D., is a professor in the Department of Family Social Science at the University of Minnesota. Her research interests are in family policy, with a special focus on the impact of governmental actions on individual and family well-being.

Acknowledgments

Many individuals and organizations have made important contributions to this book. Our first thanks go to Susan Hartman, director of CON-NECT US–RUSSIA, the inspiration and guiding light for this project. Susan and Paula DeCosse, the original codirectors of CONNECT US–USSR, and their administrative assistant, Deborah McHugh, spent countless hours planning visits, meeting with authors, transporting proposals and manuscripts between Moscow and the Twin Cities, arranging for visas and translators, and soliciting financial support for the project. We are very grateful for their vision, wisdom, and efforts, and for the support of the CONNECT board of directors.

The University of Minnesota believed in this project, and many individuals and units provided demonstrable support. We thank our colleagues in the Department of Family Social Science for backing the idea of cross-cultural education and research. Our thanks also to Harold Grotevant, head of the department, and to Kathy Witherow and the administrative staff. Vicky Weise and Micque Brickson, members of the civil service staff in the College of Human Ecology, made important contributions. Many undergraduate and graduate students at the university, as well as translators, helped make a success of the Soviet delegation's visit to Minnesota. Special appreciation goes to Family Social Science graduate students Beth-Ellen Maddock, Michelle Johnson, and Georgui Kroupine, who provided bibliographic assistance in the final stages of writing.

Mary Heltsley, dean of the College of Human Ecology, encouraged university support and participated in a number of seminars and social functions related to the project. Former Acting President Richard Sauer, Vice-President C. Eugene Allen, and Michael Page from the Office of International Education aided us in hosting the Soviet delegation. More recently, President Nils Hasselmo and the university's central administration, as well as the Alumni Association, have recognized the project and have tangibly encouraged continuing collaboration between the university and countries of the former USSR.

We are grateful for the financial support for this project provided by the Department of Family Social Science, the College of Human

Ecology, the Office of International Education, and the Agricultural Experiment Station at the University of Minnesota. Other generous contributions were made by the Rockefeller Foundation (New York City), the Charles Stewart Mott Foundation (Flint, Michigan), the Soras Foundation (New York City), and the Amherst H. Wilder Foundation (St. Paul, Minnesota).

Thanks to Mary Jo Czaplewski and the staff of the National Council on Family Relations for their endorsement and help in hosting the Soviet delegation's visit to the United States. We also appreciate the ongoing interest and encouragement of Marian Hill, who with her late husband, Reuben Hill, long ago recognized the importance of cross-cultural family research.

Particular thanks to Sharon Panulla, our editor at Guilford Press, whose interest, support, and patience were deeply appreciated during the long and challenging months needed to complete the manuscript. Professors David Klein of the University of Notre Dame and Bert Adams of the University of Wisconsin–Madison served as editorial consultants, providing us with valuable feedback and encouragement.

Our most enduring gratitude is to our colleagues at the former Soviet Academy of Sciences, who agreed to come to the United States to begin a dialogue about families. We have wonderful memories of stimulating conversations and of warm hospitality shown us during our visit to Russia. We are privileged to know these scholars and their families. And to our own families, we add a special thanks for your interest and involvement in this project.

James W. Maddock
M. Janice Hogan

Preface

This book is the result of lengthy dialogue between a group of faculty members in the Department of Family Social Science at the University of Minnesota and a number of Russian family scholars who were, when the project began, members of the Institute of Sociology in the Soviet Academy of Sciences. Also contributing on the United States side were Susan Hartman, who initiated the project as executive director of CONNECT US–USSR, and then Lieutenant Governor Marlene Johnson of Minnesota, who joined the project to support our university's efforts to explore problems of families cross-culturally. Meeting in both the United States and Russia, Soviet and American authors worked in teams to write the chapters that follow—a form of collaboration that was both stimulating and exhausting. We hope, however, that this approach will prove more useful to readers than simply having individuals from each society contribute chapters to a book edited by a third party. Through our meetings and correspondence, we reached a deeper understanding of the impact of social structure on family life in two very different cultural milieus. Furthermore, we came to recognize and appreciate the impact of these cultural differences on our thinking and working as social scientists. In many ways, our collaborative efforts to write these chapters resembled anthropological investigations by cross-cultural visitors or journalistic narratives by writers covering "stories" in distant places. An overview of the project's background and history is provided in Susan Hartman's introduction to the book.

When the project began, we had hoped to conduct a thorough analysis of the methodological similarities and differences in family science in our two societies. That goal proved to be elusive. No central source of information on scientific methodology existed in the former Soviet Union, where the differences in perspective and approach among family scholars were even greater than in the United States. Finally, despite the presence of highly motivated and brilliant thinkers in Soviet social science, the absence of technological tools and support systems has seriously curtailed research efforts. Therefore, readers will have to infer some of the methodologies reflected in the various kinds of data reported here.

The bicultural teams of authors have written in their various areas of expertise. The selection of topics for this book evolved from our first week together, when we identified the dominant family issues in both of our countries. Each chapter of this book explores a topic that we consider to be significant for understanding some of the unique aspects of family life characterizing Soviet socialist society through much of the twentieth century. Furthermore, each represents an important issue confronting post-Soviet families and the society that will emerge from the turmoil of the current period. In addition to a comparative overview of families (Chapter 1), the teams of authors have explored gender roles in marriage relationships (Chapter 2); divorce and remarriage (Chapter 3); sexual issues related to family life (Chapter 4); intergenerational relationships at two critical periods–adults with adolescents leaving home, and adults with aging parents (Chapter 5); the lives of women at the interface of work and family (Chapter 6); and issues of family policy, illustrated by the problem of day care for children (Chapter 7). We conclude with an overview and brief analysis of the themes that emerge from a comparative examination of Soviet and American family life, along with a few thoughts about the future of families in our societies.

Some topics are not covered thoroughly simply as a matter of priority. For example, we have intentionally omitted a chapter on "childhood" (care of infants, socialization patterns, discipline, school-related issues, and the like), because other past and recent writings have dealt with this topic rather extensively. The same is true for such topics as the transition to parenthood, the adolescent subculture, and certain family rituals and customs. Some other exclusions reflect family-related topics that have not yet been adequately addressed in the context of the contemporary post-Soviet situation, for example, family violence and alcoholism. Finally, some omissions represent the biases of individual authors, a lack of meaningful data on a particular topic, and the practical limitations of book space and time schedules.

Most of the original Russian sources cited have not been translated into English. However, we have translated some of the references into English to help the readers understand the contents of these sources.

We began our work on this project when the USSR still existed as a geopolitical state. Unless otherwise specified, our use of the adjective "American" in this book refers to the United States, while "Soviet" refers to the present-day Russian Republic and any other republics that were part of the former USSR, some of which are still politically associated with Russia. These terms are used for convenience.

The Editors

Contents

Introduction

Susan Hartman

When the United States/Soviet Family Project began in 1985, no one could have imagined the overwhelming changes that would occur by the time this book—one of the tangible outcomes of the project—would be published. The collaboration is a remarkable story in itself. The fact that both Soviet and American societies have placed increasing emphasis on the issues of the family may well have saved this project, even as the political framework for our cooperation seemed to be dissolving.

The Family Project (as it was ambiguously titled) began in 1985 as a major program of CONNECT US-USSR, a small, newly formed, nonprofit organization, staffed entirely by volunteers. The goal of this organization, cofounded by Paula DeCosse and me, was to develop constructive relationships between *people* in the United States and the Soviet Union. The CONNECT philosophy was grounded, in part, in my work with family violence as a therapist and as a family life educator. I had discovered that teaching men to stop acting abusively and women to protect themselves was not enough to create permanently nonviolent relationships; in addition, "replacement behaviors" were needed. When couples were taught ways to relate respectfully and communicate clearly, violence was much more likely to stop permanently. CONNECT took these lessons from a micro level (family) to a macro level (international), attempting to facilitate constructive and respectful relationships between the United States and the Soviet Union as replacement behaviors for the negative, adversarial stances that were so prevalent in the Cold War years.

Our philosophy evolved in the months following the shooting down of the Korean Air Lines passenger jet in Soviet air space—an event that was considered a major setback in Soviet-American relations. We were already aware that the level of political distrust in both countries, along with stultifying governmental bureaucracies, made meaningful programmatic cooperation nearly impossible. One topic seemed to offer some hope for constructive interaction, since it could be considered important to the welfare of each society and politically safe for cooperative efforts: *the family*.

With this idea, I contacted Professor Reuben Hill, a world-renowned family sociologist at the University of Minnesota and my own former teacher and mentor. Dr. Hill had maintained communication with top Soviet sociologists throughout several decades, even during the bleakest political times. He generously shared his contacts with me, knowing full well that good contacts are critical to any successful endeavor, particularly in the Soviet region of the world. Two of his famous Soviet counterparts, Dr. Anatolyi Kharchev (a family special-ist) and Dr. Igor S. Kon (a specialist in child development and sexol-ogy), were willing to meet with me. That they were permitted to talk with me during these pre-*perestroika* years was testimony, I believe, both to the perception that CONNECT was a nonthreatening entity and to the recognition that joint work on family issues was critical to the improvement of Soviet society. In recently reminiscing about our first meeting, Dr. Kon recalled being told by government officials that I was a "nice woman who might be potentially helpful."

Responsibility on the Soviet side for getting this collaborative project approved and moving forward resting with Dr. Kharchev, then the head of the Family Department of the Institute of Sociology, in the Soviet Academy of Sciences.[1] Were it not for his vision, commit-ment, and courage, the project could never have transpired. Before his untimely death in 1987, followed shortly by Reuben Hill's, he had gathered the critical permissions and prodded the mammoth bureau-cracies enough so that the collaboration had its place in the plans of the institute. Those of us who worked over the years to develop rela-tionships and programs with the former Soviet Union have often com-mented on the importance of personal relationships. The primacy of the personal relationship between Kharchev and Hill clearly played a major part in allowing CONNECT to be trusted as a facilitator of co-operative work by the Soviet and American scholars who have written this book.

My experience with joint Soviet–American projects has taught me that people on both sides either "get it" or "don't get it" when pre-sented with a proposal for collaboration. An immediate, gut-level, affirmative response is critical to a program such as the Family Project because of all the obstacles to be overcome. This response seems to signify that an elemental chord has been struck, that one's values can support the concept. A belief in its fundamental importance can carry a collaborative effort through many crises.

My alma mater, the Family Social Science Department at the University of Minnesota, clearly "got it." The commitment of Dr. M. Janice Hogan, then head of the department, was immediate and, I believe, visionary. She recruited another faculty member, Dr. James W. Maddock, and we began a laborious process of planning and organizing. Their skills in maintaining a long-range, world-view perspective even while struggling for time, money, and other resources helped keep the project on course as we walked the tightrope with our Soviet counterparts during precarious years of change.

Other organizational support also proved critical. The College of Human Ecology at the University of Minnesota backed its family department with both encouragement and financial support. Likewise, the Charles Stewart Mott Foundation acknowledged the project's potential to shed new light on the family and to develop new bridges between the Soviet Union and the United States. They risked funding a young, idealistic organization and supporting a family symposium in each country when there were as yet no clear outcomes and no guarantees of meaningful results. The National Council on Family Relations, based in Minnesota, added depth and breadth to the American symposium by hosting the Soviets at their annual conference in 1988. For the first time in decades, top Soviet scholars reached a broad professional audience of North Americans with information about family life in their culture, and in turn were given an opportunity to participate in open discussions on a wide range of family issues.

The negotiations between CONNECT and the Institute of Sociology were carried on during the earliest years of Gorbachev's *glasnost*, from 1985 to 1987. Old governmental structures and suspicions remained in the Soviet Union. Decisions were made by persons not directly involved in the project, part of a hierarchy mostly hidden from me. Progress in developing the collaboration was painfully slow, especially after Kharchev's death broke our primary connection with the Soviet Academy of Sciences. Nevertheless, the fact that the Institute of Sociology directly informed me of Kharchev's unexpected demise was a clue to their commitment to the project. At each negotiating session in Moscow I met with a larger circle of people; yet I knew none of them as individuals.

Finally, the detailed symposium agenda and travel itinerary we had worked on for months was accepted by the Soviets, and our first meeting was scheduled for November 1988, to coincide with the annual conference of the National Council on Family Relations in Philadelphia. The background for our first face-to-face meeting was an improving climate of trust between our countries and a symbolic setting of a city recognized as one of the "cradles" of American democracy. The seven Soviet family scholars were euphoric about being in the United States, a first visit for all but one. Various combinations of them gave presentations at the conference, anxious to share as much information as they could about the status of families in their country. Formal and informal dialogues took place, cramped by the restrictions of language. Fortunately, several of the Soviets spoke competent English, and they were willing to be burdened with the tasks of translating individual conversations and formal papers. At the end of the five-day conference, which included a day-long sightseeing trip to Washington, D.C., we escorted our visitors back to Minneapolis/St. Paul for more detailed discussions and the opportunity to build relationships on a one-to-one basis.

Another week of meetings at a local retreat center followed, with small subgroups of Soviet and American researchers together examining various family-related topics. Despite obvious differences in personality and background, the Soviet delegations seemed to form a solid front with regard to family issues. Information was plentiful; candid opinions were scarce—or perhaps we had not yet learned to distinguish between these. The two cultural groups were generally polite and accommodating, with little challenge of viewpoints either within or between delegations. The symposium concluded with two things resolved. One was an agreement to hold another meeting in the Soviet Union; the second was a decision to produce something concrete as a result of our discussions—a book about Soviet and American families.

The symposium ended on the day before Thanksgiving, and the Soviet visitors were invited into our homes to celebrate with our families one of the most American of holidays. Here, we came to know our guests more personally as individuals, and our insights into the lives and ideas of Soviet citizens were greatly enriched. They, in turn, were able to experience American family life in concrete rather than abstract terms. Not surprisingly, our interaction with the Soviets began to take on qualities of friendship, and bidding them farewell at the end of the weekend was a more emotional event than we might have anticipated.

Following another period of planning and organizing—this time primarily by the Soviet family scientists collaborating closely with CONNECT—a second symposium was scheduled for Moscow in September 1989. By the time we arrived, an increasing sense of individual freedom had taken hold in the Soviet Union. Yet the stifling bureaucracies and rules remained. Quickly, we came to recognize what an incredibly complex and demanding task it was for our Soviet hosts to arrange meetings and tours for American academicians and professionals. Not the least of the problems was the financial burden, heavy even prior to the collapse of the USSR. Political concerns were also apparent. For example, a trip by overnight train to the industrial city of Vologda occasioned considerable difficulties for our Soviet colleagues and local hosts. Until some costumed Russian woman boarded the arriving train to present us with traditional friendship gifts of bread and salt, our Soviet colleagues hadn't known for certain whether we would be permitted to stay in this city, previously closed to Western visitors. Though the processes by which our Soviet hosts accomplished a magnificent ten-day symposium and tour remained mysterious to us, we knew that each bus, meal, guide, and hotel accommodation took enormous energy and personal sacrifice to arrange.

Our reaction was not only gratitude, but also a sense of supportive kinship with our Soviet partners. We now better understood what it was like to function on a day-to-day basis in such a rigidly structured society, and we admired even more our colleagues' ability to carry on meaningful academic and professional endeavors. Our first working meetings were held in one of the classroom/office buildings of Moscow State University. Now that we had a concrete goal of writing a book together, discussions were more probing, communication more open, and ideas more personally expressed. Opinions grew to be freely exchanged, and some heated debates occurred. Late one evening in our hotel in Vologda, the entire group assembled and began to talk; there was no structure, no agenda, and no clearly stated goal. What emerged was a freewheeling discussion, in which we revealed our personal differences and diverse philosophies. Some of the greatest disagreements were within rather than between delegations. For example, the Americans argued about how issues of sexism should be addressed in the context of our book project. At the same time, the Soviets revealed radical, nonnegotiable splits in their beliefs about social policies affecting families. This process both raised and lowered tensions. Conflicts were difficult to deal with; however, the richness of diversity was now revealed and could inform our work more directly. In addition, letting conflict into our relationships without abandoning one another seemed to increase our sense of intimacy, even across cultural lines.

Thus, by the end of the second symposium, we had evolved into a single binational group, with its own roles, alliances, rituals, and even "insider humor." Although some substantial cultural differences remained, there was now a sense of loyalty and commitment to each other and to our joint endeavor. And our celebrations were memorable.

Following the two symposia, work on this book and several joint research projects proceeded at an excruciatingly slow pace. Of course, our efforts were disrupted by geopolitical events in what was the Soviet Union. The exchange of ideas and materials was delayed at the mechanical level—lost mail, shortages of FAX paper, canceled visits, employment changes, long waits for news of visitors to either country who might be recruited to carry chapter drafts. Some of these problems could be traced to bureaucratic snarls; most, however, stemmed directly from lack of money. Despite some generous financial support, more was needed. Nevertheless, the editors were able to exchange brief visits for consultation, and Dr. Kon provided additional assistance to the editors during an extended trip to the United States. On trips to Moscow several times each year, I carried manuscripts by hand and met with the authors of various chapters. Mostly, the project required patience and dogged persistence.

The factors connected with the political and economic situation in the former Soviet Union had two substantive effects on the cooperative book project. The first was to alter the plan from simultaneously publishing a single book in Russian and English editions to producing two closely related books—one, a book in English about Soviet families with some comparative American data; the other, a book in Russian about American families with some comparative Soviet data. The second major effect was to force the authors and editors to arbitrarily choose a time period at which to "freeze" their analyses of the Soviet cultural situation, in light of the extent and pace of social change. Therefore, the title of this book and the contents of the following chapters reflect a focus on the cumulative effects of the period of Soviet family life dominated by the centralized government of the Communist party and its accelerating erosion during the late 1980s.

Despite the obstacles to continuing direct contact, the American authors of these chapters have attempted to remain true to the information and sense of perspective supplied by their Soviet counterparts. Many of the research populations were difficult to compare, and research methodologies differed substantially across the two societies. Questions that seemed important to American researchers were sometimes left unanswered in Soviet projects. Solid conclusions were often hard to draw without returning to original data that were now unavailable. And, of course, there were the problems of translation. Subtleties of meaning and interpretations are difficult to convey when working across languages and cultures. Both Soviet and American authors labored diligently to overcome these handicaps. At times in these pages, individual scholars speak for themselves with controversial opinions. All in all, I believe that readers will find in this book a faithful rendering of the fabric of at least some aspects of Soviet family life. Naturally, all of us connected with this project wish that time, energy, and money could have permitted the investigation of even more family phenomena. Most notably missing are materials on general childrearing practices, on certain aspects of married life, and on family rituals and spiritual practices. In addition, as all of the authors are quick to point out, data on the diversity of Soviet ethnic groups and family forms are largely absent—a problem familiar to American family scholars and readers as well. All in all, however, this book contains a wealth of information and some proactive insights into Soviet family life.

A common response when Soviet and American groups first meet is amazement at our similarities. The emphasis on how we are alike often fuels a euphoria that serves to sweep aside old perceptions and to provide strong motivation for collaboration. The notion that we are alike draws us initially to each other; however, recognizing and accepting our cultural differences can be extraordinarily beneficial as well. This level of awareness is rarely reached by American visitors to the Soviet region. The struggle of the American authors of these chapters to understand these differences and their implications is enormously important to this book's ability to meaningfully compare Soviet and American family experiences.

One cultural difference we discovered, has many ramifications. While Americans emphasize the importance of individuality, personal rights, and privacy, Soviets have been steeped in the belief that society is primary, and they do not even have an exact word for "privacy." Paradoxically, however, Soviet citizens appear to make their greatest investments of time and energy in a small circle of relatives, very close friends, and work associates. Although most live in enormous housing complexes, they take greatest pride in the beautiful interiors of their own apartments and do little to maintain communal space. And although they work in large bureaucracies, they have few skills in group interaction and problem solving. For example, while the Soviet family scholars demonstrated some allegiance to the Institute of Sociology, they were far more eager to initiate independent research projects with their American counterparts than to conduct large-group collaborations. During the years of this project, tensions between the public and private, the group and the individual, were high for our Soviet colleagues, mirroring the political struggles of their society.

Despite the widely touted public benefits of life under a centralized socialist regime, the Soviets have had to acknowledge the failure of their society to make good on its promises of equal rights for women, high-quality day care and education for children, adequate health care for all citizens, and economic security for the elderly. In short, the research reported here reveals that, even at its best, the Soviet socialist system did not live up to its potential to support family life. The harsh reality is that families in both post-Soviet and American societies face serious problems and difficult challenges. Perhaps by joining together in studying families and discussing family issues, former "enemies" can become more effective in improving the quality of family life in both societies. Just as our eight-year collaboration on this project built bridges between individuals as scholars and as friends, my hope is that this book will contribute to ongoing connections between our societies in the struggle to survive as a universal human family.

NOTE

1. Prior to 1989, the Institute was known as the Institute for Sociological Research at the USSR Academy of Sciences. The name was changed to the Institute of Sociology and, since 1991, the Institute has been part of the Russian Academy of Sciences. To avoid confusion, we have referred to the Institute of Sociology throughout this book.

Chapter 1

Soviet and American Families: A Comparative Overview

David H. Olson
Mikhail S. Matskovsky

> What will destroy us, both as families and as a
> society, is not change, but the inability to change.
> –Herbert Otto[1]

Change characterizes family life in both Soviet and American societies. Whereas the nature of social change in the United States might best be described as evolutionary, social changes in the former USSR have been truly revolutionary. These changes have significant impact on the psychological, social, and economic life of families.

Families are especially important in times of cultural crisis, serving as one important buffer between the individual and the forces of social change. Perhaps the most ancient of all social institutions, the family unit has survived in some form across all known cultures and historical periods. It has also proven to be a very adaptable and functional social system.

The purpose of this chapter is to provide a comparative overview of family life in two societies that appear to be significantly different. The twentieth-century histories of the United States and the former Soviet Union have been intertwined, because of their historical conflicts as world "superpowers." These two societies clearly have unique histories, differing political systems, and somewhat opposing ideologies. However, in spite of these differences Soviet and American families are similar in certain important ways.

In this chapter, we will focus primarily on general patterns of similarity, considering such basic issues as the composition of families, gender roles, patterns of sexual behavior, the dynamics of marriage, the launching of adolescents, and patterns of divorce and remarriage. The chapters that follow explore these issues and others in more detail, comparing a number of specific characteristics of families in the two societies.

THE FAMILY ENVIRONMENT

The size and complexity of the United States and the former Soviet Union make comparative generalizations very difficult. The United States is a large country; the area occupied by the former USSR was even larger than all of North America. The country covered eleven time zones, compared to only four for the mainland of the United States. The former USSR extended 2,500 miles from north to south and approximately 5,600 miles from east to west. Russia alone occupies 6.6 million square miles—more than 75% of the Soviet territory.

Although Soviets were often referred to in the West as "Russians," nearly 50% of the population of the former USSR was non-Russian. There were over eighty different cultural groups in the former USSR, each with its own language. Out of approximately 287 million Soviet citizens, 147 million were Russians, 43 million were Ukrainians, and 55 million were Turks. The remainder were divided among scores of smaller ethnic groups, some separated by the geographic and political boundaries of the republics, but many—particularly Russians—spread throughout the country.

Under the Soviet regime, ethnic Russians sometimes enjoyed certain advantages over other ethnic groups, particularly if they lived in urban centers, where health care, housing, income, and cultural arts were generally better than in other areas. The Russian language predominated as the official state language. Citizens of other nationalities were expected to learn Russian, however, relatively few Russians learned the native languages of other Soviet regions.

In each of the fifteen former USSR republics, there were indigenous populations that maintained a strong identification with their ethnic and national backgrounds. Following *perestroika*, these "hidden nations" began to reassert themselves.[2] Their nationalism, along with the chaos of radical economic reform, brought about the breakup of the USSR.

Great differences in urban and rural living conditions also characterized the Soviet Union. Despite official Communist Party doctrine and the efforts of centralized planning, huge inequities existed in services such as education and health care. Urban areas were generally better off than rural areas and had better organized Party bureaucracies. Collective farming worked poorly, though some rural villages became self-supporting. During the period of *perestroika* in the middle to late 1980s, urban conditions deteriorated. The collapse of the Soviet Union and the move toward a free-market economy have created severe shortages of nearly all goods and services in major metropolitan areas. Rural areas now have the advantage of direct access to food supplies, although shortages of heating oil and auto fuel are an ever-present threat.

The United States is also a notably heterogeneous country, with a heritage rooted in ethnic diversity. Unlike the Soviet Union, however, it was settled largely by voluntary immigration rather than by conquest—with the notable exception of its native and African slave populations. Although the predominant ethnic groups today are Caucasian Europeans, the proportions of African-Americans, Hispanic-Americans, and Asian-Americans are rapidly increasing. For example, predictions are that California will become a state with no single ethnic or racial majority by the year 2020.[3] More specifically, it is predicted that California's population in 2020 will be 41% white, 38% Hispanic, 14% Asian, and 8% black. The white majority will increasingly become the white minority.

Like Russians in the former Soviet Union, European-Americans have been a dominant group in American society. That dominance is now being challenged, for reasons that are both similar to and different from the factors that are currently restructuring Soviet society. On the one hand, both societies must struggle to accommodate genuine cultural diversity amidst rising feelings of national identity and ethnic pride. On the other hand, the United States has a history of greater openness and peaceful assimilation of ethnic subgroups than the former USSR—with the notable exception of Native Americans and African-Americans.

Although both countries are suffering from economic hardships, the problems in the United States seem minor, compared with the almost total collapse of the Soviet society. The former USSR truly has vast challenges facing it as it moves from a socialistic monolith to a group of more democratic societies, both politically and economically.

Some of the most striking similarities in American and Soviet societies today are the issues facing families. Among the most prominent are gender role changes, conflictual sexual mores, intergenerational conflicts, divorce, and care of dependent family members. In spite of dramatic differences in cultural ideology in the two societies, families have encountered remarkably similar types of problems. Both societies are large, complex, diverse, and industrialized. Both have been "superpowers" for the past fifty years, albeit at opposite ends of the political and economic spectrum. Perhaps being bound together as the major "enemies" in the Cold War world order over the past fifty years has created commonalities of culture that are recognizable only now that fundamental geopolitical and economic reorganizations are occurring throughout the world.

FAMILY VALUES

The Locus of Moral Responsibility

In the former USSR, the *perestroika* years brought an increasing emphasis on the moral development of family members. During the preceding decades of unchallenged Communist government, the state attempted to be the ultimate authority on right and wrong. However, over time Soviet families have once again come to have the dominant responsibility for teaching values.

This shift toward Western democratic values represents a significant adjustment for Soviet citizens. At the same time, this democratization of ethics in Soviet society highlights conflicts within the culture, particularly between individualism and allegiance to religious institutions, notably Islam and the Eastern Orthodox faiths. These manifestations of religious diversity put pressure on families in relation to personal decision making and the religious upbringing of children in much the same way that family members in the United States are confronted with moral dilemmas on issues such as abortion and birth control, the role of women in the home and at work, and the religious education of children.

Attitudes toward Marriage and Family Life

In 1986, a representative study of values among all nationalities in the USSR (Russians, Ukrainians, Moldavians, Jews, Uzbeks, and others) found that "family" was rated the most important value, followed by "work" and "respect from others."[4] For example, Uzbeks ranked "family" first (72%), followed by "respect from others" (59%), "a peaceful life" (54%), "financial well-being" (49%), "interesting work" (45%), and "creative activity" (29%) (see Table 1.1).

A 1989 survey by M. S. Matskovsky and colleagues on "The Family as a Mirror of Public Opinion" was conducted with over 3,000 citizens ages sixteen to sixty living in fifty-one cities of Estonia, Latvia, Lithuania, Byelorussia (now Belarus), Ukraine, Moldavia (now Moldova), Georgia, Armenia, Kazakhstan, and Uzbekistan.[5] The study focused on

TABLE 1.1. Values and Preference in the USSR

Rank	Russians	Percentage	Uzbeks	Percentage
1	Family	85	Family	72
2	Interesting work	78	Respect of people	59
3	Financial well-being	74	A peaceful life	54
4	Respect of people	70	Financial well-being	49
5	A peaceful life	25	Interesting work	45
6	Creative activity	21	Creative activity	29

attitudes toward the single life versus marriage and family life. Results confirmed that the family is one of the most important values of Soviet citizens. Approximately 90% of the respondents positively valued marriage and childrearing. "Creating a good family" was valued by 86%, followed by "remaining in good health" (83%), "living in harmony with others" (75%), "having good friends" (73%), and "having interesting work" (66%). While "achieving economic well-being and comfort" ranked only seventh in this survey, the severe economic disruptions of the past several years may well have increased its relative value since then (see Table 1.2).

A similar study in the United States was reported in 1990.[6] Individuals were asked to rank the most important values in their lives, and "the family" consistently had the highest ratings. Reported values associated with family life included the following: "providing emotional support to family," "respecting one's parents," "having a happy marriage," "respecting one's children," and "communicating feelings to family members" (see Table 1.3).

TABLE 1.2. Family and Life Value Systems in the USSR

Value orientation	Percentage
Bring up children; secure their future	90
Create a good family	86
Remain in good health	83
Live in harmony with conscience	75
Have good friends	73
Have interesting work	66
Achieve economic well-being and comfort	50
Achieve spiritual perfection	37
Travel; see many new and interesting things	32
Achieve success in profession or job	31

TABLE 1.3. Family Values in the United States

Value orientation	Rank[1]
Being responsible for actions	4.35
Provide emotional support to family	4.32
Respecting one's parents	4.32
Respecting other people	4.30
Having a happy marriage	4.30
Respecting one's children	4.27
Being able to communicate feelings to family	4.23

[1]5 = very important; 4 = somewhat important.
Source: Adapted from M. Mellman, E. Lazarus, and A. Rivlin, "Family Time, Family Values," in D. Blankenhorn, S. Baymer, and J. B. Elshtain (eds.), *Rebuilding the Nest* (Milwaukee, WI: Family Service of America, 1990), 83.

In the Matskovsky et al. survey, the vast majority of Soviet respondents answered "yes" to this question: "Do you agree with the belief that every individual should sooner or later get married and have a family?" The older the respondents, the greater the agreement with the choice of "family" as the most appropriate life style. Negative answers to the question were given by approximately 23% of the respondents below age twenty, 15% of those in their twenties (ages twenty to twenty-nine), 13% of those in their thirties, and 9% of those in their forties.[7]

Reported reasons for marriage varied (see Table 1.4). Having children (56%) and closeness with the marital partner (45%) were reported to be the two most important values of family life. Getting married

TABLE 1.4. Reasons for Getting Married and Having a Family in the USSR

Value orientation	Percentage
Have children; continue one's family	56
Be with a person who can understand and be supportive in any circumstance	45
Feel that somebody needs you; have an opportunity to take care of someone	37
Having family and children is a moral duty of an individual	27
Not to be lonely	26
Have a cozy home, comfortable everyday life	24
Not to part with your beloved	19
Have a permanent sexual partner	7
It is traditional to get married	2
Difficulty to answer	2

was much less strongly related to the need for a permanent sexual partner (7%) or to the requirements of tradition (7%). Marital status was associated with differing values. Over 60% of married and widowed persons related the value of marriage to the need for children and the continuation of the family, while only 40% of single persons did so. Ten percent of the single and divorced individuals cited primarily the need for a permanent sexual partner, while only 5% of the married individuals mentioned this.

Not surprisingly, the older the respondents, the more important was creating a family for the sake of the children, personal comfort, or prevention of loneliness. The needs for mutual understanding or sexual relations were seen as relatively less important. The importance of children was of special significance for religious individuals, particularly Muslims and Catholics (60% and 63%, respectively, compared with 55% among "nonbelievers"). Some considered the creation of a family through childbearing to be a moral duty (35% of the Muslims and 20% of the Catholics).[8]

Results of the Matskovsky et al. survey also reflected the negative aspects of family life in Soviet society (see Table 1.5). These were most often associated with the difficulties and material discomforts of everyday life—conditions that have drastically worsened in the several years since the survey. Most often cited as negative aspects of family life were, first, the necessity of working so hard outside the home to secure material well-being for one's family (44%); and, second, the overwhelming demands of household chores in addition to outside work (40%). Problems in the relationships between spouses and between

TABLE 1.5. Negative Aspects of Family Life in the USSR

Value orientation	Percentage
It is necessary to work too much to secure the material well-being of the family	44
Household chores occupy too much place in family life	40
Family restricts personal freedom	20
Difficult to answer	20
There is too much monotony in family life; one and the same duties	18
Children cause much trouble and distress in the family	17
Family life imposes too much responsibility for the well-being of others	16
Deception, betrayal and conflict are unavoidable in the family	15
Family life interferes with professional growth	4
It is impossible to preserve love in the family	2

ildren were also cited, though less often. Despite the
:ern that family life is an obstacle to one's career (a
 .y expressed in the United States), only a small percent-
 soviet respondents pointed to this as an actual problem (7%
 .cn and 8% of women). However, more than twice as many individuals with university education as graduates of vocational–technical
schools indicated that family life did, in fact, interfere with their professional growth.[9]

Clearly, the majority of contemporary Soviets espouse family-
oriented values and prize many aspects of family life, even more than
social or professional values. Like their American counterparts, most
Soviet adults do not view families as hindering career goals or personal
fulfillment, even though a certain number of married couples wish to
remain childless. And, as in the United States, public opinion on marriage and family relations varies among Soviet ethnic and religious
groups as well as geographic regions.

COMPARATIVE TRENDS IN MARRIAGE AND FAMILY LIFE: AN OVERVIEW

The similarities in patterns of family life in industrialized societies are
readily apparent, even when those societies have been characterized
as opponents on the world political scene. Initially, we had little difficulty identifying a variety of family-related characteristics common to
the United States and the former Soviet Union: rising rates of illegiti-
macy, gender role changes in marriage, higher divorce rates, adolescents living at home for longer periods, and so on. However, further
discussion revealed that the meaning and significance of these patterns
could be very different in the two societies. For example, some demographic trends that appear similar at this point in time are, in fact,
moving in opposite directions in the two societies. Other similarities
in behavior are accompanied by substantially different attitudes between
Soviets and Americans. Furthermore, the nature of the data available
to Soviet and American family researchers is vastly different, making
accurate and meaningful comparisons very complicated. Both societies are so diverse that generalizations even within one culture must be
made carefully, let alone comparisons across two societies that have
been closed to each other for so long a time. Finally, the dramatic shifts
in the Soviet political and economic systems have had an enormous
impact on everyday life in that society over the past five to ten years.
These revolutionary changes strongly influence the reports of citizens

on their life experiences, and also color the interpretations made by social and behavioral scientists.

Despite these limitations on cross-cultural comparisons, we have agreed on eight major trends of parallel change in the two societies that are significantly influencing the nature of family experience: family composition; gender roles; sexual behavior; the nature of marriage; familes and parenting; the launching of adolescents; divorce, and remarriage; and older couples and families.

Family Composition

According to the Soviet census of 1989, 89% of the population lived within "families." The other 11% lived alone or in various collective arrangements, a figure that remained stable between 1979 and 1989. Over the same time period, the number of persons living in hostels grew from 6 million to 11.5 million. In 1979, about 66% of the Soviet population lived in nuclear families, with or without children, up slightly from 63.5% in 1970. About 13% of these were single-parent families.[10]

Over the past thirty years in the United States, traditional nuclear families have become the minority. By "traditional," we are referring to families in which a husband and wife live with their own children, with the husband being the primary breadwinner and the wife a homemaker. In 1950, 70% of American households were such traditional nuclear families. In 1989, only about 30% of households in the United States fit this description.[11] Family composition is becoming more varied—a change generated primarily by the high rates of divorce and remarriage, but also by the growing number of women who choose to have children without being married. Of the families in the United States in 1989, only 62.8% involved couples in their first marriage; 17.1% involved remarried couples; 11.3% were single-parent families; and 8.8% reflected other types of family structure.[12]

In the United States in 1990, single-parent families accounted for almost 25% of the population with children under the age of eighteen.[13] The figures were even higher for Hispanic-Americans (30%) and African-Americans (54%). It has been estimated that up to 60% of today's two-year-old American children will live in a single-parent household before their eighteenth birthdays.[14]

According to recent available estimates of Soviet families, only about 10% of children under age eighteen live in single-parent families, while 2% live in families without either biological parent. The vast majority of children live with both parents, and often grandparents, in the household.[15] Nevertheless, a poll of workers conducted in Moscow and Lvov in 1988 indicated that only 8% of respondents (all males) disapproved of a woman's giving birth to a child without being married, while a sizable 54% indicated actual approval if the woman became pregnant intentionally rather than accidentally.[16] Soviet single mothers had a number of recognized privileges: preferential housing and child care placements, as well as protection from dismissal from employment.

Postdivorce blended families are increasing in both Soviet and American societies. In one Soviet study, 73.6% of men and 62.9% of women were remarried within fifteen years after a divorce; many of these married again within just a few years. Similarly, nearly 75% of divorced adults in the United States eventually remarry.[17] Currently, about 17% of American families involve remarriage by one or both of the partners, and the number has been rising.

Family size is decreasing in both Soviet and American societies. In the former USSR, the total fertility rate dropped from 2.8 children per woman in 1958–1959 to 2.4 in 1969–1970 and 2.2 in 1980–1981. By 1987, the rate had increased to 2.5, but it dropped again to 2.45 by late 1988. Among the urban populations, the fertility rate in 1988 was 2.0 children per family.[18] In a parallel though more striking way, the fertility rate in the United States dropped from a peak of 3.6 children in 1957 to under 2.0 by 1985. The fertility rates are somewhat higher among certain ethnic minority groups (e.g., 2.3 for African-Americans and 2.8 for Hispanic-Americans).[19]

Gender Roles

Both Soviet and American societies have large numbers of two-earner families. Even in the conservative eastern republics of the former Soviet Union, the majority of women were employed. By the late 1970s, 92% of Soviet women between the ages of sixteen and fifty-four worked outside the home. However, in the years since, Soviet women have begun a gradual shift away from outside employment—or at least full-time employment—in favor of more emphasis on childrearing. The vast majority of women (80% in 1983) do not work during the first year after childbirth, and—thanks to new legislation during the 1980s—many extend their maternity leaves for an additional period of time.[20] Of course, this trend may now begin to reverse itself in the harsher economic climate of the 1990s.

These patterns contrast somewhat with those of the United States, where the employment of women lagged far behind that of the Soviet Union and only gradually caught up. In 1940, only 27% of all women were in the American labor force. By 1988, this figure had increased to 56%. Currently, nearly as many American as Soviet women in the prime working years of twenty-five to fifty-four are employed—more than 37 million, or over 75%.[21]

More details on family structure and employment are presented in Table 1.6. Today, fewer than one-third of American families reflect the traditional pattern of fully employed fathers and full-time home-making mothers. The most typical arrangement (45%) is that in which both parents work outside the home, either full-time or part-time. Families in which single mothers are employed account for 10% of the total; families with unemployed single mothers account for 7%; and families with employed single fathers account for 2%.[22]

Gender discrimination continues to restrict a woman's pay and career advancement in both countries. Women comprise more than half of all Soviet laborers, office employees, and farm workers. In contrast, the share of women among high-ranking officials is only 5.6%, varying from 9.5% in industry to 0.6% in transportation. In practically all branches of Soviet industry, women do less managerial work and receive lower wages. Although women make up 61% of all specialists with higher education, their salaries are much lower than those of their male counterparts.

While the number of employed women in the United States has increased dramatically, the majority still have "pink-collar" jobs that pay low wages; only about 10% of women hold managerial positions. In addition, women are still paid less than men for doing many of the same jobs.

Both Soviet and American families have moved from a more authoritarian to a more democratic style of functioning. In the former

TABLE 1.6. Diversity of Families with Children in the U.S.

	Number (thousands)	Percentage
Father works; mother at home	4,957	33.3
Both parents work full-time	4,277	28.8
Father works full-time; mother works part-time	2,343	15.8
Mother—single parent		
Employed	1,506	10.1
Unemployed	1,089	7.3
Father—single parent employed	300	3.0
Couple—neither employed	402	2.7
Totals	14,874	100.0

Source: Bureau of Labor Statistics (March, 1987).

Soviet Union, the high rate of women's employment and increased urbanization helped promote a more egalitarian approach to spousal relations. Soviet studies have indicated that, depending upon geographic location, decisions on the most important family problems are typically made by both spouses, sometimes by the husband only, and only seldom by the wife alone. Similarly, more egalitarian functioning in American families is attributed to the fact that more wives are returning to full-time employment. Despite the broad social trend in the United States, however, some ethnic and religious groups continue to support a more authoritarian, male-dominated approach to family life.

In both societies, younger husbands are gradually becoming more involved in household tasks, reflecting increased cooperation between spouses regarding household duties. In a family study conducted in Moscow, 33% of the respondents stated that both spouses participated equally in housework. Most typically reported (45%) was a pattern of wives doing housework with "help" from husbands.[23] However, in principle, an even larger number of Soviet citizens believe in the concept of equal sharing of household duties.

Although recent studies have indicated that most American couples (up to 85%) agree that child care should be shared, and many (nearly 70%) agree that money management should be shared, a much smaller number (fewer than 40%) agree that housework should be shared.[24] American husbands are often more willing to participate in child care than in housework. While more husbands are actually helping with housework than in the past, research clearly indicates that many wives wish their husbands would contribute equally to household responsibilities.[25]

An egalitarian view of marriage is emerging strongly as an ideal in American families, though it is still far from realization.[26] Soviet marriage and family relationships may be actually more egalitarian overall than those of Americans because of the relatively long-standing financial independence of women, as well as the internalization of socialist values.

Sexual Behavior

Premarital cohabitation is less common in Soviet than in American society. In the United States, the rate of cohabitation has increased at least fivefold since the 1960s. Over half of the couples cohabiting are adults who have never been married.[27] Delay in the age of first marriage and the growing number of divorces have led to increasing acceptance of sexual involvement outside of marriage. Correspondingly, cohabitation increased from less than 0.5 million in 1960 to 2.5 mil-

lion in 1988. Both incidence of sexual intercourse and rate of cohabitation increase greatly as couples in the United States move toward
engagement.[28]

By contrast, nonmarital cohabitation has not been customary in
Soviet regions, for reasons ranging from religious constraints to lack
of adequate housing. In 1967, a test census of the population conducted
in three republics indicated that only 15% of 1,070 women of fertile
age (up to age fifty) were cohabiting.[29] Smaller local studies have been
conducted also, providing clear evidence of an increase in nonmarital
sexual activity, but less clarity on rates of actual cohabitation.[30]

Rates of premarital sexual involvement have increased dramatically
among women in the United States over the past half century. A recent
survey of 2,765 women currently between the ages of eighteen and
twenty-six found that about 60% of them had experienced intercourse
while unmarried by the age of seventeen. This represents an increase
of 25% since the early 1980s, when surveys revealed a rate of about
one-third of unmarried women reporting premarital intercourse.[31] In
addition, the rate of illegitimate births, which is particularly high among
young Americans, also has increased dramatically in the past few
decades. In 1988, 25% of all births in the United States occurred to
unmarried women, up from a rate of only 5.3% in 1960.[32]

In sharp contrast, Soviet statistics indicated that the share of children born to unmarried women increased just slightly from only 8.8%
in 1980 to 10.2% in 1988. Of these children, 43% were accepted by
their fathers and thus registered as legitimate. As in the United States,
the share of children borne by unmarried women in urban areas is
generally higher (about 11%).[33]

The Nature of Marriage

In the United States today, the median age of first marriage is 26.0
years for men and 23.5 years for women—the oldest average age of
marriage in U.S. history. In 1960, the median age of first marriage was
22.8 for men and 20.3 for women.[34] This upward trend in marital age
does not appear to be present in Soviet society. According to the Soviet
census of 1989, the mean age at first marriage was 23.0 years for men
and 21.7 years for women, almost exactly the same figures as in the
previous census of 1979.[34a]

In both societies, however, marriages are becoming more heterogeneous in terms of background characteristics of the partners.
Whereas similarity in life circumstances is still a good predictor of
marriage in the United States, there is now more openness to mar-

riage between people of different ethnic and religious backgrounds.[35] While overall patterns of ethnic and religious diversity in the United States are most accurately described as a "mosaic," families still serve as a kind of "melting pot" for blending a variety of cultural character- istics. A comparison of marriages in the former Russian Republic between 1978 and 1988 shows an increasing number of marriages be- tween members of different nationalities. In 1988, 9.7% of Russian men and 11.1% of Russian women married persons of another nationality. In the Ukraine that same year, 22.4% of women and 20.9% of men were in ethnically mixed marriages. The highest frequency of mixed marriages in Russia is observed among three ethnic and religious groups: Germans (64.4% of women and 67.6% of men), Jews (47.6% of women and 58.3% of men), and Tatars (42.2% of women and 40.9% of men).[36]

A summary of some important trends in American marriages over the years is presented in Table 1.7, which compares five key indicators of change between 1960 and 1985.[37] In general, these trends indicate a major decline in traditional forms of marriage and family life in the United States.

The significance of intimacy in marriage varies greatly, as indicated by the widely reported diversity of motives for marriage in the United States. Over the course of the twentieth century, Americans have come to place a high priority on intimacy, as evidenced by the rising divorce rate. In fact, intimacy has grown to be such an important priority that couples often divorce if they do not feel emotionally close, even if they have no financial or practical problems.

In Soviet society, too, a clear relationship exists between marriage and intimacy. In a majority of studies, the dominating motive for marriage is reported to be "love." According to a study conducted in Moscow, Perm, Yaroslavl, and other cities (11,843 respondents), love was described as "critical" to marriage by 81% of both married men and married women.[38] Similar interests and values—more ratio- nal components of behavior—are also important in the marital choices of Soviets.[39]

Despite emphasis on the importance of love and intimacy in mar- riage, the emotional quality of intact marriages is often low in both American and Soviet societies. A 1989 Gallup poll in the United States found that most married individuals were "satisfied" with their mar- riages, although more in-depth questioning often revealed serious prob- lems. Thus, though 85% of couples reported that they were "very sat- isfied" with their marriages, 40% had considered leaving their partners; 20% had a "bad marriage" half the time; and 28% had already been divorced at least once.[40] Newlywed couples in the United States may

TABLE 1.7. Changes in Five Key Indicators of Marriage in the United States

Value orientation	1960	1985
Percent of childbirths outside of marriage	5	22
Percent of teenage mothers who are unmarried	15	58
Divorced individuals per 1,000 married individuals	35	130
Percent of children living with only one parent	9	25
Percent of adult life spent with spouse and children	62	43

Source: D. Blankenhorn, "American Family Dilemmas," in D. Blankenhorn, S. Bayme, and J. B. Elshtain (eds.), *Rebuilding the Nest* (Milwaukee, WI: Family Service of America, 1990), 15. Reprinted by permission.

have problems that are quite serious during the first year of marriage.[41] Even though half of American marriages survive without divorce, the quality of those marriages ranges from poor to very good.

Considerable evidence exists in the United States that the first few years of marriage are quite difficult for couples. Divorces are frequent.[42] Teenage marriages are more than twice as likely to end in divorce as marriages of individuals in their twenties. This is as true in Soviet as in American society, even though the rates of divorce are somewhat lower in the former USSR than in the United States.[43]

In spite of their high rates of divorce and remarriage, neither Soviet nor American society invests time, energy, and money to prepare individuals for marriage. Some evidence exists that Americans who have personally experienced a divorce are more open to counseling prior to a subsequent marriage, and effective marriage preparation programs have gradually become more widely available to the public. Soviet family scholars and educators have long recognized a similar need for marriage preparation; however, few such programs are available. Over the past several decades, some attempts have been made to implement family life and sex education courses in Soviet schools. As in the United States, these attempts have been frustrated by lack of financial support, bureaucratic entanglements, and social controversy occasioned by efforts to devise programs suitable to an extremely diverse population.

Families and Parenting

Although the birthrate for single parents in the United States has increased dramatically, reflecting a sizable number of "accidental" conceptions, American couples typically can and do plan their childbearing rather methodically. Because of the relative ease with which they can control conception, couples often delay childbearing for some time after marriage, particularly if the wife has full-time employment outside the home. The number of children per family in the United States has also decreased in the past fifty years, at least until recently, when the birthrate began to rise again.[44]

The former Soviet Union was a nation of extremes and contradictions. Among these were the differences seen in approaches to family planning. In the largely Muslim eastern regions, contraceptives have been little used, and traditional "natural" methods of family planning have predominated. By contrast, the Europeanized western regions have relied on abortion as the primary method of birth control. Thus, the former Soviet Union ranked first in the rate of abortions among developed countries with similar birthrates. In 1988, there were almost 7.5 million abortions, compared to about 5.4 million births. This high rate of abortion reflects both cultural values and practical reality. Reliable contraceptives have always been in short supply in Soviet society. Birth control pills have long been regarded as medically unsafe; mechanical devices such as condoms and IUDs have been poorly manufactured or unavailable.[45] The net result is that more than 10% of all Soviet women of reproductive age have abortions annually.[46] Interestingly, the practice of delaying first childbirths is not widespread in Soviet society. By the end of the 1970s, an average interval between marriage and the first child was only 1.25 years.[47]

Contemporary couples in both societies have had progressively less time for child care at home. The number of Soviet children in day care has been high for decades. Recently, day care has increased dramatically in the United States, nearly equaling the Soviet rate. Ironically, the past few years have seen a return to care at home for Soviet children, especially preschoolers, as growing numbers of women have taken part-time jobs and/or obtained increased parental leave.[48]

As more women in the United States are employed full-time, the need for day care services has increased. Today, the majority of children growing up in the United States will spend at least some period of time being cared for by an adult other than a parent. The impact of nonparental day care on children is still controversial in the United States. Some parents maintain that the *quality* of time spent with their children is increased when quantity is decreased. Others dispute this, claiming that the loss of substantial amounts of time with parents may harm children. Soviet and American family researchers agree that in both societies, more individual attention is given to each child today as a result of smaller family size.[49] The issue of quality versus quantity of time between parents and children needs further research.

The importance of family relationships over work and other activities has begun to increase in Soviet society. As noted earlier, a representative sampling of Russians and other ethnic groups rated "family" as the most important value, followed by "work" and "respect from others" (see Table 1.1).[50]

The rearing of young children has grown steadily more rational and democratic in Soviet society, as families become more child-oriented. Books by noted American pediatrician Dr. Benjamin Spock have become very popular, just as they were in the United States during the 1950s and 1960s. However, both societies are characterized by great diversity in childrearing practices; this is particularly noticeable when ethnic groups within the same geographic region are compared. In both societies, more parenting is done by mothers than by fathers. Soviet fathers have even less everyday contact with their children than do American fathers. As in the United States, most responsibility for educating Soviet children lies with mothers and female teachers. Like their American counterparts, the majority of Soviet children who are not raised on farms learn the skills of employment and adult living from persons outside their families.[51] It remains to be seen whether Soviet males will match the very recent trend of American fathers toward greater involvement in childrearing.

Launching of Adolescents

As is typical of industrialized cultures, both Soviet and American youths mature earlier, but leave home later. Thus, adolescence is a protracted stage of life. American adolescents have long expected freedom and independence from their families of origin, even though they may receive financial support for higher education well into their adult years. College life affords many young people an opportunity to live away from home and to decrease their emotional connection to parents, though they may remain financially dependent. Recently, however, a growing number of young Americans, both single and married, have found that they cannot afford to live on their own after high school, or even after college.[52] They continue to live at home while gaining an education or beginning a career, or they return to the family home after having lived away for a time. This trend, combined with the rapidly rising number of aging adults being cared for by their children, has increased the prevalence of the multigenerational family household—a phenomenon that was previously shrinking through the twentieth century.

Leaving home is particularly difficult for contemporary Soviet youths, both psychologically and physically. Severe housing shortages make it almost mandatory to live with parents. Virtually all dating couples are living in their family homes, making privacy a rare commodity. Even after marriage, 60% of newlyweds live with the parents of one spouse.[53] Psychologically, too, there are problems. Like their American counterparts, many Soviet young people expect financial assistance from their parents, even after marriage. Many young adults retain close ties with their families of origin, relying on their parents for everything from emotional support to child care and help with household tasks.[54] The recent collapse of the Soviet Union and the resulting financial crisis have elevated this problem to disastrous proportions in many parts of the former USSR.

The general nature of adolescence in Soviet and American societies appears very similar. Partly, this results from a trend toward "democratization" of parent–child relationships that characterizes the highly technologized cultures of Western Europe and Japan, as well as the United States and the former Soviet Union.[55] Adolescents have more freedom to create semi-independent subcultures reflecting the values and issues of their stage of life, fueled by media images and by material goods reflecting the entreprenurial successes—and excesses—of a growing global capitalism. Researchers have found that youths in many cultures seem to struggle in some way as they enter adulthood, trying to synthesize clashing ideologies and to merge the world as they understand it to be with the world they desire to have.[56] Thus, interaction between parents and their adolescent or young adult children requires considerable effort to balance power and control, dependence and independence, closeness and distance. Research in the United States has suggested that parents who are too rigid and inflexible with their adolescents or too laissez-faire and lenient tend to have more family problems than those who are successful in striking a balance.[57]

Divorce, Child Support, and Remarriage

In both societies, the divorce rate increased through the 1960s and 1970s, but stabilized in the 1980s at about 50% in the United States and approximately 40% in the former Soviet Union.[58] A growing number of women have sought divorce in both societies.

Contemporary marriage in the United States is a risky endeavor, with the odds of divorce now about fifty-fifty. Yet marriage continues to be a popular institution—over 90% of Americans marry at least once.[59] The odds of divorce following remarriage are even higher; about 60% of remarried Americans eventually divorce. Similarly, the Soviet divorce rates are 1.75 times higher for remarriages than for first marriages. The lack of stability is even higher when both sets of parents have children that they bring into the new marriage.[60] This social cycle of marriage and remarriage that the late American anthropologist

Margaret Mead labeled "serial polygamy" seems to characterize the highly technologized urban cultures of the world.[61]

In both Soviet and American societies, more divorces are occurring among parents of young children and adolescents than in the past. A Russian study in 1988 found that only 377,000 out of 950,000 divorcing couples (40%) had no children. A similarly high number of divorces in the United States involve children, and the number of single-parent families and stepfamilies has increased manyfold over the past several decades.[62]

In both societies, the majority of divorced individuals remarry, with men remarrying more quickly and more often than women.[63] The rate at which Soviet and American women remarry is to some extent related to the number of children they have: The greater the number of children, the less the likelihood of remarriage.[64] Nevertheless, divorced American women with children are now remarrying more quickly than they did in the past.[65] In 1980, about 50% of remarried American households contained one or more stepchildren under the age of eighteen.[66] Divorced Soviet women under age thirty with only one child are also very likely to remarry. However, older women with one or more children have little chance of remarriage.[67]

Causes of the rising divorce rates in Soviet and American societies are varied and complex. Certainly, one reason is that both Soviets and Americans have become more tolerant of divorce. A 1988 study conducted in Moscow and Liov found that 37% of respondents regarded divorce as an "ordinary" phenomenon, 42% did not approve of it, and 21% were uncertain. Only 3% of the respondents thought that a high divorce rate proved that marriage and family life are relatively unimportant. Most respondents believed that a divorce does not affect a person's reputation.[68] Although divorce is still seen as problematic in the United States, most Americans have accepted it as a fact of contemporary life.

Among other contributors to divorce in the United States appear to be the willingness and ability of more women to support themselves and their children financially. A similar trend may be occurring among Soviet women, although the pattern is not yet as clear. Marital dissatisfaction, based upon higher expectations for the rewards of a close relationship, is clearly a factor in divorce in both societies. Various power and control struggles between men and women have become more visible in both societies. Alcoholism and family violence—issues being addressed more frequently in American society—are also cited more often by Soviet women as major sources of marital conflict leading to divorce.

The emotional and financial consequences of divorce are difficult for all parties concerned, although lessening social stigma is helpful. Studies in both societies show that children suffer from the divorce of their parents, but that the impact decreases over time and many children prove to be quite resilient.[69] Ongoing conflict between the divorced parents—a common phenomenon in both societies—can harm the children, in addition to making postdivorce adjustment problematic for one or both parents.[70]

In the United States, many divorced fathers have little meaningful involvement in their children's lives, and a significant number fail to provide adequate financial support. Gradually, these patterns are changing, partly because of a growing commitment of fathers to more active parenting and partly because of better legislation and enforcement of child support payments. However, "serial parenting" still accompanies "serial polygamy": Noncustodial parents (usually fathers) play an active role in raising and supporting the children of the partners they are currently married to, while dropping their ties to children from a previous marriage.

Here, too, the Soviet situation parallels that of the United States. Following divorce, Soviet fathers are often removed from their children's lives, either by choice or through the active alienating efforts of the mothers. The younger the child, the less likely the father is to be involved in childrearing activities on a regular basis. A father is also less likely to be involved if the child is a girl.[71] Thus, a society that has already endured generations of life without men because of losses during the two World Wars is still at risk of losing the contributions of fathers to children's lives through a rising divorce rate. In addition, the current economic crisis of Soviet society could lead to especially severe deprivation for children of divorce, particularly those in single-parent families.

Older Couples and Families

Middle-aged parents in the United States are sometimes called the "sandwich generation," referring to the pressures placed upon them to provide practical and financial support for both their adolescent children and their aging parents. The same dynamic is present in Soviet society; indeed, it is made even more extreme by the economic circumstances that have led to insufficient household income and crowded living conditions.

Independent living for older Americans is becoming increasingly difficult because of the rising costs of medical care and the intermittent periods of economic inflation and recession, which seriously affect those on fixed incomes. The costs of educating children, especially through college, have also risen dramatically, leaving middle-aged parents feeling more financially squeezed than ever. In the United States, older couples are likely to live in their own homes or apartments, at least until one partner dies. After that, much caretaking of aging parents is the responsibility of the children, although government-supported medical care and social security programs are designed to help ease the burden.[72]

Historically, the Soviet Union has had an extensive program of social support for its aging citizens. However, economic problems and lack of advanced health care have led to marginal existence for the elderly. Thus, Soviet families have had to assume major responsibility for care of sick or aging parents, despite the existence of social welfare programs. As indicated above in our discussion of young adults, Soviet families are characterized by multigenerational households over much of the life span. For example, census figures reveal that nearly 60% of widows and 58% of divorced women, even as young as age fifty, live with one of their adult children. Remarriage by older adults is not common in Soviet society.

The quality of life for aging individuals in most societies is problematic, because of their growing need for medical care and practical services for tasks they can no longer accomplish on their own. Despite the socialist framework of Soviet society, the lives of the elderly have grown more difficult. In some regions, a sizable number have continued to work at menial tasks such as street cleaning and coat checking; some beg on the streets or in churches. For many elderly citizens, particularly those without immediate family support, life has deteriorated even further since *perestroika* and the ensuing economic collapse. Retirement pensions barely reach subsistence level. For example, in 1987, 41.5% of retired laborers and office workers and 92.8% of farm workers received a monthly pension of less than eighty rubles—barely enough to enable them to survive then, and now dangerously low in a climate of rapid inflation.

Both Soviet and American elderly must depend upon younger family members for much of their practical and economic support. The diminished size of the family in both societies has seriously affected this situation. Fewer young workers paying taxes and generating income mean less money for government programs and pension funds. In addition, the aging parents in both societies have fewer children to rely on financially and emotionally.

Through the twentieth century, ideals of "family togetherness" have diminished in both Soviet and American societies, particularly across generations. In both countries, geographic mobility and family instability (i.e., divorce and remarriage) appear to have weakened family ties. This is particularly true in the United States, where the emphasis on individualism has combined with other social factors to produce a pattern of isolated nuclear families as a kind of cultural ideal.

The family pattern in Soviet society is more varied. Having few children favors nuclearization of the family, whereas the cultural ethic, along with economic necessity, encourages intergenerational contact. At the same time, the rapid pace of change in social conditions and cultural values disrupts continuity between the generations. In both Soviet and American societies, older family members are more likely to hold traditional values that clash with those of younger generations, leading to alienation and breakdown in communication.[73] Age is no longer automatically respected, as in more traditional cultures; the elderly are often seen as a burden rather than an asset, even within families. Thus, a variety of factors interact to isolate the older generation, creating a major social issue not yet successfully addressed by either society.

CONCLUSION

In this chapter, we have attempted to provide an overview of two very different societies that have been operating under contrasting political systems, yet bear a striking resemblance to each other. Even in the few years since we began planning for this book, Soviet culture has undergone a revolutionary transformation, much of which has had a negative impact on families. While economic instability and unemployment have also plagued families in the United States, many Soviet families have been dramatically plunged into abject poverty and social chaos, sometimes in the context of civil war. Despite the obvious cultural differences, families in both societies have adapted to the growing stresses in some similar ways. Some of these adaptations may eventually contribute positively to social organization; others must be characterized negatively as "family breakdown."

We have highlighted eight major areas of change in marriage and family life. From these, it is apparent that success or failure in coping with family problems is directly proportional to the level of economic adversity in our two societies. Furthermore, family life is clearly becoming more complex in both cultures, with structures and roles shifting. Women's issues inside and outside of families—and the resulting changes in men's lives—predominate in both societies, affecting rates of premarital sexual activity, patterns of marriage and divorce, parenting practices, and intergenerational relationships, as well as social policies and programs related to health care, contraception/abortion, employment, and day care. Pluralism is an overriding theme in both societies, viewed positively by some social commentators and family scholars, but negatively by others. Cultural diversity exists in both societies; how it will eventually be accommodated remains to be seen.

Many of the issues described above are explored in more depth in the remaining chapters of this book, where research results are presented and analyzed. To set the stage for this endeavor, we should note that our collaborative efforts to examine family life are not only complicated by contrasting philosophical assumptions, differing social histories, and idiosyncratic cultural conditions; they are also made more difficult by different research tools and methodological approaches.

Meaningful sociological studies were almost nonexistent during much of the history of the Soviet Union, since most analyses of life conditions were conducted under the mandate of political ideology, and there were to be no social problems in this "ideal society." Similarly, only certain strands of psychological thought were compatible with political requirements, limiting theory construction and making difficult any research efforts into a variety of interpersonal and social issues. Therefore, Soviet family researchers have had to rely primarily on demographic studies and, more recently, surveys of public attitudes and broad behavioral trends.

Family research in the United States has a stronger and more diverse theoretical base and has been privileged with a range of research methodologies. Understanding the dynamics of family life and the variables influencing behavior in close relationships is still a challenge to researchers in both societies, though some noteworthy efforts have been made in the United States. Future cooperation between family scholars in our two societies will enable us to combine research expertise and methods, so that studies will eventually be more comprehensive and comparisons more meaningful. Our hope is that the efforts we have made here will contribute to further cooperative projects. To paraphrase the statement of Herbert Otto with which we have begun this chapter, the ability to change will help preserve both families and societies.

NOTES

1. H. A. Otto, *The Family in Search of a Future* (New York: Appleton-Century-Crofts, 1970).
2. N. Diuk and A. Karatnycky, *The Hidden Nations: The People Challenge the Soviet Union* (New York: William Morrow, 1990).

3. Commission on the Family, State of California, *California Report on the Family* (Sacramento: Author, 1989).

4. Y. V. Arutunayan, "Similarities and Differences among Ethnic Cultures," in Y. V. Arutunayn (ed.), *Sociocultural Images of Soviet Nations* (Moscow: Nauka, 1986), 251.

5. M. S. Matskovsky, G. A. Zaikina, Y. V. Foteyeva, and V. V. Bodrova, "The Family as a Mirror of Public Opinion," survey conducted in collaboration with the All-Union Center for Public Opinion (1989).

6. M. Mellman, E. Lazarus, and A. Rivlin, "Family Time, Family Values," in D. Blankenhorn, S. Bayme, and J. B. Elshtain (eds.), *Rebuilding the Nest* (Milwaukee, WI: Family Service of America, 1990).

7. Matskovsky et al., *op. cit.*

8. *Ibid.*

9. *Ibid.*

10. Families in the USSR (Data of the 1989 General Census)." (Moscow: *Finansy i Statistica*, 1991), 20. See also G. P. Kiseleva and A. B. Sinelnikov, "Marriages, Divorces, and One-Parent Families," in T. D. Ivanova (ed.), *Population and Social Development* (Moscow: Nauka, 1988), 115.

11. P. C. Glick, "Remarried Families, Stepfamilies and Stepchildren: A Brief Demographic Profile," *Family Relations, 38* (1989a), 24–27.

12. *Ibid.*

13. U.S. Bureau of the Census, *Statistical Abstract of the United States: 1992* (Washington, DC: U.S. Government Printing Office, 1992).

14. A. Brophy, "Children under Stress," *U.S. News and World Report* (October 27, 1986), 58–63.

15. Kiseleva and Sinelnikov, *op. cit.*

16. G. A. Zaikina, "Liberation of Sex Morals and the Family," in M. S. Matskovsky and T. A. Gurko (eds.), *Formation of Marriage and Family Relations* (Moscow: Institute of Sociology, Soviet Academy of Sciences, 1989), 59.

17. See M. Coleman and L. H. Ganong, "Remarriage and Stepfamily Research in the 1980s: Increased Interest in an Old Family Form," in A. Booth (ed.), *Contemporary Families: Looking Forward, Looking Back* (St. Paul: National Council on Family Relations, 1991), 192–225.

18. Kiseleva and Sinelnikov, *op. cit.*

19. D. Popenoe, "Family Decline in America," in D. Blankenhorn, S. Bayme, and J. B. Elshtain (eds.), *Rebuilding the Nest* (Milwaukee, WI: Family Service of America, 1990), 39–51.

20. Kiseleva and Sinelnikov, *op. cit.* See also "Labor in the USSR." (Moscow: *Financy i Statistica*, 1988), 107.

21. K. A. Matthews and J. Rodin, "Women's Changing Work Roles: Impact on Health, Family and Public Policy," *American Psychologist, 44*(11) (1989), 1389–1393.

22. J. Pleck, *Working Wives/Working Husbands* (Beverly Hills, CA: Sage, 1985); J. Pleck, "American Fathering in Historical Perspective," in M. Kimmel (ed.), *Changing Men* (Newbury Park, CA: Sage, 1987); United States Bureau of Labor Statistics (Washington, DC, 1987).

23. Z. A. Yankova, E. F. Anguildieva, and O. K. Loseva, *The Man and the Woman in the Family* (Moscow: Finansy i Statistica, 1983).

24. D. Y. Hiller and W. W. Philliber, "Division of Labor and Contemporary Marriage: Expectations, Perceptions and Performances," *Social Problems, 33*(3) (1986), 191–201.

25. E. Anderson, "Shifting Feelings about Who Does What," *Minnesota Science* 44, (Agricultural Experimental Station, University of Minnesota, Summer 1989), 1, 4.

26. *Ibid.*

27. Glick, 1989a, *op. cit.*

28. *Ibid.*

29. L. E. Darsky and G. A. Boudarskaya, "Marital Status of Women and Birthrates in the USSR," Proceedings of *The All-Union Scientific Conference, Prognosticating Social Development and Demographic Processes under the Conditions of Scientific and Technological Revolution Acceleration,* Section III (Erevan: 1988), 44.

30. For example, from 1960 to 1981 in the city of Perm, the proportion of childbirths during the first eight months after marriage among married women ages twenty to twenty-four increased from 28% to 37%. See S. I. Golod, *Family Stability: Sociological and Demographic Aspects* (Leningrad: Nauka, 1984), 6.

31. The current information on premarital sexual activity among young women is reported in S. Janus and C. Janus, *The Janus Report on Sexual Behavior* (New York: John Wiley, 1993). These data can be contrasted with the data in the original Kinsey studies of the 1950s. See A. Kinsey, W. Pomeroy, C. Martin, and P. Gephard, *Sexual Behavior in the Human Female* (Philadelphia: W. B. Saunders, 1953).

32. Blackenhorn, *op. cit.,* 41.

33. Darsky and Boudarskaya, *op. cit., 82.*

34. Glick, 1989a, *op. cit.*

34a. "Demographic Annual of the USSR," (Moscow: *Finansi i statistika,* 1990), 228–229.

35. B. J. Fowers and D. H. Olson, "Predicting Marital Success with PREPARE: A Pedictive Validity Study," *Journal of Marriage and Family Therapy, 12* (1989), 403–413.

36. M. S. Toltz, "Marriages between Different Nationalities," *The Soviet Culture,* (June 5, 1990), 5.

37. D. Blankenhorn, "American Family Dilemmas," in D. Blankenhorn et al. (eds.), *Rebuilding the Nest* (Milwaukee, WI: Family Service of America, 1990), 3–25.

38. Z. I. Fainburg, "Emotional and Cultural Factors of Family Functioning," *Sociological Studies, 1* (1981), 145.

39. A. G. Kharchev, *Family and Marriage in the USSR,* 2nd ed. (Moscow: Mysl, 1979), 192.

40. "Marriage Satisfaction," Gallup poll (distributed by the *Los Angeles Times* Syndicate, 1989).

41. One study of several hundred newlywed couples found that 63% had serious problems related to their money; 51% had serious doubts that their mar-

riages would last; 49% had significant marital problems; 45% were not satisfied with their sexual relationship; 42% found marriage harder than they expected; and 35% said that their mates were often critical of them. See M. A. Arond and S. L. Parker, *The First Year of Marriage* (New York: Warner Books, 1987).

42. A. J. Norton and J. E. Moorman, "Current Trends in Marriage and Divorce among American Women," *Journal of Marriage and the Family, 49* (1987), 3–14.

43. Within a cohort of Soviet women married in 1959, 17.1% of those who married before the age of twenty-two were eventually divorced. See L. R. Kuznetsov, "Divorce Rates: Dynamics, Factors, Tendencies," in A. G. Volkov (ed.), *The Methodology of Demographic Prognosis* (Moscow: Nauka, 1988), 95.

44. S. J. Ventura, "Trends and First Births to Older Mothers, 1970–1979," *Monthly Vital Statistics Report* (1982), 31–32.

45. E. B. Babin, "Contraceptive Behavior of Spouses in Urban Families," in L. L. Ribakovskiy and A. I. Antonov (eds.), *Family Activity: Yesterday, Today, Tomorrow* (Moscow: Mysl, 1986), 51.

46. A. A. Avdeev, "Abortions and Birthrates," *Sociological Studies,* 7 (1989), 55.

47. M. V. Kurman, "Dynamics of the Average Number of Children in the Family," in T. V. Rabushkin (ed.), *Soviet Demography throughout 70 Years* (Moscow: Nauka, 1987), 215.

48. *Statistics Herald, 1* (1990), 42.

49. A. Vasilevsky, "A Human Factor in Demographic Measurement," *Communist, 17* (1986), 77.

50. Arutunayan, *op. cit.*

51. O. B. Bozhkov and V. B. Goldfast, "Distribution of Labor in an Urban Family," *Sociological Studies, 4* (1986), 72.

52. P. C. Glick, "The Family Life Cycle and Social Change," *Family Relations, 38* (1989b), 123–129.

53. According to a 1984 survey conducted by the USSR Central Statistics Board, only 13% of 87,200 dating couples lived outside their family homes. *Statistics Herald,* 3 (1987), 59.

54. V. A. Sysenko, *Young People Get Married* (Moscow: Mysl, 1986), 130.

55. I. S. Kon, *Child and Society* (Moscow: Nauka, 1988), 234.

56. For more in-depth discussion, see E. H. Erikson, *Identity: Youth and Crisis* (New York: Norton, 1968); for a more recent view of the topic, see M. Buchmann, *The Script of Life in Modern Society: Entry into Adulthood in a Changing World* (Chicago: University of Chicago Press, 1989).

57. D. H. Olson, C. S. Russell, and D. H. Sprenkle, "Marital and Family Therapy: A Decade Review." *Journal of Marriage and Family Therapy* (1980), 973–993.

58. Kiseleva and Sinelnikov, *op. cit.*

59. Glick, 1989a, *op. cit.*

60. *Ibid.*

61. M. Mead, *Growing Up in New Guienea* (London: William Morrow).

62. Kiseleva and Sinelnikov, *op. cit.*

63. *Ibid.*

64. P. C. Glick and S. Lyn, "Recent Changes in Divorce and Remarriage," *Journal of Marriage and the Family, 48*(4) (1986), 737–747.

65. P. C. Glick, "Fifty Years of Family Demography: A Record of Social Change," *Journal of Marriage and the Family, 50* (1988), 861–873.

66. A. Sherlin and J. McCarthy, "Remarried Couple Households: Data from the June, 1980 Current Population Survey," *Journal of Marriage and the Family, 47* (1985), 123–130.

67. In one follow-up study nearly twenty years after divorce, remarriage rates were as follows: 51% of childless women, 41% of women with one child, and 36% with two or more children. See V. A. Belova and E. M. Moreva, "Remarriages of Women: Situations and Factors," in A. G. Volkov (ed.), *The Methodology of Demographic Prognosis* (Moscow: Nauka, 1988), 109.

68. Y. V. Foteyeva, "Divorce Ideas of Workers and Intelligentsia," in M. S. Matskovsky and T. A. Gurko (eds.), *Formation of Marriage and Family Relations* (Moscow: Institute of Sociology, Soviet Academy of Sciences, 1989), 64, 67.

69. Kon, *op. cit.*

70. Glick, 1989a, *op. cit.*

71. *Ibid.*

72. L. E. Troll, S. J. Miller, and R. C. Atchley, *Families in Later Life* (Belmont, CA: Wadsworth, 1979).

73. For an analysis of the patterns in American families, see D. H. Olson, H. I. McCubbin, H. Barnes, A. S. Larsen, M. Muxen and M. Wilson, *Families: What Makes Them Work*, rev. ed. (Newbury Park, CA: Sage, 1989). The issue in Soviet society is discussed in Bozhkov and Goldfast, *op. cit.*

Chapter 2

The Relationships of Men and Women in Marriage

Pauline G. Boss
Tatyana A. Gurko

Although precise comparisons between American and Soviet societies are impossible—particularly now that the former Soviet Union is undergoing radical political and cultural change—we do our best in this chapter to explore commonalities and differences in how men and women in these two societies live together in marriages and families. Clearly, large-scale social changes affect families in a variety of ways; therefore, an analysis of relationships can never be "final." Our goal is to illuminate gender issues in couple relationships in both societies. We attempt to identify factors that can help us understand why marriage is so often a different experience for women and men, and we point to areas where important questions remain for further research.

Three things must be stressed initially. First, we are using the term "comparison" loosely; though we have selected topics for which there are existing data on both Soviet and American families, much information comes from studies that are not strictly comparable. This selectiveness illuminates many gaps that still exist in our ability to make scientifically valid comparisons. Second, we note that the Soviet data presented in this chapter are limited largely to Russia and the Baltic republics. Relatively little information about male–female relations in central Asian families is available, beyond the widely recognized fact that these families are patriarchal in structure. We have noted ethnic differences whenever possible; however, the cultural diversity of our respective societies is not yet well represented in family research. Finally, we touch only briefly upon the important topics of sexuality, work, and finances in relation to gender, since these topics are covered more fully in other chapters.

GENDER AND CIVIL RIGHTS IN THE UNITED STATES

The United States Constitution and the subsequent Bill of Rights created a system of justice based upon English common law and eighteenth-century ideals of liberty and equality for *men*. Explicit references to civil rights for women were specifically omitted, although these documents left open future possibilities of voting rights and the privilege of running for federal office. It was not until 1920 that women's right to vote was finally secured, following a battle of fifty years that culminated in the Nineteenth Amendment. Elizabeth Cady Stanton and Susan B. Anthony were two of the best-known leaders of the early fight for women's equal rights in marriage, education, employment, and politics.[1] Following the victory of voting rights, women's political issues were swept aside by several decades of social turmoil, including the Great Depression and World War II. They emerged again in the "women's movement" of the 1960s, when some further progress began to be made in bringing women into public life outside the home, particularly into politics.[2]

Despite significant progress in the legal status of American women from 1963 on, females still lack parity with men in important areas of social life, such as education, employment, and health care. Over 200 years after the drafting of the Constitution, gender inequality still exists. However, it is too simplistic to say that all women in the United States want equal rights and all men are against them. The situation is considerably more complex, reflected in the fact that attempts to pass an Equal Rights Amendment have been defeated, or even passed and then rescinded, by voters of both genders in the past two decades. Debate continues over the exact nature and extent of gender inequities, as well as over the best means to resolve the social problems of women.[3] As one feminist scholar has put the question: "Do we want equality of the sexes—or do we want justice for two kinds of human beings who are fundamentally different?"[4]

GENDER AND CIVIL RIGHTS IN SOVIET SOCIETY

Russian women were first granted certain civil rights by the Zemsky Reform of 1864 and then by the Manifesto of October 17, 1905. Following the October Revolution of 1917, decrees were issued on marriage, divorce, and employment for men and women. Indeed, the first Soviet constitution, adopted in 1918, gave women equal rights with men in all spheres of economic, cultural, social, and political life. However, legal equality for women does not always mean actual equality.

In terms of level of women's employment, the former USSR was one of the leading countries in the world. A large number of women received (and continue to receive) advanced professional training. As of 1988, women comprised 40% of all scientists. Fourteen percent of these female scientists held doctorates, and 28% were candidates for advanced degrees. Thirty-six percent of all engineers were women, as were 50% of those working in the arts.[5] Nevertheless, even in the present period of tumultuous change, women's professional activities still reflect the stereotypes of "female roles." Women in traditionally "male" professions and employment settings are typically allotted the least prestigious and most monotonous tasks. On the whole, women's wages are much lower than men's within the same industries. Virtually no women serve as diplomats or work in the field of international relations, with one recent exception: The Soviet ambassador to Switzerland in 1988 was a woman.[6]

A sizable number of women held political office and served in bodies of governmental authority in the former Soviet Union. In 1984, women comprised 33% of the USSR Supreme Soviet, 35% of the Supreme Soviets of the republics, and about 50% of local Soviet bodies. However, the high proportion of women was based upon legal formulas for appointment rather than elected representation. Only 15% of those elected in 1989 to the first Congress of People's Deputies of the USSR were women, along with 18% of the USSR Supreme Soviet; and only one woman was elected to the USSR Council of Ministers.[7]

Recently, Soviet women have become more active in exercising their rights, including wider participation in state administration. Created by the 1989 USSR Supreme Soviet, a special Committee on Family, Children and Women had as one of its goals the development of a program to encourage more active participation by women in Soviet political life. Informal women's groups, such as the Association of Women's Creative Activity, are being set up to assist women of all ages.

Until recently, the Soviet Union was oriented exclusively toward women with regard to childrearing privileges and responsibility. Recently, however, the system of privileges and grants for families with children has begun to include men as well. In 1990, the USSR Supreme Soviet passed a law permitting employed men to take a partially paid leave of absence for child care until the child is three years old. Recently, some Soviet men have expressed concern about the established practice of courts' granting divorces without even considering the possibility of granting custody to a father, unless the mother is alcoholic or legally insane. In about three-quarters of all cases, a father's participation in childrearing after divorce is limited to paying child support. This policy doubtless reflects the low value accorded males in relation to family life, since fatherhood has little prestige in Soviet society.

THE SOCIAL CONTEXT OF GENDER RELATIONS

The roles of husband and wife are everywhere defined by culture and history as well as by the law. However, traditional definitions no longer seem to reflect the actual behaviors of married men and women in many areas of our two societies. Indeed, wives and husbands who hold onto traditional roles may find them to be obstacles to a satisfying marriage in these times of rapid social change.

In the United States, traditional marital role expectations were once interpreted by family sociologists in terms of small-group dynamics: In efficient families, it was said, wives are in charge of the within-family emotional environment (the "expressive" role), while husbands are in charge of breadwinning and connections to the outside world (the "instrumental" role).[8] However, because marriage roles are so often enacted in ways other than those prescribed by society, role theorists have been criticized for limiting the definitions of gender roles and for artifically relegating women and men to separate spheres of life. This division of roles isolates men from the emotional warmth of children and family life, and women from full participation in the larger society. In addition, this separation of spheres does not accurately portray the reality of women's participation in the work force outside the family. Furthermore, such role differentiation does not reflect the adaptive blending of marital roles in ethnically diverse American families, in which wives earn the major income and husbands are heavily involved with child care.[9]

Since World War II, both Soviet and American women have increasingly assumed both "expressive" and "instrumental" roles within and outside of their families, while men have largely continued to focus their energies on the world of work and have remained tangential to family life. Though some men have recently begun to be more invested in child care and in household duties, heavy male involvement in family life is not yet a trend in either of our societies.

Earlier writings on American families did not highlight gender differences. A notable exception was Jessie Bernard's classic book, *The Future of Marriage*.[10] Bernard was the first American sociologist to point out that a husband's version of marriage differs from his wife's; she found that men were more satisfied with and benefited more fully from marriage than did women. Bernard also found that American husbands were healthier and less prone to depression and suicide than were their wives, while the opposite was true for single American women and men. The institution of marriage, she declared, held more benefits for men than for women. Bernard's study stimulated more research in the United States—first a trickle and then a deluge of literature analyzing gender differences.

In the United States today, our attention is often on "the struggle between the sexes." By contrast, the numerous social conflicts and ethnic struggles in the former Soviet Union have tended to mask the serious tensions that also exist between the sexes. However, the very processes of *perestroika* and *glasnost*, and the resulting social upheavals of recent years, have increasingly brought these tensions to the surface, revealing growing dissatisfaction between women and men.

Today, the majority of Soviet scholars assume that both sexes should equally share most social and marital roles.[11] Many social scientists stress the need to make married women's lives easier by improving household services, getting spouses to share everyday family responsibilities and child care, and bettering the system of preschool nurseries. To some extent, this attitude reflects the continuing influence of Soviet socialist ideology, emphasizing full employment of the adult population, "collectivist" notions of children's upbringing, and legal equality of men and women. However, it also represents the very critical challenge in Soviet life to meet the economic needs of families and to help women with their double burden of work—a job inside and a job outside the home.

Across the former USSR, responsibility for private and public spheres of life varies greatly as a result of cultural differences. In the regions of Central Asia and the Caucasus, many women work outside the home; however, men are still considered to be the family breadwinners. Women's employment is not taken seriously, and their jobs are not supposed to interfere with the family's interests. Public attitudes, particularly in the working class, support the traditionally prescribed norm: "Home is where women belong." For example, interviews were conducted in 1980 with approximately 3,000 respondents in Riga (Latvia) and Dushanbe (Tajik, now Tajikistan). Both laborers and professional employees were included, representing both native nationalities and ethnic Russians. In Dushanbe more than two-thirds of the respondents supported the connection of women to the home, while in Riga, the findings were nearly the opposite, even among married workers.[12]

Soviet family sociologists point out a peculiar kind of "sexism" in research; that is, most studies question husbands and wives on the degree of married *women's* participation in work outside the home, and the problems that ensue as they try to balance work and family life. However, the activities of married *men* with children, and their orientation toward the balance between employment and the family, have not been examined. Not surprisingly, this same bias exists in American family research.

Despite considerable effort at change, the Soviet "women's problem" remains complicated and unresolved. On the one hand, since 1970 fewer than 10% of able-bodied Soviet women have been engaged in full-time homemaking—largely because it is impossible for most families to live on a single salary.[13] On the other hand, the development of supportive public services such as day care has lagged far behind the growth of women's employment. (For a more complete discussion of each of these issues, see Chapters 6 and 7.) These trends negatively affect Soviet life in a variety of ways. Despite a very low birthrate, there is evidence of inadequate care of children. At the same time, economists speak vaguely of the "low labor productivity" of women with young children and have begun to encourage the transfer of mothers to part-time employment (on a voluntary basis).[14] Some family sociologists argue that, contrary to certain ideas advanced by Western feminists, emphasis needs to be put on the idea that family, home, and children are important elements in the development of a woman's personality. In the mid-1980s, the pre-eminent Soviet family sociologist A. Kharchev contended that "being a mother is the most important form of women's creative activity for the destiny of the country and socialism."[15]

In the context of Soviet history, this orientation of social scientists is quite understandable. After the October Revolution of 1917, the primary emphasis was on the role of *woman as worker.* Currently, the central question is whether the necessary social conditions exist to allow women to take an active role in *both* economic production and family life. Of course, serious Soviet scientists do not believe that a woman should be "kept in her place" inside the family. Rather, these viewpoints reflect the reorientation of Soviet society from a monolithic structure to pluralism in both opinions and patterns of behavior.[16] In general, Soviet family scholars agree that women should be granted the freedom to choose combinations of employment, family life (including motherhood), and community activity as they desire. Just as in the United States, however, many Soviet women do not have real options: Economic conditions force them to work full-time outside the home.

Once again, we remind the reader that the demographic trends and psychological features of marital relations differ widely across the various geographic regions of the Soviet Union. Religious differences have an enormous impact, especially between predominantly Muslim and Christian regions; however, the particularities of ethnicity and history also produce dramatic differences in the social roles and psychological characteristics of Soviet men and women. For the sake of expediency—most large-scale studies of Soviet marriage have been conducted in Russia—most of what follows concerns the western, or European, regions of the former USSR.

GENDER ISSUES IN MARRIAGE

Partner Selection and Attitudes toward Marriage

Studies conducted in Russia through the 1970s showed a gradual decrease in the age of men and women at their first marriage. By 1979, the average ages were approximately twenty-two years for women and twenty-four years for men. Since then, the pattern has stabilized; in fact, the corresponding figures for 1989 were practically the same.[17] In contrast, the median age at first marriage in the United States rose noticeably during the period from 1955 (twenty years for women and twent-three years for men) to 1980 (twenty-four years for women and twenty-five years for men).[18] Thus, contemporary Russian women marry earlier than their American counterparts, whereas Russian and American men marry at about the same age.

In the former USSR, selection of mates and subsequent marital relations of men and women are affected by such factors as the ratio of the sexes at the customary age of marriage and the educational levels of potential marriage partners. From the middle twenties on, there are more women than men in all age categories.[19] In addition, the educational level of women in the European part of the former USSR is very high: 56% of students enrolled in institutions of higher education, and 58% of students in specialized (technical) secondary institutions, are women.[20] Young women usually want their future husbands to be educated as well as or better than they are, whereas young men often prefer brides at lower or equal educational levels. A significant problem in mate selection is thus created.

Of course, these demographic factors are not the only things influencing the attitudes and actions of men and women regarding marriage. Contemporary Soviet men often accuse women of lacking "femininity" and "softness," charging them with assuming male vices along with traditional male social roles. Interestingly, some women acknowledge these "deficiencies" of their own gender, citing cruelty, aggressiveness, judgmentalism, and ruthlessness in career advancement as frequently displayed negative characteristics.[21] Other women counter with complaints about men who provide no protection or support and husbands who share no household or child care responsibilities. In addition, a substantial amount of alcoholism among men has been revealed, and this affects both mate selection and marital satisfaction.[22]

Soviet women generally expect fewer advantages from married life than do Soviet men. The failure of available men to meet requisite standards as marriage partners has led to an increasing number of unmarried women, including intentionally unwed mothers. One of us (Gurko) surveyed 175 couples who were getting married in Moscow in 1980. In response to the question "Do you think your (groom) (bride) fits you?", 85% of the grooms but only 60% of the brides answered "yes." To the question "Would your (groom) (bride) make a good (husband) (wife)?", 60% of the grooms but only 39% of the brides answered "yes." Prior to marriage, Soviet women have more decision-making power, particularly in relation to the decision to marry at all; however, surveys of married couples find wives ten times more likely than their husbands to give in during disagreements or arguments.[23]

Numerous studies conducted in the former USSR have shown that love, emotions, and spiritual values are rated most highly in the choice of a marriage partner by both women and men. However, social conditions or personal circumstances force a sizable number of young people to marry. Among the reasons given are "expecting a child," "wish to leave parental home," and "wish to improve living conditions."[24] The fact that birth control supplies are not readily available may very well influence the early marriage age of Russian women. However, the interrelationships among mate selection preferences, courtship customs, sexual behavior, and social conditions (such as crowded parental households) have not been adequately studied by Soviet social scientists. Thus far, researchers stress that the reasons for marriage differ between men and women, and that compatibility is related to satisfaction with the marriage. More and more Soviet citizens are also pragmatic about terminating a marriage. Many men and women planning to marry do not believe that their marriages will last. Approximately 40% of both women and men surveyed just before their weddings agreed that "divorce is a good way out of an unsuccessful marriage even if there are children."[25]

Gender Role Expectations in Early Marriage

In a study of 175 Muscovite couples preparing to marry in 1981, Gurko found that prospective spouses' expectations about a wife's career

coincided in only about half of the cases. Of those couples whose
expectations were the same, 9% expected equal involvement of husband and wife in professional work, 34% believed that a woman should
work as long as it is not detrimental to family interests, and 5% stated
that a married woman should be primarily a mother and homemaker.
The remaining couples held differing expectations; of these, 41% of
the brides expected to have a professional career, while only 11% of
the grooms anticipated this. Three-quarters of the couples studied
agreed on who should do household work; of these, 59% expected equal
participation by wife and husband. In a very small number of couples
(7%), the brides but not the grooms anticipated a strict division of marital roles. These women expressed the wish that their husbands would
provide for them financially, enabling them to avoid employment.[26]
This attitude may very well be a reaction to the difficult conditions
under which working Soviet women now live. Of course, the attitudes
toward women's employment tend to vary according to nationality, level
of education, and place of residence.[27] This same series of studies
demonstrated that in the process of living together over time, the
notions of what it means to be a husband and a wife are often radically altered. For some couples, this is a positive process of adaptation,
resulting in congruence between role expectations and actual family
behavior. For other couples, however, the original divergence in role
expectations remains, becoming a source of marital dissatisfaction and
conflict. Furthermore, on the basis of men's answers to questions asked
just before marriage and again three years later, it appears that Soviet
men's expectations tend to become more traditional as their marriages
continue. Responses indicated that these husbands now believed that
their wives should be doing the household tasks that both partners had
originally considered to be joint, or even male, responsibilities.[28]
Research across several cultures has suggested that spouses' behavior
tends to become more traditional after the birth of the first child, and
that this pattern may continue through most of the life cycle.

A comparative study of "younger" families ($n = 233$) and "older"
families ($n = 319$) carried out in Moscow in the 1980s found great similarity in the patterns of cooperation on household tasks. Spouses in
younger families were slightly more likely to share household tasks
equally (37%) than spouses in were older families (29%); however, the
major difference was the greater sharing of tasks by the *parents* of
younger couples.[29] Sociologists in Estonia have also noted that the
division of household tasks differs generationally. Household work is
more traditionally divided in the families of older parents than in their
children's families, although a somewhat more equal division of work
between the genders has begun to appear.[30] In the predominantly Mus-

lim regions of Central Asia and the Caucasus, husbands seldom do "women's work" in the household. A recent small study of young families in Uzbekistan by Gurko found that a young husband is often "prevented" from doing household work by the presence of older parents who directly or indirectly discourage him from helping, even though many wives are also employed and/or studying in institutions of higher education.[31]

Longitudinal research on Soviet families is still needed to document changes in the division of labor between husbands and wives over time. On the whole, however, the limited Soviet research suggests that men appear to be adjusting very slowly to new roles within families in which both spouses are employed full-time—even though the employment status of women has been fairly stable for several decades. Some variation in family patterns is just beginning to emerge. Thus, it remains true that a Soviet women "is given the right to equality with men in professional activities and the prerogative to work about the house."[32]

Clearly, the problem of the "double working day" of women is a continuing feature of both Soviet and American family life. And the participation of men in family life remains limited.

Marital Communication

American family specialists have often emphasized the need for good communication in successful marriages. In the mid-1980s, one study of fifty married couples (from newlyweds to couples married for thirty-six years) examined the congruence of husband–wife perceptions of communication.[33] "Agreement" and "feeling understood" were significant predictors of communicative satisfaction for both partners. "Communicative satisfaction" was defined as husbands' or wives' satisfaction in successfully communicating to their spouses or in successfully being communicated with by their spouses. However, the *wives'* "realization" (recognizing that they understood or misunderstood their spouses) and "understanding" (correctly imagining what their spouses thought) were linked to their husbands' marital satisfaction, whereas the reverse was not true. The researchers speculated that this gender difference might be attributable to the connection between understanding and the balance of power in the relationships: "If the wives have less power within the relationships, their understanding of their husbands would be important. In other words, it is more important for someone who does not have power to understand the person who does have it than vice versa."[34]

This and similar studies suggest that research on marital communication is most fruitful when gender differences and power dynamics are also assessed.[35] Although findings on marital communication are similar in the United States and the former USSR, the interpretations have differed. Soviet scholars are more likely to explain gender differences in communication as biologically determined, whereas American scholars view them as results of a socialized power imbalance between husbands and wives. This is a complex issue for which more research in both countries would be useful.

Like their American counterparts, Soviet family specialists often stress the importance of effective spousal communication for marital quality. In a society characterized by confusion and conflict, clear communication, empathy, and mutual understanding are at a premium. In one recent study of young families in Moscow, gender differences were discovered in the specific perceptions by husbands and wives of their relationships.[36] Wives more often reported understanding their husbands than husbands reported understanding their wives; wives were more often perceived as "a mystery" by their husbands. Predictably, wives more often than husbands reported sharing their emotions, stresses, and problems with their partners (82.4% and 65.7%, respectively). However, other relational characteristics investigated in the study (complying with each other's wishes, providing psychological support, and showing affection) revealed no essential differences between the genders (see Table 2.1).

The correlation between gender and various aspects of marital communication is apparent. These young Soviet wives were concerned

TABLE 2.1. Correlations between General Satisfaction with Marriage and Specific Relational Characteristics among Young Soviet Spouses

| | General satisfaction with marriage | | | |
| | My spouse in relation to me | | I in relation to my spouse | |
Relational characteristics	Men's answers	Women's answers	Men's answers	Women's answers
Understanding	.50	.38	.54	.34
Psychological support	.49	.37	.58	.34
Adaptiveness, flexibility	.47	.45	.53	.23
Manifestation of good feelings	.67	.35	.53	.35
Confidentiality, sincerity	.55	.39	.35	.25

Source: T. A. Gurko, *Formation of a Young Family in the Big City: Conditions and Factors of Stability*, unpublished doctoral dissertation, Institute of sociology, Soviet Academy of Sciences (Moscow: 1984).

TABLE 2.2. Correlations between General Satisfaction with Marriage and Specific Relational Characteristics among Experienced Soviet Spouses

| | General satisfaction with marriage | | | |
| | My spouse in relation to me | | I in relation to my spouse | |
Relational characteristics	Men's answers	Women's answers	Men's answers	Women's answers
Understanding	.57	.48	.35	.38
Psychological support	.45	.40	.26	.15
Adaptiveness, flexibility	.33	.36	.18	.15
Manifestation of good feelings	.37	.37	.58	.49
Confidentiality, sincerity	.41	.38	.26	.31

Source: T. A. Gurko, "Satisfaction with Marriage as an Index of Spousal Relations," in M. S. Matskovsky (ed.), *Family and Social Structure* (Moscow: Institute of Sociology, Soviet Academy of Sciences, 1987).

less with the way they behaved toward their husbands and more with their husbands' attitudes toward them. The wishes for flexibility and sincerity were emphasized. Young Soviet husbands appeared to be equally concerned with their own attitudes toward their wives and with the wives' assessments of their (the husbands') behavior. Perhaps these young husbands were, in some sense, more "altruistic" than their wives. They wanted to be able to support their wives psychologically, to understand them, and to be responsive to their needs. Conversely, they want their wives to experience "good feelings" toward them (probably reflected in sexual interest) and to be sincere and understanding. Interestingly, older spouses who had been married longer showed fewer gender differences. Of greatest importance for both men and women were the manifestation of good feelings toward spouses, psychological support from spouses, and the ability of spouses to understand each other (see Table 2.2).

In some interesting research on male–female relationships, N. N. Obozov found that husbands gave more accurate appraisals of their wives when the wives were similar to them in personality, whereas wives demonstrated understanding even of partners with dissimilar personalities. Furthermore, adequate understanding of wives by their husbands showed a positive effect on marital compatibility, while husbands' understanding of their wives did not appear to have the same influence on the lives of the spouses. In commenting on these findings, the researcher wondered whether the men were better at strictly differentiating personal and professional spheres of life (i.e., not letting their marital problems have a negative impact on their jobs), whereas wives' problems with nonunderstanding husbands were more likely to be carried over into the workplace.[37]

Marital Power and Decision-Making

In marriage, whoever has more choices available also has more power. The opportunity to make major decisions is one example of marital power. In any assessment of the power relations between women and men in families, the larger societal and economic contexts must be considered. Alexis de Tocqueville, the nineteenth-century French social philosopher, wrote that the American character is shaped by values first inculcated in family life—a sphere he saw as belonging to women. Because these values center on the social functions of love and marriage, he called them "habits of the heart."[38] This view of separate private and public spheres of life—the family as a "haven in a heartless world" of business and politics—has gradually become a cornerstone of American social ideology.[39] Many Americans see the home as a respite from the world of competition, and still consider it women's responsibility to establish and maintain the proper atmosphere of family life.

In their large study of American couples in the early 1980s, Phillip Blumstein and Pepper Schwartz stated: "In marriage, adherence to the male-provider philosophy grants greater power to husbands. . . . The balance of power in marriage is affected not only by income but also by a very central aspect of marriage: the traditional male-provider role. Because of it, husbands are generally accorded more power than wives."[40] The degree to which these American couples accepted the validity of the male-provider role varied greatly. Blumstein and Schwartz found that when either husband or wife, or both, approved of the male-provider role philosophy, the husband had more power no matter how much income each spouse earned: "Even if a wife earns a great deal of money—perhaps even more than her husband—she will not necessarily acquire a proportionate amount of power."[41]

In a recent review of family power theory and research, United States sociologist Maxine Szinovacz notes the extreme complexity of the topic and calls for additional family studies that take account of the power differential between males and females in the larger society.[42] She argues that the structure of family life within the larger society invariably leaves women with fewer choices than men. Gender role socialization, economic dependence, responsibility for childrearing, and discrimination in education and employment all act as background factors that reduce the decision-making power of women in marriage. "Homemaking" in the United States is a relatively low-status position, and women have been found to suffer significant disadvantages as a result, ranging from self-esteem problems to poverty to physical harm at the hands of violent husbands.

For a long time, the Soviet sociological literature used the term "head of the family," reflecting a patriarchal view that implied submission of all family members to the husband/father or some other elderly (male) person representing the family in society. Contemporary Soviet researchers generally agree that the traditional notion of "family head" is now outdated. Most Soviet citizens in the western regions view family leadership as more dependent upon personality and/or situation than upon gender. However, despite a tendency to espouse more democratic social ideals in general, many people throughout the former USSR still consider the "head of the family" to be the husband. In a recent Russian study, 18% of Muscovite grooms and 9% of brides, as well as 26% of young husbands and 6% of young wives, held this view. The association of males with household leadership is especially characteristic of Soviet men who were born in rural areas and have only an average level of education (over 40% of males in this study).[43] The traditional stereotype of male superiority is also still widely held by the populations (both rural and urban) of Central Asia, which are mostly Islamic. For instance, according to data from a pilot study in the city of Tashkent, 7% of young wives and 47% of husbands agreed with the statement that "the husband should make most family decisions." In Moscow, some spouses—especially women—claimed that the wife should be the preferred head of the family; in Tashkent, not one person gave such a response. Overall, however, the majority of participants in the study were oriented to joint decision making or to husbands' and wives' separate responsibility for different spheres of family life.[44]

Despite these professed attitudes, how does family decision making actually occur? Table 2.3 shows that in Moscow, wives made decisions in practically all spheres of family life more often than did husbands, although in many families both spouses made decisions. The role of women in family decision making has increased in the past several decades. Studies in Leningrad in 1965 and in Tallinn in 1975 indicated that husbands were more likely to be responsible for financial decisions (e.g., distribution of money, purchases of expensive items), while wives were more likely to be responsible for childrearing, community activities, and social life. In the past decade, it has been suggested that wives dominate virtually all areas of family life.[45] However, the domestic situation of women in Soviet society is a complex

TABLE 2.3. Family Decision Making at Various Stages of Family Life Cycle (in percentages)

Family problems	Husbands[1]		Husbands[2]		Wives[1]		Wives[2]		Both spouses[1]		Both spouses[2]		Parents[1]	
	Husb. resp.	Wife resp.	Husb. resp.	Wife resp.	Husb. resp.	Wife resp.	Husb. resp.	Wife resp.	Husb. resp.	Wife resp.	Husb. resp.	Wife resp.	Husb. resp.	Wife resp.
Disposes of money	8.2	9.4	1.9	1.6	30.5	30.0	52.4	53.0	58.4	58.8	44.5	42.6	0.9	—
Arranges spending of spare time	15.9	13.7	12.9	8.8	19.7	21.0	19.4	27.9	0.0	52.7	62.7	52.7	—	—
Solves household problems	6.0	4.7	3.4	1.9	29.2	36.5	38.2	37.6	57.5	52.8	54.2	52.4	2.6	3.0
Determines upbringing of a child	5.3	3.6	—	—	25.5	26.4	—	—	69.7	68.9	—	—	0.4	1.0
Has the final say in discussing most other problems	22.7	15.5	—	—	13.3	20.2	—	—	57.1	58.8	—	—	1.3	1.3

Note. The countrywide percentages are less than 100 because other respondents did not answer the question.
[1]An unpublished study of 233 young Moscow families in 1989.
[2]An unpublished study of families with older children or adolescents who responded only to the first three items.

matter, and it is unclear just how much power women actually have in Soviet marriages.

In urban Soviet families (particularly in the western regions), the power of men in families appears to have gradually eroded; the family has, in fact, become a sphere of women's activity almost exclusively. A man's social status outside of his family no longer ensures his authority, if only because his wife also works and may very well have the same social status. In numerous families, the wife's level of education is higher than that of her husband (despite the general educational preferences noted earlier), further strengthening her position. Many Soviet women are employed in positions of authority that require administrative, supervisory, and disciplinary skills, as well as psychological sophistication. In addition to being teachers, nurses, or directors of child care centers, many women are physicians, judges, and even engineers. These women are likely to involuntarily transfer their professional behaviors into their homes.

The history of revolution and war yields insights into the family leadership role of Soviet women. The loss of 20 million men from 1941 to 1945 meant that a great many of today's husbands were raised by widowed mothers. Some have speculated that the single mothers in the Soviet Union developed strong attachments to their sons and were overprotective because of their war-related losses; however, this has not been documented in any reliable way. In the post-World War II era, the number of employed women rose precipitously as they replaced males lost in the war. Widows became "heads of families" by default, taking over as sole providers for their children amidst terrible economic and social circumtances.[46]

Although World War II left a particularly heavy mark on Soviet family structure, other sociohistoric factors also contributed to lessening the authority of men in families. During the long Stalinist–Brezhnevist period, very few Soviet men had a chance for self-affirmation outside their families without compromising their own consciences. Passivity became an important coping mechanism for dealing with the huge social bureaucracy, which was both unresponsive and dangerous. Perhaps this accounts for the lack of self-confidence and cautiousness of many Soviet men, even today. The combination of social isolation and distance from family activities left men with few avenues for self-fulfillment. Alcohol abuse became an escape for many. Perhaps more inclined to compromise, women remained relatively self-assured in their roles as mothers and were able to derive more personal rewards from family interaction.

Men's wages in the former Soviet Union today are very low, particularly when compared with incomes in Western industrialized countries. When they first marry, men are likely to have very low social status and poor income. Thus, the social power of young husbands is minimal. Add to this the fact that most young families in the former USSR live with one spouse's parents and depend on their financial help. The result is that many young men may actually behave in a somewhat "childlike" manner in their families, thereby disappointing their wives, who expect them to be "adult" and "virile." Thus, as young wives struggle for independence from their families of origin, they may more easily assume the role of family "leaders."

How does this distribution of family power and leadership affect satisfaction with marriage? Undoubtedly, the coordination of the husband's and wife's expectations for power is of primary importance. However, it is interesting to note that *both* wives and husbands show less satisfaction with a wife-led marriage. Similar findings have been reported by some American researchers.[47]

For some Soviet women, functioning as "family leaders" may represent a further burden on them, added to an already heavy load of housework and childrearing. Soviet wives have been heard to complain, "I'm sick and tired of making all the decisions by myself." They lament men's lack of initiative, passivity, even indifference to important aspects of family life. A vicious circle is created: Women strive for more power in shaping their own destinies, while tiring of the burden of being "in charge."

The view is sometimes expressed in both Soviet and American societies that certain women go "too far" in the fight for their independence and power in the family. The stereotype of the contemporary "superwoman"—capable of handling everything, always right, and somewhat intimidating to others (including her husband and children)—is an unfortunate by-product of the struggle for gender equality in the family. There has been relatively little change in the actual decision-making patterns of husbands and wives in American studies of marital power relations[48] (see Table 2.4). Although husbands' automatic right to have the final say in decisions is increasingly questioned, their position as the ultimate authority has not been rejected.[49] Both Soviet and American wives have been gaining power in the family; however, equality in decision making has yet to be achieved.

Marital Satisfaction

Research in the United States suggests that American women are less satisfied with marriage and family life than are men.[50] A study by R. A. Bell and colleagues described the strategies couples considered important in maintaining their marriages: "... honesty, listening, open-

TABLE 2.4. Reported Joint Participation in Family Decisions, 1955–1975 (in Percentages)

						Decision area				
Reference	Year of study	Sample	Car	Life insurance	House	Husband's job	Wife's work	Money for food	Doctor	Vacation
Blood and Wolfe (1960)	1955	Wives	25	41	58	3	18	32	45	68
Centers et al. (1971)	1964	Husbands and wives	21 27	28 33	54 64	4 5	24 22	33 32	56 56	71 69
Kandel and Lesser (1972)	1969	Wives	31	51	61	8	37	36	52	75
Duncan et al. (1973)	1971	Wives	26	36	63	4	24	34	—	—
Hesselbart (1976)	1975	Men and women	—	—	—	15	38	35	—	—

Note. For full information on references, see note 48.

ness, physical and verbal affection, physical attractiveness, self-concept, confirmation, sensitivity and supportiveness."[51] In other studies,[52] similar behaviors have been reported to be important in maintaining marital quality, and the characteristics listed are more often associated with females. Furthermore, the Bell et al. study found that the women who participated in the study felt more responsible than their husbands for the maintenance of their marriages, and placed more importance on being the *recipients* of these maintenance behaviors than did their husbands. The exact interpretation of these findings is uncertain. Do women actually *do* more to maintain marital quality than their husbands, or do they simply *perceive* themselves as more responsible than their husbands for marital quality? On the basis of inferences from a number of studies and anecdotal evidence, it is tempting to conclude, with sociologist Jessie Bernard,[53] that women are indeed expected to assume a greater burden than men for maintaining their marriages. Perhaps this accounts for why American women rather consistently report being less satisfied with marriage than do men.

To make marriage equally satisfying for both women and men, changes are needed in societal and institutional structures as well as in individual orientations.[54] In an extensive review of literature on changing family roles and interactions, sociologist Maxine Szinovacz summarized the findings as follows:

> Women's increased participation in the labor force has lightened men's economic burden somewhat but not to the extent of shared responsibility. The new social norms stress autonomy and self-fulfillment for both sexes. However, men's greater resources and their societal dominant position enable them more than women to define relationships, rules, and obligations, and to use (or abuse) emerging societal norms of autonomy for their own interests rather than to the mutual advantage of all family members. Such on-sides application of autonomy standards is probably enhanced by women's increasing demands for equality and the resulting conflict and power struggles in intimate relationships. To achieve sex-role transcendence and true equality between the sexes, increased pressure must be exerted on social institutions and organizations to adapt to family needs, and men will have to be convinced (and prepared through socialization) that they can, indeed, profit from such changes.[55]

As America ages demographically, more attention is being given to older families.[56] In small nuclear families in the United States, spouses are expected to provide companionship and support throughout the later years. It appears that those couples who have vital and rewarding relationships earlier are the ones whose relationships continue to be satisfying into old age. Even changes accompanying retirement or illness do not necessarily decrease marital satisfaction. Here, too, however, gender differences can be seen. Some research has indicated that an employed wife with a retired husband experiences lower marital satisfaction than either a wife in a dual-retired situation or a wife who has retired first.[57] A study conducted in 1980 reported that women experience more difficulty with retirement than do men, stressing that understanding is necessary from the husbands as well.[58] When husband and wife support each other, research indicates that they will both be able to adjust to the inevitable changes that occur after retirement; however, further research is needed in this area, especially regarding gender differences.

Most Soviet studies have also concluded that wives are less satisfied with their marriages than are husbands, and the numbers of dissatisfied wives appear to be growing. Furthermore, the divergence in level of satisfaction between husbands and wives is greater in older than in younger families (a pattern found also in the United States). Once again, there is no single clear explanation for these results, particularly since reliable studies of marriage are lacking in the former USSR.

A study of 233 young couples in Moscow examined the relationship between reports of overall marital satisfaction and satisfaction with particular aspects of the lives of husbands and wives. For *husbands*, the major factors producing overall marital satisfaction were (in rank order): (1) satisfaction with wife's attitude toward husband; (2) satisfaction with sexual relations with wife; (3) satisfaction with job; (4) satisfaction with ways of spending free time; (5) satisfaction with the range of spouse's friends and acquaintances; and (6) satisfaction with the way decisions are made within the family. The major contributors to *wives'* overall marital satisfaction were (in rank order): (1) satisfaction with husband's attitude toward wife; (2) satisfaction with sexual relations with husband; (3) satisfaction with assistance spouse's parents provide in child care; (4) satisfaction with the way husband spends his free time; (5) satisfaction with housing conditions of family; and (6) satisfaction with distribution of household roles.[59]

What do these results imply? For both young husbands and young wives, satisfaction with the emotional and sexual relationship and manner of communication are of primary importance. But there are also gender differences. Young husbands find it important to be satisfied with their jobs and how they spend their free time. Family values are more significant for women—the upbringing of children and the way the husband spends his free time (answers focused primarily on husbands' staying home and helping the wives).

Additional Soviet research has reported that wife's satisfaction with marriage depends heavily upon the material resources of the family[60] and/or on the educational and social status of the husband.[61] A young wife wants her husband to be educated and to earn a substantial amount of money (remember that education and income are often unrelated in the former USSR), to help with child care, and to do housework. A Soviet man prefers his wife to be reasonably well educated (but not more so than himself), to have a wide range of interests, and simultaneously to be a good homemaker and loving mother. A study of spouses applying for help from a family consultant indicated that young wives had higher expectations of their husbands than husbands did of wives; at the same time, wives appraised their capacity to meet marital expectations more highly than did their husbands.[62]

Of particular interest are the changes in men's and women's satisfaction with marriage over the life span. One study in the mid-1980s examined a random sample of 200 married couples living in Moscow. Overall, satisfaction varied with the duration of the marriage, with women becoming progressively less satisfied than men. Couples married from twelve to eighteen years were least satisfied; after that, satisfaction rose again.[63] The researchers found that the most significant nonmarital variables affecting marital satisfaction were, first, the presence or absence of a child in the family (and his/her age); and, second, the nature of the spouses' employment and social life.

As for variables within the marriage itself, the longer the duration, the more spouses' involvement with each other *decreased*. However, the decrease occurred for different reasons and produced different experiences for husbands and wives. On the one hand, after women became mothers, their attitudes toward family roles became more traditional (a pattern identical to that in the United States). At the same time, women reported an increasing desire for both emotional and practical contact with their husbands as their children grew older. On the other hand, men reported *less* desire for such contact with their wives, as they too became more traditional in their orientation toward family roles. As a result of the interaction of these trends, marital satisfaction seemed to be determined primarily by wives' indulgence of their husbands' autonomy, in combination with the husbands' assessment of the way wives performed their family roles as companions and as mothers. After as little as five years of marriage, husbands began to detach from their wives, relating to them primarily as housekeepers and as passive "friends." This divergence between men and women during the childrearing years led to the lowest levels of satisfaction with marriage for both spouses, particularly women, as children entered adolescence. After nearly twenty years of married life, however, increased satisfaction was reported by both spouses. However, this appeared to occur at the expense of mutual involvement; husbands and wives now lived together but led separate lives.[64]

The Soviet sociologist S. I. Golod conducted a similar study of 260 couples in Leningrad (now St. Petersburg), with similar results. Golod interpreted his findings as a dialectical process of evolution in the marital relationship. During the early years of marriage, considerable adaptation is required of both spouses; then a sense of "companion-ship" becomes important to both spouses; finally, needs for autonomy arise in each spouse: "Until a certain moment of married life, this or that combination of adaptation or intimacy elements creates a favor-able situation, but then such a state in the development of an indi-vidual family is reached when it is not enough to be together; the resources of married life have been exhausted."[65] According to Golod, this autonomy need of the spouses helps ensure the permanency of the marriage by motivating each spouse to reach beyond the marriage. Unlike some other Soviet researchers, Golod has emphasized the *equal* need for autonomy by men and women. However, in reality husbands are less responsive to these needs on the part of their wives than vice versa—thereby setting the stage for women's satisfaction with marriage to decrease more substantially than men's. Golod's view of the need for autonomy to ensure marital success is intriguing. Are there, in fact, not other alternatives to marital longevity? Can a lasting balance of closeness and autonomy be achieved by *both* wives and husbands over the course of marriage? These questions reflect a need for greater understanding of marital dynamics, regardless of cultural context.

Extramarital Relations

The majority of adults in contemporary Western societies engage in courtship behaviors and eventually marry. Pairing activities typically occur with only one person at a time. Americans continue to report that they view marriage as a lifetime commitment, even though the high rate of divorce suggests a pattern of "serial polygamy."[66] Yet here, too, there are distinct gender differences. Despite the widely acclaimed "sexual revolution" of the past several decades—and some noticeable changes in the sexual behavior patterns of females in the United States—the "double standard" remains a reality with regard to extramarital sex. Men (both heterosexual and homosexual) engage in sexual activity outside of their primary relationships more often than women.[67] Even in Western Europe, where sexual standards are more permissive than in the United States, women are less likely than men to engage in extramarital intercourse and tend to perceive sexually open relationships more negatively then do men.[68]

Studies of premarital and extramarital sexual behaviors in the former USSR are almost nonexistent because the subject was "closed" to Soviet researchers until recently. Sociologist S. I. Golod observed a distinct pattern of transition in sexual behavior in the 1970s, noting that women's behavior seemed to be changing more than men's and that the changes were occurring more quickly in urban than in rural areas.[69]

Of course, patterns of extramarital sexual behavior, and attitudes toward it, vary greatly among the ethnocultural regions of the former USSR. In the republics of Central Asia where Islam dominates, one seldom comes across a man who would admit to his wife's having an affair, even if one were to occur. And, indeed, Muslim women are considerably less likely to engage in extramarital liaisons than their more European-oriented counterparts in the western regions. Muslim women also reject the idea of cohabitation before marriage, even with their husbands-to-be—a rather common occurrence in urban areas of Russia.

In Gurko's 1989 research on Moscow couples referred to earlier, only 11% of young husbands acknowledged that their wives had had extramarital relations, while 31% said that they themselves had had such liaisons. Wives' reports were more uniform: 18% admitted to their own extramarital liaisons and 16% to their husbands'.[70] These figures probably reflect some reporting biases—or perhaps husbands are better at keeping their affairs secret from their wives. Most likely, however, the dual standard of sexual behavior for men and women is still characteristic of Soviet culture.

Another study providing information on extramarital sexual relations was conducted in the early 1980s in Moscow.[71] Subjects (500 men and 200 women) were married individuals of varying ages who had applied to a clinic for treatment of skin diseases. About 60% of the men and 30% of the women reported being, or having been, involved in an extramarital affair—figures that are quite comparable to reports in the United States. Furthermore, the Soviet authors discovered certain patterns in sexual attitudes and behavior that also have been found by American researchers: Attitudes toward extramarital sex and the occurrence of actual extramarital relations were not highly correlated. About 20% of the Soviet respondents involved in extramarital liaisons could not justify them; in fact, some of those most strongly opposed to such relationships also engaged in them. In addition, respondents' involvement in extramarital relations was only partly related to satisfaction with their marriages. Forty-nine percent of the husbands and 21% of the wives reporting satisfactory marriages had nevertheless engaged in extramarital affairs.[72]

This study also tried to identify what led respondents to engage in extramarital relations. For men, the primary reasons were ranked as follows: sexual needs, long absence from wife, alcohol intoxication, love for the other woman, and curiosity. Only 10% of the husbands reported dissatisfaction with marital sex as a major reason for an affair. By contrast, sexual dissatisfaction in the marriage was reported by wives to be the most important reason for an extramarital relationship. In addition, wives gave such reasons as infatuation, frequent quarrels with husband, and need for tenderness. One of the researchers concluded that women involved in extramarital relations seek "first of all love."[73]

The longer the marriage, the greater the possibility of extramarital sexual experience. In both the former Soviet Union and the United States, the percentages of those involved in extramarital affairs rise with the duration of the marriage. In both countries, "adultery" is often given as a major reason for divorce by young spouses, while older spouses may tolerate extramarital involvements despite the resulting unhappiness when affairs are discovered. Soviet women, like American women, are more likely than their husbands to remain in a marriage in which the spouse has engaged in extramarital sex. Here, too, is evidence of a double standard accepted by women as well as men: Extramarital relations are more expected of men than of women—and therefore may be more tolerated.

Chapter 4 of this book covers the subject of sexual behavior in more detail. Here, we simply conclude with a comment about research on extramarital relations: One must differentiate explicitly between males and females, as well as between attitudes and behaviors, before drawing any conclusions.[74] Clearly, gender is a key variable in our understanding of this phenomenon.

GENDER ISSUES IN THE FAMILY

Childrearing

Despite a great deal of rhetoric about American men and women sharing family roles, most American men are still resistant to regular involvement in housework and child care. A noted family researcher considers this a form of ambivalence, and she hypothesizes that it arises from fear that becoming more emotionally and verbally expressive may make men more vulnerable in the highly competitive American workplace.[75] This ambivalence has been documented by the eminent sociologist Mira Komarovsky,[76] who found that many young men were torn between the emerging values of gender equality and an internalized need to feel dominant over women. At the same time, many young women clearly expect changes in the traditional mode of marriage. The statement of one college student is illustrative:

> My parents have a good marriage, but it's rather traditional. My mother cooks my father a separate dinner—she makes chicken for the kids, but my father hates chicken and won't eat it, so she cooks him a steak separately. . . . My mother doesn't think twice about it, but when I see it I think about it for myself. I wouldn't want my husband to act that way. My father is spoiled and somewhat of a big baby. . . . I would expect equality in the domestic tasks. . . . My father never cooks and insists that my mother cook special meals for him. I would want my husband to share in the cooking and cleaning up afterward.[77]

In Komarovsky's view, the equality that young women seek in marital relationships cannot be realized by the vast majority as long as society maintains gender role segregation within marriage and offers no real alternatives. She has summarized her study of changing male and female roles as follows:

> We have been trapped on the horns of false dilemmas by the traditional stereotypes of femininity and masculinity. If men continue to be socialized to suppress emotional expressiveness at the threat of appearing "sissified", they will be deprived of the capacity for emotional intimacy. If women are made to feel that self-confidence and ambition to succeed in work are "abrasive" and "castrating", they will continue to fail to develop their full human potential. . . . The changes in psychological sex stereotypes will continue to be resistant to change as long as society maintains the traditional ideology concerning role segregation of the sexes within the family. Such changes are needed for many reasons, including the huge increase in the proportion of working mothers that generally places upon women the triple burden of working, child rearing, and homemaking.[78]

Komarovsky has called for a variety of social changes that will reduce this dilemma and ease the nearly intolerable workloads of many American women. She notes that these gains for women need not come at the total expense of men. Her own research and that of others has found that the most poignant regrets expressed by many men about family relationships have to do with their experience of distance from their fathers.[79] Many young people in the United States, particularly young women, envision a society in which the fathers are involved in childrearing and in which the demands of work and family life are balanced by institutional reorganization and social innovations. This call for increased participation of males in family life is echoed in the former Soviet Union.

Contemporary child care patterns in the former Soviet Union reflect a number of social influences. Women usually stay home to care for newborns until they are from eighteen months to two years old. After that, children are typically placed in a child care center, or they are cared for by relatives helping the mothers, who continue to juggle their household and employment responsibilities. Naturally, working mothers (most Soviet women) would appreciate child care help from their husbands, particularly in families where there is more than one child.

How great is the actual participation of Soviet fathers? In western, European-oriented parts of the former Soviet Union, fathers are fairly often involved *with their wives* in playing with, or caring for, the children. However, very few fathers take on this role alone. A study of 233 young Moscow families with children[80] showed that, individually, fathers were the providers of child care even less often than the grandparents (see Table 2.5).

Some researchers have concluded that spousal cooperation in childrearing is a major contributor to the stability of Soviet marriages. Child care is typically valued much more highly by Soviet wives than is husbands' help with daily household tasks. Both husbands and wives agree that unsatisfactory parenting by fathers contributes strongly to the development of family problems.[81] Ironically, however, Soviet women sometimes express greater dissatisfaction with the lack of sufficient help in childrearing from their husbands' *parents* than from their husbands. This expectation is understandable, given the significant degree of involvement of grandparents in childrearing throughout the former Soviet Union (see Chapter 5). Due either to extended family traditions (more prominent in central Asia and the eastern regions)

TABLE 2.5. Participation in Playing with and Caring for Children (in Percentages)

	Husband performs	Wife performs	Both spouses perform	Mostly spouses' parents perform	No response
Playing with a child	5.9	17.6	69.2	4.8	2.5
Child care	1.0	45.2	47.9	3.2	2.7

or to the recognition that public day care facilities are inadequate (more prominent in Russia and the western regions), grandparents—including grandfathers—are likely to be heavily involved in child care at some point, particularly in those families of lower socioeconomic status (a pattern similar to that of African-American families in the United States).[82]

One study of Muscovite parents and adolescents found that mothers interacted with their teenage children more often than fathers did in all areas of life except providing help with homework (see Table 2.6). The same study revealed that fathers discussed career choices with their sons more often than with their daughters, but that such career discussions still occurred more often between the teenagers and their mothers without the involvement of fathers.[83]

Overall, then, Soviet children have more contact with mothers than with fathers, and they report being closer to their mothers than their fathers throughout childhood and adolescence. Although most Soviet women have been involved in socially productive employment for many years, very few men are comparably involved in childrearing. The reasons for this are complex, and they are probably similar to the factors that prevent American fathers from participating more fully in family life.

Under the old Soviet regime, social policy focused most attention on the mother's role in childrearing. Women received official child allowances and employment benefits that facilitated child care. In addition, employed women were also given certain informal privileges. For example, married men were required more often than married women to work overtime or to engage in employment-related social activities. Furthermore, women worked mostly in those occupations where the work day did not exceed 6 hours or where hours were not fixed. (Whether the new political order will result in any changes in these policies remains to be seen.) Finally, the attitudes of both genders continue to support a distinction in the family responsibilities of women and men.

Some of the reasons for men's lack of involvement in childrearing may also be specific to the Soviet situation. Sociologist I. S. Kon has emphasized that historical records from the traditions of virtually all Soviet peoples indicate minimal involvement of men in the raising of children, other than those activities directly related to teaching children (usually boys) useful skills of farming or the trades.[84] Yet this situation is very similar to that of the United States. Other than teaching their skills to the children who followed them into the world of work, have American fathers ever participated fully in the care and rearing of their children? One factor that *is* perhaps unique to the Soviet situation is the loss of so many men in fighting before and during World

TABLE 2.6. Participation in Interaction with Teenagers (in Percentages)

Sphere of interaction between a parent and a teenager	Husband		Wife		Both spouses		Other relatives or acquaintances	
	Husband response	Wife response	Husband response	Wife response	Husband response	Wife response		
Who has more authority?	15.9	13.2	21.0	26.3	31.0	31.3	33.0	29.5
Whom does a teenager turn to for support and sympathy?	9.4	6.3	33.9	49.2	43.3	33.5	13.4	11
Teenager's frankness: "tells me almost everything that is important and interesting to him"	27.6	24.8	49.2	55.8	—	—	—	—
Usually helps a teenager to do his homework	51.4	—	—	38.9	—	—	—	—
With whom does a teenager usually discuss . . .								
His studies?	48.3	—	—	87.5	—	—	—	—
His relations with his friends?	27.9	—	—	78.1	—	—	—	—
What he does in his spare time?	39.5	—	—	79.9	—	—	—	—
Choice of profession?	47.3	—	—	88.7	—	—	—	—

Source: Unpublished study of 319 families with adolescent children by Institute of Sociology, USSR Academy of Sciences, 1980.
Note. More than one response given to most questions.

War II. Many of today's husbands were raised without any regular contact with an adult male in the home; small wonder, then, that they neither expect nor know how to function effectively as fathers.

After retiring on a pension, reorientation to family activity occurs among both men and women in many parts of the Soviet Union. The results of a 1978 study of pensioners conducted by the Institute of Gerontology in Kiev (Ukraine) found that 49% of women and 40% of men reported taking an active part in bringing up their grandchildren. This involvement was not necessarily based upon what these elderly people wished to do, but what their children expected of them.[85]

Household Work

Studies of household work in American marriages are discouragingly consistent: Women carry the major burden of household responsibility, even if they are employed full-time. In fact, employed women spend only slightly less time in housework, meal preparation, and child care than do full-time homemakers.[86] To help facilitate changes in these patterns, research needs to focus on the advantages for men of participating more fully in family work. For example, in a 1989 study of married couples, John Gottman found that men who do housework are physically healthier than men who do not. He explained this by speculating that husbands who withdraw and "stonewall" their wives about household issues internalize stress more than those who communicate, rationally resolve conflict, and negotiate a compromise solution. The latter are the men who are more likely to participate in housework.[87]

Work inequality between Soviet men and women differs from that of Americans in several ways. First of all, Soviet women are employed full-time nearly as often as men. They work out of necessity, since very few Soviet men can financially support a family on a single income (an economic reality that is increasing in the United States as well). Women cannot obtain a retirement pension unless they engage in some kind of work, and most Soviet women can expect to outlive their husbands. Therefore, Soviet women have virtually no time to devote to their children, to pursue their own interests, or to spend in leisure activities. Of course, many Soviet women desire to work. Over the past seventy-five years, regular employment of women came to be a cultural norm in much of the former USSR. However, as we have indicated, the Soviet culture also presumes that the *household* is primarily the concern and responsibility of women. Thus, the stage is set for stress and conflict between the genders in relation to work—both in the labor market and in the home. Without equity in the division of household responsibilities, equal opportunities for women in the realm of employment are difficult to obtain. Here, of course, the situation in our two societies is similar.[88]

The urbanization of the former Soviet Union is sometimes thought to account for much of this problem. In cities as opposed to rural farms, men are particularly unable to use the skills they have been socialized to believe are connected with "hard, masculine" jobs. This encourages men to physically remove themselves from their homes because they believe that there is "nothing to do." We remind the reader that virtually all urban Soviet families live in rented "flats," or apartments, whose maintenance (what there is of it) is centrally controlled. Furthermore, few materials are available for home "remodeling," or even necessary repairs, so that these contributions to the household are blocked for all but the most highly motivated and enterprising of men. Naturally, this contributes to alienating men from their families. Father absence, which we have described earlier, can be interpreted as "exploiting" an overworked wife; however, the reverse is also true. Husbands are exploited by an economic system that does not permit a man, on the one hand, to earn enough money to ease the employment requirements of his wife, or, on the other hand, to contribute meaningfully to family life by making the necessary time and materials available to him.

In Russia and the western republics, men claim to take seriously the idea of women's equality. By this, they typically mean that they support their wives' having careers. At the same time, many of these men would like their wives to be employed less outside the home; however, they see no way to alter the situation under current societal circumstances. And an increasing number of women report that *they* would like to be able to work less outside the home and to devote more time to childrearing and household tasks. For the foreseeable future, the economic instability of the former Soviet Union is unlikely to permit a large-scale reorganization of employment patterns that could ease these gender-linked problems.

Despite many differences between Soviet and American societies, both appear to have an abundance of overworked women. Regardless of political ideology over the past seventy-five years, our cultures have come to expect women to be responsible for marriage and family life, as well as to become income earners in the outside world. No such dual role expectations have been placed upon men—although signs of such expectations are beginning to occur in the United States. Does this situation account for women's diminished satisfaction with marriage? Will more and more women in the future see fewer and fewer reasons to get married or stay married? Will homes come to be seen not as "havens," but as sources of more work and stress for most women, and perhaps also for men? Clearly, the answers to these questions will have an enormous impact upon the character of family life in the future in both our societies. Additional discussion of the relationship of household work and employment outside the home can be found in Chapter 6.

Family Violence

The family cannot be a "haven" for either gender if than the misuse of power by stronger members (usually men) leads to the exploitation or abuse of those with less power (typically women, children, or the elderly). Family violence has come to be recognized as a major problem in large, industrialized countries. Indeed, domestic abuse may be characteristic of many cultures of the world, linked as it is to conflicts between the genders.

In the United States over the past twenty-five years, family violence has emerged as a major social problem. Many marital conflicts involve physical assault by either or both parties, and significant numbers of wives are regularly battered by their husbands. A growing number of women are revealing circumstances under which they have been physically forced or psychologically coerced to have sexual contact with their husbands, boyfriends, or even casual dates. Numerous children have been found to be physically beaten by one or both parents, with injuries far beyond anything that could be thought to be reasonably associated with "discipline." A startling number of children have been discovered who have been sexually abused, often by members of their own household or extended family. Feeble or invalid elders have been starved, beaten, confined, or tortured by their adult children or other family members. A considerable amount of research has been conducted on these phenomena, and they are now widely written about in both professional and popular publications. Physical and sexual abuse of women, children, and the elderly are now open topics of discussion in much of the public media, although controversy still exists over the exact nature and extent of such experiences.

Most disturbing of all is the recognition that the family is so often the context for violence, and, in some sense, a mechanism for the transmission of violence and abuse within the context of the larger society. The following are some sample statistics from the United States in the 1980s:[90]

- Battering is the leading cause of injury to women in the United States; on the average of every fifteen seconds, a woman is beaten by her husband or boyfriend.

- In 1986, 30% of female homicide victims were killed by husbands, exhusbands, or boyfriends.
- Fifty-three percent of battering husbands abused their children.
- There are over 1,200 battered women shelters and safe-home programs in the United States. In 1987, over 375,000 women and children were served by these programs.
- Twenty percent of all adult women are raped during their lifetimes; in 75% of these assaults, the rapists are known to the women, and a high percentage of these are relatives, boyfriends, or dates.
- Four out of five women murdered are murdered at home.
- Research from 1978 to 1988 show us that battered women who leave husbands are 75% more at risk for being murdered than battered women who stay.
- One out of 4 female suicides is a victim of battering (this figure is double for black women).
- A woman is more likely to be assaulted, injured, raped or killed by a male partner than by any other assailant.

On a more hopeful note, national surveys were conducted in 1975 and again in 1985 to determine rates of family violence in the United States. While the numbers of women and children beaten remained high, the studies found a slight decline over the ten-year period. Researchers guardedly concluded that people are beginning to understand that violence in families is dysfunctional. Changes in both attitudes and behavior are beginning to occur in the United States.[91]

The empirical documentation of domestic violence is giving direction to much-needed intervention programs and policy changes. However, more research is needed before we will fully understand the underlying motivations and influences that promote these troubling behaviors. In a major review of the scholarly literature, Richard Gelles and Jon Conte point out the complexity of patterns for transmitting abuse in families from generation to generation:

> Evidence from studies of parental and marital violence indicate that while experiencing violence in one's family of origin is often correlated with later violent behavior, such experience is not the sole determining factor. Moreover, the forces by which violence is transferred from one generation to the next is more complex than simple modeling of behavior. When the cycle of violence occurs, it is likely the result of a complex set of social and psychological processes.[92]

Clearly, gender plays a key role in the dynamics of family violence. Indeed, differential socialization patterns of the genders, along with a lack of recognized power for women in societal institutions, may serve to set the stage for the kinds of conflict patterns that promote violence and abuse (see Chapters 4, 5, and 6 for further discussion of these issues). Fueled largely by feminist scholars and writers, research on gender dynamics associated with violence is rapidly growing in the United States.[93] Research is also needed to assess the outcomes of social interventions into family violence (e.g., arrests of offenders, changes in laws and public policies), along with evaluating the outcomes of family therapy and the effectiveness of re-education about male and female relationships in the family.

In the former USSR, family violence has not yet been studied objectively. The primary reason for this under the Soviet regime was official prohibition of such discussions, rather than a lack of scientific interest. We can infer the extent of Soviet family violence only from general crime statistics—that is, those extreme situations when violence within a family has led to an officially recorded offense or demographic statistic. For example, according to the Ministry for Internal Affairs, 65,000 Russian teenagers left home in 1990. The reasons for leaving home given by these adolescents were a family's "unsatisfactory" living conditions, "conflicts" between parents, parental alcoholism, and "unsatisfactory" relations between teenagers and parents. Undoubtedly, many of these answers imply violence and abuse within the families. A significant number of such female runaways become prostitutes, while the boys become thieves.[94]

Overall family-related crime statistics for the former Soviet Union or even the Russian Federation are not available. From the Moscow Criminal Investigation Department Information Center, we obtained statistics on family crimes for the 1982–1986 period. The reported figures for criminal behaviors are undoubtedly lower than the actual occurrences of such behaviors, since (as in the United States) family members are much less likely to notify the police than are other victims of violence—and the actual prosecution of offenders by family members is even lower. A total of 1,287 crimes involving family members were reported in Moscow in 1986.[95] Current or ex-husbands are responsible for most of the violence—divorcing and divorced spouses often continue to live together because of the extreme scarcity of housing. Wives are sometimes reported for violence, as are other family members, including in-laws.

The only full-scale research on family violence published to date was conducted by V. M. Kormstchikov with families in the Ural region during the mid-1980s. Kormstchikov studied teenagers who had been charged with some sort of criminal offense. Interviews revealed that most of these adolescents were members of what they reported to be "unhappy" families. The parents were described as criminal offenders themselves, often alcoholic, and frequently involved in extramarital affairs. Forty-three percent of the teenagers reported having been present during their parents' quarrels, and noted that they either were turned out of the house or ran away; 19% of those interviewed indicated that this occurred "regularly." In addition, about 20% of the adolescents suffered from neglect, deprived of food and clothing.[96] This limited research and the anedotal evidence available do not permit us to generalize about the level of family violence in the former Soviet Union. However, on the basis of these indications and of what we know about the problem in American and European families, additional research efforts are certainly warranted.

CONCLUSION

In our view, the widespread ethnic and regional strife in the former USSR may have served to mask the most important conflict of all—the struggle between men and women. Serious research and concentrated efforts are needed in both societies in order to make the relationship between the genders a secure and trusting alliance, both in the workplace and in the family.

The American sociologist William Goode has hypothesized that men will resist sex role changes in marriage until they can see the advantages for themselves in egalitarian relationships.[97] New approaches to marital research have begun to document these gains for both genders as roles become more flexible and shared in marriage. Maxine Szinovacz states that the "major issue in the achievement of egalitarian relations is not the pursuit of autonomy and personal self-fulfillment, but spouses' willingness and ability to negotiate and implement mutually satisfactory arrangements."[98] What this means is that husbands and wives will have a fuller relationship if they work together and communicate—even when they disagree. Living separate lives within marriage is not a real marriage.

NOTES

1. M. Osmond and B. Thorne, "Feminist Theories: The Social Construction of Gender in Families and Society," in P. Boss, W. J. Doherty, R. La Rossa, S. Steinmetz, and W. Schum (eds.), *Sourcebook of Family Theories and Methods: A Conceptual Approach* (New York: Plenum Press, 1993).

2. For a full review of relevant legislative and political issues, see J. Hoff-

Wilson, "The Unfinished Revolution: Changing Legal Status of U.S. Women," *Signs*, *13*(1) (1987), 7–36.

3. Osmond and Thorne, *op. cit.*

4. W. *Williams*, "The Equality Crisis: Some Reflections on Culture, Courts and Feminism," *Women's Rights Law Reporter*, 7 (1982), 200.

5. Office of Finances and Statistics, *Women in the USSR* (Moscow: USSR Government Publications, 1988), 30.

6. O. A. Voronina, "A Woman in a Men's Society," *Sotsiologisheskie Issledovaniya*, No. 2 (1988), 104–106.

7. Office of Finances and Statistics, *op. cit.*, 26.

8. T. Parsons and R. F. Bales, *Family, Socialization, and Interaction Process* (New York: Free Press, 1955).

9. See H. P. McAdoo (ed.), *Black Families* (Beverly Hills, CA: Sage, 1981); B. Thorne and M. Yalom (eds.), *Rethinking the Family* (New York: Longman, 1982).

10. J. Bernard, *The Future of Marriage* (New York: World Press, 1972).

11. See A. G. Kharchev and M. S. Matzkovsky, *Modern Family and Its Problems* (Moscow: Statistitka, 1978); V. I. Prevedentzev, *Young Family Today* (Moscow: Znaniye, 1987); Z. A. Yankova, *The Urban Family* (Moscow: Nauka, 1979); and others.

12. O. B. Bozhkov and V. B. Goldfast, "Division of Labor in an Urban Family," *Obshestvenniye Nauki*, 4 (1986), 71.

13. In the European part of the Soviet Union, the figures are even lower. See, e.g., V. Kostakov, "Basic Trends and Problems of Population and Occupation," in L. L. Ribakovsky (ed.), *USSR Population for 70 Years* (Moscow: Nauka, 1988), 195.

14. *Ibid.*

15. A. G. Kharchev, "Family Studies: On the Threshold of a New Stage," *Sotsiologisheskie Issledovaniya* (1986), 33. See also A. I. Antonov, "Possibilities and Ways of Enhancing the Social Potential of a Family," in A. I. Antonov (ed.) *Social Potential of a Family* (Moscow: Myls, 1988), 26, 29.

16. At the same time, it has been suggested that at least some government officials may want women to return to homemaking, largely as a means to achieve full employment of males.

17. M. S. Toltz, "Evolution of Marriage and Birth Rates in the Soviet Period," in L. L. Ribakovsky (ed.), *USSR Population for 70 Years* (Moscow: Nauka, 1988), 80; M. S. Toltz, "Fate on Scales of Demography," in T. A. Gurko (ed), *Marriage Ties, Freedom Ties* (Moscow: Molodaya Gvardia, 1990), 6.

18. P. Glick, "Marriage and Family Trends," in D. H. Olson and M. K. Hanson (eds.), *2001: Preparing Families for the Future* (Minneapolis: National Council on Family Relations, 1990), 2.

19. This has especially been the case in Russia, Byelorussia (now Belarus), and Ukraine; see Toltz, 1988, *op. cit.*, 55, 59. Soviet demographers have identified several types of marriage in the former USSR by age at first marriage, age differences between bride and groom, and age at termination of celibacy. See M. S. Toltz, "Modern Problems of Demographic Typology of Marriage," in M. S. Matskovsky and T. A. Gurko (eds.), *Formation of Marital/Family Rela-*

tions (Moscow: Institute of Sociology, Soviet Academy of Sciences, 1989). In the former USSR in general, irrespective of regional differences, the proportion of never-married individuals aged forty to forty-nine in 1979 was 2% for men and 4% for women (Toltz, 1988, *op. cit.*). In 1989, among Russians in this same age group, the never married comprised 3.2% of the men and 3.3% of the women (Toltz, 1990, *op. cit.*). In the United States, by contrast, the share of forty-year-old persons who had never married increased sharply from 12% in 1960 to 28% in 1988 (Glick, *op. cit.*).

20. Office of Finances and Statistics, *op. cit.*, 16.

21. R. I. Muksinov, "Social Status of a Woman and Her Self-Perception," in E. Tiit (ed.), *Problems of Family Functioning* (Tartu: Tartu State University, 1988), 77.

22. Toltz, 1990, *op. cit.*, 91.

23. T. A. Gurko, "Formation of a Young Family in the Big City: Conditions and Factors of Stability," unpublished doctoral dissertation, Institute of Sociology, Soviet Academy of Sciences (Moscow, 1984).

24. T. A. Gurko, "Emergence of a Young Family in a Large City: Conditions and Factors of Stability," abstract of doctoral dissertation, Institute of Sociology, Soviet Academy of Sciences (Moscow, 1983), 14.

25. S. I. Golod, *Family Stability: Sociological and Demographic Aspects* (Leningrad: Nauka, 1984), 26; Gurko, 1983, *op. cit.*, 14.

26. T. A. Gurko, "Effect of Premarital Behavior on Stability of a Young Family," *Obshestvenniye Nauki*, 2 (1982).

27. T. A. Gurko, "Role Expectations of Young Spouses in Various Types of Families by an Educational Index," *Sotsiologisheskie Issledovaniya* (1990).

28. Gurko, 1983, *op. cit.*

29. Comparison by T. A. Gurko, unpublished (1989), using data from M. Y. Arutunyan, "Division of Duties within a Family and Spousal Relations," in M. S. Matskovsky (ed.), *Family and Social Structure* (Moscow: Institute of Sociology, Soviet Academy of Sciences, 1987), 56.

30. E. Haavio-Manila and E. Rannik, "Family Life, Labor, and Leisure in Finland and Estonia," in A. G. Kharchev and E. P. Roos (eds.), *Sociology and Social Practice* (Moscow: USSR Academy of Sciences, 1988).

31. The data were collected in a pilot study in Uzbekistan by T. A. Gurko, results unpublished.

32. Arutunyan, *op. cit.*, 68.

33. A. Allen and T. Thompson, "Agreement, Understanding, Realization, and Feeling Understood as Predictors of Communicative Satisfaction in Marital Dyads," *Journal of Marriage and the Family*, 46 (1984), 915–922.

34. *Ibid.*, 920.

35. See, e.g., discussions in D. Tannen, *You Just Don't Understand: Women and Men in Conversation* (New York: Ballantine Books, 1990); L. B. Rubin, *Intimate Strangers: Men and Women Together* (New York: Harper and Row, 1983).

36. T. A. Gurko, "Satisfaction with Marriage as an Index of Spousal Relations," in M. S. Matskovsky (ed.), *Family and Social Structure* (Moscow: Institute of Sociology, Soviet Academy of Sciences, 1987).

37. N. N. Obozov, *Interpersonal Relations* (Leningrad: Nauka, 1979).

38. Quoted in R. N. Bellah, R. Madsen, W. M. Sullivan, A. Swidler, and S. M. Tipton, *Habits of the Heart: Individualism and Commitment in American Life* (New York: Harper and Row/Perennial Library, 1985).

39. C. Lasch, *Haven in a Heartless World* (New York: Basic Books, 1977).

40. P. Blumstein and P. Schwartz, *American Couples* (New York: William Morrow, 1983), 56.

41. *ibid.*

42. M. E. Szinovacz, "Changing Family Roles and Interactions," *Marriage and Family Review*, 7 (1984), 163–201.

43. Gurko, 1984, *op. cit.*

44. Unpublished data by T. A. Gurko from a pilot study in Tashkent in 1990 and a study of 233 young couples in Moscow in 1989.

45. A. Kelam, "Structure and Functions of a Family," in V. Pilter (ed.), *Female Labor and the Family* (Tallinn: ESSR Academy of Sciences, 1978).

46. F. Gray, *Soviet Women: Walking the Tightrope* (Garden City, NY: Doubleday, 1990).

47. See, e.g., G. W. McDonald, "Family Power: The Assessment of a Decade of Theory and Research," *Journal of Marriage and the Family*, 42(4) (1980), 841–854.

48. Szinovacz, 1984, *op. cit.*, 178; R. O. Blood and D. M. Wolfe, *Husbands and Wives* (New York: Free Press, 1960); R. Centers, B. H. Raven, and A. Rodrigues, "Conjugal Power Structure: A Reexamination," *American Sociological Review*, 36 (1971), 264–278; D. B. Kandel and G. S. Lesser, "Marital Decision-Making in American and Danish Families: A Research Note," *Journal of Marriage and the Family*, 34 (1972), 134–138; O. D. Duncan, H. Schuman, and B. Duncan, *Social Change in a Metropolitan Community* (New York: Russell Sage Foundation, 1973); S. L. Hesselbart, "Does Charity Begin at Home? Attitudes toward Women, Household Tasks, and Household Decisionmaking," paper presented at the annual meeting of the American Sociological Association (New York, 1976).

49. Szinovacz, 1984, *op. cit.*

50. See, e.g., J. Verhoff, E. Douvan, and R. A. Kulka, *The Inner American: A Self-Portrait from 1957 to 1976* (New York: Basic Books, 1981), 147.

51. R. A. Bell, J. A. Daly, and M. C. Gonzalez, "Affinity Maintenance in Marriage and Its Relationship to Women's Marital Satisfaction," *Journal of Marriage and the Family*, 49 (1987), 451.

52. W. Ickes (ed.), *Compatible and Incompatible Relationships* (New York: Springer-Verlag, 1985); B. M. Montgomery, "The Form and Function of Quality Communication in Marriage," *Family Process*, 39 (1981), 21–30.

53. Bernard, *op. cit.*

54. Szinovacz, 1984, *op. cit.*; J. Pleck, "The Work-Family System," *Social Problems*, 24, 417–427; J. Pleck, *Working Wives/Working Husbands*, (Beverly Hills, CA: Sage, 1985); J. Pleck, "American Fathering in Historical Perspective," in M. Kimmel (ed.), *Changing Men*, (Newbury Park, CA: Sage, 1987).

55. Szinovacz, 1984, *op. cit.*, 189.

56. T. H. Brubaker, *Later Life Families* (Beverly Hills, CA: Sage, 1990).

57. *Ibid.*; G. R. Lee and C. L. Shehan, "Retirement and Marital Satisfaction," *Journal of Gerontology, 44* (1989), 226–230.

58. M. Szinovacz, "Family Power Relations and Processes," in M. B. Sussman and S. Steinmetz (eds.), *Handbook of Marriage and the Family* (New York: Plenum Press, 1987).

59. T. A. Gurko, unpublished data (1989).
Contributors to marital satisfaction of husbands
Satisfaction with spouses' attitude ($r = 0.61$)
Satisfaction with sexual relations with wife ($r = 0.49$)
Satisfaction with one's job ($r = 0.48$)
Satisfaction with the way of spending free time ($r = 0.47$)
Satisfaction with the range of spouse's friends and acquaintances ($r = 0.42$)
Satisfaction with the way decisions are made within family ($r = 0.41$)

Contributors to Marital Satisfaction of Wives
Satisfaction with husband's attitude ($r = 0.5$)
Satisfaction with sexual relations with husband ($r = 0.43$)
Satisfaction with assistance spouse's parents provide in child care ($r = 0.42$)
Satisfaction with the way husband spends his free time ($r = 0.40$)
Satisfaction with housing conditions of family ($r = 0.37$)
Satisfaction with distribution of household roles ($r = 0.33$)

60. I. Zarinsh, "Satisfaction with Marriage and Factors of Potential Stability of a Family," in I. K. Kirkovsky (ed.), *Factors and Motives of Demographic Behavior* (Riga: Zinatne, 1984).

61. D. Kutsar, "Marriage Quality in Terms of Personality and Its Determinants," in E. Tiit (ed.), *Problems of Spouses' Personalities and Quality of Family Life* (Tartu: Tartu State University, 1984), 63.

62. O. E. Zuskova, "Emergence of a Family and Development of a Personality," In *Formation of Marital/Family Relations* (Moscow: Institute of Sociology, USSR Academy of Sciences, 1989).

63. L. Y. Gozman and Y. A. Aleshin, "Contacts and Development of Spousal Relations," in G. A. Andreeva and Y. Yanoushek (eds.), *Communication and Optimization of Joint Activities* (Moscow: Moscow State University, 1987).

64. *Ibid.*

65. Golod, 1984, *op. cit.*, 82.

66. Blumstein and Schwartz, *op. cit.*

67. *Ibid.*, 303; See also I. L. Reiss, *Family Systems in America*, 3rd ed. (New York: Holt, Rinehart and Winston, 1980).

68. B. Buunk, "Extramarital Sex in the Netherlands," *Alternative Lifestyles, 3* (1980), 11–39; B. Buunk, "Jealousy in Sexually Open Marriages," *Alternative Lifestyles, 4* (1981), 357–372.

69. S. I. Golod, "Prostitution in a Context of Changing Sexual Morals," *Sotsiologisheskie Issledovaniya, 2* (1988), 68.

70. Gurko, 1990, *op. cit.*, 62.

71. T. V. Vasiljev, O. K. Loseva, and Y. F. Safro, "Marriage Stability of Syphilis-Infected Persons," *Biulleten Dermatologii e Venerologii, 8* (1982), 30.

72. *Ibid.*, 32.

73. O. K. Loseva, "Sex? Not Only, But . . ." In T. A. Gurko (ed.), *Fate on Scales of Demography: Marriage Ties, Freedom Ties* (Moscow: Molodaya Gvardia, 1990), 150.

74. J. M. Saunders and J. N. Edwards, "Extramarital Sexuality: A Predictive Model of Permissive Attitudes," *Journal of Marriage and the Family, 46*(4) (1984), 833.

75. A. Skolnick, *The Intimate Environment*, 5th ed. (Boston: Little, Brown, 1992); A. Skolnick, *Embattled Paradise: The American Family in an Age of Uncertainty* (New York: Basic Books, 1991).

76. M. Komarovsky, *Women in College: Shaping New Feminine Identities* (New York: Basic Books, 1985).

77. Quoted in *Ibid.*, 149.

78. *Ibid.*, 316.

79. M. Komarovsky, *Dilemnas of Masculinity: A Study of College Youth* (New York: Norton, 1976); Komarovsky, 1985, *op. cit.*

80. T. A. Gurko, unpublished data (1989) There were no significant differences between the responses of husbands and wives.

81. A. Keyerberg, "Man's Role in Carrying Out Routine Family Activities," in *Problems of Family Functioning* (Tartu: TGU, 1988), 68; Yankova, *op. cit.*, 108; Zuskova, *op. cit.*, 82.

82. L. Burton, "Black Grandparents Rearing Children of Drug-Addicted Parents," *The Gerontologist*, 32, (1992), 744–751; L. Burton and P. Dilworth-Anderson, "The Intergenerational Family Roles of Aged Black Americans," *Marriage and Family Review*, 16, 311–330; G. Lesnoff-Caravaglia, "The Black Granny and the Soviet Babushka: Commonalities and Contrasts," in R. Manuel (ed.), *Minority Aging: Social and Psychological Issues* (Westport, CT: Greenwood Press, 1982), 109–114.

83. N. G. Aristova, "Socialization of a New Generation," M. S. Matskovsky (ed.), in *Family and Social Structure* (Moscow: Institute of Sociology, Soviet Academy of Sciences, 1987), 110.

84. I. S. Kon, *Child and Society* (Moscow: Nauka, 1988), 231–233.

85. N. V. Panina and N. N. Sachuk, "The Older Generation in a Family," in A. G. Kharchev (ed.), *Family and Society* (Moscow: Nauka, 1982), 49–50. The subjects were men and women of prepensionable age (59 for men, 54 for women). Interviews were conducted in two units: a hospital and an industrial establishment.

86. See, e.g., A. Hochschild, *The Second Shift: Working Parents and the Revolution at Home* (New York: Viking Press, 1989).

87. J. Gottman, "Predicting the Longitudinal Course of Marriages," *Journal of Marriage and Family Therapy, 17*(1) (1991), 3–7.

88. F. du Plessix Gray, *Soviet Women: Walking the Tightrope* (New York: Doubleday, 1989), 181–197.

89. These issues appear in virtually every chapter of T. Mamonova (ed.), *Women and Russia* (London: Basil Blackwell, 1984). Also, see T. Momonova, "Meanwhile, Back in the USSR," *MS.* (July/August, 1990), p. 42.

90. Gathered from various government agencies throughout the United States, these statistics were reported in a special publication: Minnesota Women's Fund, *Everyday Fear: A Systemic Analysis of Violence Against Women* (St. Paul, 1993).

91. M. A. Strauss and R. J. Gelles, "Societal Change in Family Violence from 1975 to 1985 as Revealed by Two National Surveys," *Journal of Marriage and the Family, 48* (1986), 465–479.

92. R. J. Gelles and J. R. Conte, "Domestic Violence and Sexual Abuse of Children: A Review of Research in the Eighties," *Journal of Marriage and Family Therapy, 52*(4) (1990), 1047.

93. M. Bograd, "Values in Conflict: Challenge to Family Therapists' Thinking," *Journal of Marriage and Family Therapy, 18* (1992), 245–256.

94. G. Bochkarev, "Russian Girls," *Trud* (August 9, 1990), 4.

95. This Statistic and the following breakdown were provided to Gurko by the Moscow Criminal Investigation Department: 67 premeditated murders, 32 attempts on a child's life, 8 incestuous rapes, 134 assaults involving "severe" physical injury, 66 assaults involving "less severe" physical injury, 909 acts of vandalsim, 10 "depraved" (sexual) acts, 61 threats of murder. We believe that these statistics represent severe underreporting. In addition, crime rates in large Russian cities have risen sharply each year since the dissolution of the Soviet Union.

96. V. M. Kormstchikov, *Criminology of Unfortunate Families* (Perm: Perm State University, 1987), 41, 50.

97. W. J. Goode, "Why Men Resist," in B. Thorne and M. Yalom (eds.), *Rethinking the Family* (New York: Longman, 1982).

98. Szinovacz, 1984, *op. cit.*, 189.

Chapter 3

Divorce and Its Aftermath

William J. Doherty
M. Janice Hogan
Ekaterina V. Foteeva
Galina A. Zaikina

INTRODUCTION

When people in Soviet and American societies talk about the deterioration of modern family life, they are often expressing concerns about divorce and its aftermath. Among all countries in the world, the United States and the former USSR have ranked first and second, respectively, in rates of divorce.[1] These high rates of divorce have led some to doubt the survival of marriage as an institution and to question the permanence of ties between children and their parents, particularly fathers. In this chapter, we undertake a collaborative process of exploring divorce in Soviet and American societies. We begin with divorce trends, followed by the legal basis for divorce, predictors of divorce, and consequences for children and adults. We also briefly discuss remarriage.

DEMOGRAPHIC TRENDS IN TWO SOCIETIES

Divorce rates increased slowly in the United States from the middle of the nineteenth century until the end of World War II, when a temporary surge of divorces resulted from the marital breakups of returning soldiers. From the early 1950s through the mid-1960s, the divorce rate returned to a level slightly above that of the prewar period. However, in the late 1960s the divorce rate began to climb to historically unprecedented levels, reaching a peak in 1981 of 5.3 divorces per 1,000 population and 22.6 divorces per 1,000 married women. This represented a 75% increase in the rate of divorce since 1968. The American divorce

rate leveled off during the 1980s, but is expected to remain at historically high levels through the last decade of this century.[2]

Divorce rates in the former USSR rose in comparable fashion to
those in the United States. Soviet figures show a threefold increase in
the number of divorces per 1,000 population from 1940 to 1987. The
rate in the United States doubled in the same period, but started from
a higher base. Whereas the sharpest increases in the USSR came
between 1950 and 1966, the biggest jump in divorce rates in the United
States was between 1965 and 1980. Both countries experienced a leveling off of divorce rates in the 1980s. By the late 1980s, the divorce
rate per 1,000 population was 4.9 in the United States and 3.4 in the
USSR.[3] In 1987, the corresponding rates per 1,000 married women (a
more reliable figure) were 20.8 in the United States and 14.1 in the
USSR. (This means that about 2.1% of all American couples and 1.4%
of all Soviet couples divorced in 1987.) Overall, the divorce rates in
the United States are nearly 40% higher than in the former USSR, and
both are higher than those in other nations of the world.

Predicting the likelihood of divorce for a new cohort of married
couples is not as straightforward as calculating current divorce rates,
because future trends cannot be forecast with complete confidence.
However, demographers such as Arthur Norton and Jeanne Moorman
predict that if current divorce rates continue, the youngest group of
married couples will experience a 54% rate of divorce. Extrapolating
to the former USSR, one might anticipate a divorce likelihood of
approximately 33% for the new group of married couples.[4]

Regional variations in divorce rates are apparent in both societies. In the former USSR, large discrepancies have occurred between
urban and rural populations. For example, in 1986–1987, the divorce
rate was 2.5 times higher in urban than rural areas. However, divorce
has increased much faster in rural areas—an eightfold increase since
the 1950s in rural areas versus a threefold increase in urban areas.[5]

Divorce rates have also varied among the republics of the former
USSR. The highest rates have been found in Russia, Ukraine, Byelorussia (now Belarus), and the Baltic region (Latvia, Lithuania, and
Estonia). These regions have relatively egalitarian norms for family life
and low birthrates. The lowest divorce rates occur mainly in the central Asian and Caucasian regions, which have more traditional, patriarchal family norms and high birthrates. Estonia, for example, has a divorce
rate four times that of Armenia. Recently, however, the more "modern"
regions have begun to experience a leveling off of their divorce rates,
while rates in more "traditional" areas have been increasing.[6]

Regional differences in American divorce rates are far less drastic
than differences in Soviet society, reflecting, no doubt, the greater

homogeneity of the United States. The West, South Central, Mountain, and Pacific census divisions have 50% higher levels of marital dissolution than the rest of the country. Sociologists N. D. Glenn and B. S. Shelton believe that these higher rates of divorce can be explained by the higher rates of residential mobility (the frequency with which people change their place of residence), which is an indicator of social integration (the extent to which there is consensus about rules of behavior and how to enforce them).[7] Thus, regional differences in divorce probably reflect cultural differences in Soviet society, whereas regional differences in American society probably reflect different levels of stability among populations. In both societies, however, these regional differences are diminishing.

The post-World War II period in the former Soviet Union witnessed a change in divorce patterns from young, childless couples to somewhat older couples with children. By the 1980s, the average length of marriage prior to divorce was higher in the USSR (9.8 years) than in the United States (6.9 years).[8] Soviet statistics on the number of children involved in divorce each year have not been gathered since the 1960s, when about half the divorcing couples were parents. In the United States, about 60% of divorces currently involve children. For the 1980s, the best estimates of the number of children involved in a divorce each year were approximately 665,000 children in the USSR and 1,038,000 in the United States.[9]

THE LEGAL CONTEXT OF DIVORCE

In both Soviet and American societies, laws regulating marital dissolution have been thoroughly intertwined with politics, economics, and tradition. The American experience has been characterized by an increasing distance between state laws on the one hand, and church doctrine and the British common-law tradition that undergirds the legal system of the United States on the other. The British common-law tradition assumed a patriarchal family structure in which men had property rights that included the children. The nineteenth-century Industrial Revolution brought fundamental alterations in husbands' and wives' roles, and with these, significant changes in divorce laws. Mothers were more often awarded custody of the children; however, divorces were still granted only for grave offenses such as adultery or desertion.[10]

Other major changes in divorce laws in the United States did not occur until the 1970s, when "no-fault divorce" legislation was introduced. This permitted either spouse to request a divorce because of "irreconcilable differences" or "irretrievable marital breakdown," without proving guilt on the other spouse's part. However, divorcing couples could still become adversarial over custody of the children and/or the terms of the financial settlement and child support. One unanticipated consequence of no-fault divorce has been that gender-neutral rules have placed custodial mothers at economic risk, stemming from their relative lack of independent financial assets and inadequate child support payments from fathers. Since mothers win nearly 90% of disputed custody awards, fathers are placed at risk in their role as parents, and frequently retaliate by withholding support payments.[11] Thus, a vicious circle of deprivation has been created—one that legal procedures to date have been unable to prevent.

In the former Soviet Union, the history of divorce laws is tied directly to the upheavals of government systems and political ideologies. Following the October Revolution of 1917, one of the first legal initiatives of Soviet power was the decree on divorce. In contrast to the rigid regulations of tsarist Russia, divorce was made available upon the request of one or both spouses.[11a] During the same period of time, the liquidation of private property altered the tradition that gave husbands ownership of family property. Under the banner of gender equality and the emancipation of women, new marriage and divorce codes emerged, the first of which (in 1926) established a relatively simple set of divorce procedures.[11b]

As the Soviet totalitarian government strengthened, the ideological orientation changed. Emphasis was once again placed on preserving a stable family. In 1936, a court trial and public disclosure of the divorce in the press began to be required. Soon divorce was considered a social offense and a form of social deviance—an attitude that still exists to some extent today.

In the 1960s, the Soviet state gave renewed attention to social policies, and divorce procedures were again simplified in 1965. For example, according to the code of the Russian Federation adopted in 1969 (and still operative today), a marriage can be dissolved upon the application of one or both spouses. However, couples who have children under age eighteen can divorce only through the courts. Furthermore, a legal hearing must be held when one of the spouses opposes the divorce, or when there are financial support or property issues to be settled. If the wife is pregnant or if there is a child under age one, a husband cannot obtain a divorce. However, the court will grant a divorce to the *woman* in this situation if she wants one. These changes were included in the Code on Marriage and Family adopted by all of the recently formed federations.

By law, Soviet judges are required to attempt to reconcile the disputing spouses. However, this mandate is rarely implemented because of large court caseloads, lack of conflict resolution training for judges, and a severe shortage of professional resources (e.g., marriage therapists). Some judges attempt to prevent couples from obtaining a divorce by creating bureaucratic obstacles. Although this is technically illegal, it reflects the opinion of many judges that divorces often occur impulsively. Recently, some judges have proposed that family professionals analyze the divorce cases and assist in the reconciliation of couples—a process similar to that of many court service agencies in the United States.

Although the legal and economic histories of divorce have been quite different in the United States and the former USSR, the contemporary legal climate is remarkably similar. In both societies, the choice to divorce is viewed as an individual right that cannot be denied by government. However, divorce procedures are often complicated when there are minor children and/or disputed property rights. In these circumstances, the legally mandated outcomes of divorce proceedings are often problems for the former spouses and for their children.

ATTITUDES TOWARD DIVORCE

In both Soviet and American societies, attitudes toward divorce have changed dramatically over the past few decades. For years, most family professionals in the United States seemed to view divorced persons as if they had personal deficits, reflecting broader societal attitudes toward divorce as deviant behavior. Moral constraints against divorce were supported by churches and other social institutions. As late as the 1960s, the divorces of American politicians seriously affected their election prospects. Although some social stigma is still present, divorce has been seen increasingly in recent years as a rather typical life transition that does not carry the implication of moral or psychological weakness.[12]

Negative attitudes toward divorce were also strong in the former Soviet Union until quite recently. Prior to the 1960s, few Soviet couples divorced; public opinion severely condemned those who "broke up" a family. These attitudes were supported by both the Communist Party and the state, and they were a powerful factor in keeping the divorce rate low. The social stigma attached to divorce began fading during the 1960s—a period of liberalization, just as in the United States. Increasingly, the values of individual freedom and gender equality came into conflict with the ideal of marital stability. Even in a society in which the state attempted to regulate every sphere of life, official were forced to recognize some of the rights of citizens to self-determination, including the right to divorce.

These changes in Soviet marriage legislation and the similar "no-fault" divorce laws passed in the United States in the 1970s mark a parallel transformation in attitudes toward divorce. In both societies, this new freedom for individuals to divorce was an expression of growing equality of men and women in marriage and family relations. In Soviet society, it was also a measure of individual freedom.

Since the rigid socialist system of the USSR did not "officially" recognize social problems for many years, the concerns of some Soviet social scientists about divorce were not discussed openly or thoroughly. The investigation of divorce issues started in the late 1960s and early 1970s. The rapid changes of the 1980s brought the issue into the open, with resulting disagreement and debate. Citing the high divorce rates of recent years, some Soviet social scientists assert that the Soviet family is in serious crisis. Other family scholars view the high rate of divorce more benignly as simply a life transition characteristic of family life in contemporary technological societies. A third group takes a middle position, viewing divorce as problematic but justified in a number of particular circumstances. All of these Soviet scientists are committed to conducting studies on divorce to determine its impact on human development and on social structure.[13]

According to recent studies of the Soviet legal system, most judges believe that the number of divorces is troubling and that some action should be taken.[14] The actions most often proposed are as follows (in rank order): (1) Improve financial and housing conditions for families; (2) build more child care centers; (3) enhance the preparation of young people for marriage; (4) treat alcoholism more vigorously; (5) make divorce procedures more complicated; (6) raise the age of eligibility for marriage; and (7) improve the lives of employed women. Although the majority of Soviet judges want the divorce rate to decrease, they, like their American counterparts, have little direct power to change the situation.

Other Soviet studies have found public opinion divided on whether or not divorce should be viewed as an ordinary phenomenon in contemporary family life. In one poll, about half of the men and women surveyed (particularly women with higher education) expressed the belief that the divorce rate reflects a demand for higher levels of marital satisfaction. Those polled were unanimous in their conviction that divorce is an important contributor to the hardships of Soviet life.[15] Conversely, many citizens believe that the high rate of divorce is also a *result* of the harsh conditions of life in Soviet society—lack of adequate housing, little or no privacy, few consumer goods, long lines for food, and the like. They believe that improved economic conditions will actually *lower* divorce rates. However, the experience of the United States challenges this notion. Americans have a higher standard of living and fewer economic hardships, but an even higher divorce rate than Soviets.

In the United States in recent decades, a White House Conference on the family has been held, Senate and House of Representatives committees on children and families have been established, and testimony on divorce and family well-being has been elicited from family professionals. During the same period, Soviets have also attempted to stem the rising tide of divorce. Most of these efforts have been in the form of resolutions by the national government and the Communist Party, as well as the appointment of special committees on family, motherhood, and childhood. To date, however, neither government has been notably successful in improving the stability of marriage for its citizens.

WHO DIVORCES AND WHY?

Because divorce is viewed as an important social issue in both Soviet and American societies, family researchers are understandably interested in its causes. These causes can be divided into three categories: (1) broad social forces that serve to increase divorce throughout a society; (2) demographic characteristics that predispose certain couples to divorce; and (3) specific reasons why particular couples decide to divorce.

Scholars in the United States have pointed to several major social trends that appear to have influenced rising divorce rates, including urbanization, farm-to-city migration, increased education, changes in women's roles in the economy, and the feminist movement. All of these factors are associated with a decrease in social control over individual behavior and an increase in the belief that marriage is designed for personal fulfillment.[16] Soviet scholars have proposed a very similar set of social factors influencing divorce trends. These include migration from rural to urban areas, changes in women's roles in the economy, increased education, declines in social control over individual and family behavior, and increased emphasis on personal fulfillment.[17] For a variety of reasons unique to the history of each, these trends appeared earlier in American than in Soviet society. Despite the numerous social problems of Soviet women, a significant feminist movement has not yet appeared; some scholars wonder whether an even sharper rise in Soviet divorce could accompany such a movement in the future.

In the United States, extensive research exists on the demographic factors that predict who is most likely to divorce. These studies indicate that the following factors are associated with increased divorce risk: younger age at marriage; divorce of one's parents; and lack of homogeneity or similarity in such characteristics as race, ethnicity, education, and social status. Other demographic factors are more complex. The presence of children has not been clearly linked to marital stability. The relation of education to divorce appears to differ by gender, with better-educated men having lower divorce rates, but women who have graduate school education showing higher divorce rates than those of women with undergraduate degrees. Income is another divorce-related factor that differs by gender in the United States. For men, there is a simple linear relationship: The higher the income, the lower the divorce rate. For women, the key seems to be the ratio of their income to that of their husbands; when women earn relatively more than their husbands, the likelihood of divorce increases. Finally, religious affiliation has been declining as a significant factor in divorce rates, although higher religious participation is associated with less likelihood of divorce.[18]

Soviet studies have also found age at marriage to be one of the strongest predictors of divorce. It appears that individuals marrying before age twenty or after age thirty have the highest rates of divorce (American studies show this relationship only for younger couples).[19] Like their American counterparts, Soviet spouses who have experienced a parental divorce are more likely to divorce themselves. In addition, the more dissimilar newlyweds are on personal, ethnic, and social characteristics, the higher their risk for divorce. For example, one study found that marriages of two Moldavians had a 19% divorce rate after ten years, whereas 33% of Russian–Moldavian marriages ended in divorce during the same period.[20]

As in the United States, other factors associated with Soviet divorces are more complex. The presence of children, for example, increases marital strain but appears to serve as a stabilizing factor—perhaps by increasing the economic costs of leaving the marriage. Little research on education and divorce exists in the former Soviet Union; however, one study found that divorced women have higher educational levels than divorced men, especially in younger groups. Thus, gender and education may be linked to divorce in both societies.[21] To date, only one Soviet study has examined the relationship between income and divorce. The findings are similar to those of American studies: Lower-income couples had higher divorce rates.[22] Religion has not been systemically studied as a factor in Soviet divorce, except for the general demographic recognition that Islamic regions have lower divorce rates than non-Islamic areas.

In the United States, there has been a trend in recent decades toward a lessening of the influence of socioeconomic factors in divorce rates. This is demonstrated in the relatively greater increases in divorce rates among individuals with higher incomes and educational levels. In other words, there appears to be a *homogenization* of divorce across different segments of American society. It will be interesting to see whether Soviet scholars find a similar trend in their studies of families over the next several decades.[23]

Turning to the specific reasons couples give for divorcing, we find a good deal of similarity between the two societies. In studies of American couples seeking divorce, extramarital sex is the factor most often mentioned as a reason for the decision. Personality and financial problems are next in frequency, followed by interpersonal complaints such as lack of communication, feeling unloved, lack of satisfying family life, and conflicts over roles. Many couples experience a long-standing period of marital decline, marked by ambivalence about separating, before making the actual decision to divorce. Thus, reasons given at the time of the divorce may in some cases reflect current complaints, rather than the long-standing problems that originally created a destructive atmosphere in the marriage.[24]

Soviet studies have found a fairly similar list of reasons given by couples for their decision to divorce: lack of common views and interests, personality differences, falling in love with another person or having an extramarital affair, alcoholism, and violence. However, Soviet couples also report that poor housing and poor financial conditions have contributed to marital breakup—explanations seldom given by American couples. These complaints doubtless reflect living conditions that do not allow many younger couples to maintain their own dwellings and establish family lives independent from their parents. Of course, cultural differences may also explain why Soviet couples are more likely than American couples to blame external conditions for their marital breakups.[25]

CONSEQUENCES OF DIVORCE FOR CHILDREN

In both American and Soviet societies, the greatest worry about divorce concerns the welfare of children; as the most vulnerable family members, they have the most to lose. Since the 1960s, a large body of research has accumulated on the consequences of divorce for children in the United States. By contrast, most of the research on divorce in Soviet families did not even begin until the 1980s.

On average, American children who experience parental divorce have slightly lower well-being than do children raised in continuously intact two-parent families. A meta-analysis of 92 studies of children's adjustment to divorce found negative outcomes in the areas of academic achievement, conduct, psychological adjustment, self-esteem, and social relations.[26] Adults who experienced divorce as children, compared with adults from families with continuously married parents, have poorer psychological adjustment, greater marital instabiity, and lower socioeconomic attainment.[27] The range of outcomes experienced by children of divorce has been linked to the absence of the noncustodial parent, the adjustment of the custodial parent, interparental conflict, economic hardship, and stressful life changes.[28]

Soviet research on divorce is currently at the stage where American research was in the 1960s—namely, small studies comparing convenient samples of one-parent and two-parent families, rather than large studies of families more representative of the broader society. In a general way, the same pattern appears in both societies: Children in one-parent families are worse off on a wide range of measures of emotional problems, behavioral problems, and academic achievement than are children in two-parent families.[29] In American studies that have applied statistical controls for family income levels, these negative findings still remain. In other words, more than just financial problems create difficulties for children in one-parent families in the United States. Presumably, similar patterns will emerge from Soviet data in the future, although other effects may be more difficult to isolate because of the extreme economic hardship that characterizes Soviet family life at this point in history.

American research over the past twenty years has paid increasing attention to studying families actually going through the process of adjustment to divorce. Although Soviet studies are much more limited, preliminary findings are consistent with results in the United States. In both societies, there appear to be distinct phases in children's reactions to parental divorce. Emotional turmoil and distress typically follow immediately upon parental separation. For most children, this acute reaction lasts just six to twelve months, followed by a period of stabilization.[30] After this, some children show a high level of resiliency, with good adaptation in major areas of their lives. Other children develop problems, such as aggressive or noncompliant behavior, difficulties in academic achievement and school adjustment, or disruptions in peer relations. Both Soviet and American research has found that boys have greater adjustment problems after divorce than girls. However, American research of a longitudinal sort finds that postdivorce adjustment problems of children may be different at different times; for example, evidence suggests that girls do less well than boys following a parental remarriage.[31]

The few available Soviet studies on outcomes of divorce for children are entirely consistent with American studies. For many children, the primary negative aspect of a divorce is loss of contact with a parent, most often the father. Indeed, studies in both societies have documented that half or more of divorced fathers have little or no involvement with their children, particularly as time passes after the divorce.[32] Studies in both the United States and the former USSR also clearly indicate that predictable and frequent contact with the noncustodial parent is an important factor in children's postdivorce adjustment.[33]

The postdivorce psychological adjustment of the custodial parent also affects children. Evidence suggests that the *divorce* event itself may not be as important for children's adjustment as the overall postdivorce environment.[34] Several studies have found that American children in low-conflict postdivorce environments are better adjusted than children in high-conflict environments. Unfortunately, Soviet parents, like their American counterparts, commonly engage in struggles over access of the father to the children after a divorce. However, such struggles are not universal and inevitable; in some countries in the world, divorce is not premised on awarding "ownership" of children to one of the parents.[35]

The quality of a custodial parent's childrearing is also an important factor in children's postdivorce adjustment. Studies in both countries have documented single mothers' problems with disciplining their children after divorce; these mothers report more difficulty in being patient, consistent, and firm with rules. No doubt these difficulties are tied to the emotional challenge of postdivorce adjustment and the loss of support from the other parent. However, evidence from American studies to date suggests that even the extra burden of household responsibilities can contribute to a child's self-esteem and maturity when the single parent maintains a nurturing and firm stance.[36]

In recent years, researchers in the United States have begun to study children's adjustment in families *prior* to divorce. These studies indicate that a good many (but not all) of the negative effects of divorce are already occurring *before* the actual marital separation—presumably because of the tension and conflict created by the marital distress. Since the psychological experience of divorce for American and Soviet children appears to be so similar, we expect that future Soviet research will reveal the same pattern. As researchers continue to examine the process of divorce and family transition, they are learning that the same factors affect children, regardless of family structure: quality of parental nurturance and control, contact with both parents, and extent of parental conflict. If divorce has negative consequences for many children, the most likely reason is that these children are placed at risk for experiencing distressing family processes both before and after the divorce—the same processes that might have harmed the children had their parents stayed married in a conflictual relationship. Clearly, more research is needed in both societies on the long-term outcomes for children whose parents continue to live together in such troubled relationships, so that these outcomes can be compared with the outcomes of divorce.[37]

CONSEQUENCES OF DIVORCE FOR ADULTS

In Soviet society, little empirical knowledge exists regarding the impact of divorce on former spouses and on other adults involved (e.g., grandparents). However, research on the psychological and physical health status and the economic well-being of divorced individuals in the two societies indicates more similarities than differences.

In numerous studies, American researchers have reported a higher incidence of disease morbidity and mortality, suicide, alcoholism, and homicide among divorced persons. Divorced and separated individuals are overrepresented in the statistics of all types of mental illness. Physical illness often follows the stressful events in the marital dissolution process.[38] In the United States, research has emphasized the negative impact rather than the developmental impact of divorce on the formerly married. Yet spouses who initiate divorces often have a *positive* perspective on the consequences of their decisions.[39]

Data indicate that American women's economic well-being decreases when they divorce and increases again if they remarry.[40] Men's economic well-being, on the other hand, appears to be less vulnerable to divorce. Marital dissolution has been shown to be a major contributing factor to families' living in poverty; one-third of divorced women in the United States end up living below the officially recognized line of poverty.[41] This movement into poverty is related to many women's inability to earn enough to compensate for the loss of husbands' earnings, to the child custody arrangements, and to the low and infrequent child support payments from fathers. Women with higher levels of education, work experience, and few or no preschool-age children evidence some ability to minimize the economic losses.[42]

The few Soviet studies available on the psychological well-being of divorced couples have also found negative consequences of divorce. For example, Z. I. Fainburg compared the life satisfaction levels of divorced men and women with those of married and never-married men and women. About 35% of the divorced men and 47% of the divorced women were reported to view their life situations as negative—more than double the percentage for men and women who were married or had never married. These findings are supported by other Soviet researchers, who report that some ex-husbands and ex-wives regret their divorces and would like to return to their spouses.[43]

In a recent Soviet study, couples who applied for divorce were asked for their assessment of the situation. Men were somewhat more likely to regard divorce as liberating than were women (28% and 24%, respectively); conversely, women were somewhat more likely to regard divorce as a grave life crisis than were men (17% and 14%, respectively). Divorced women were more likely than men to have lower self-esteem and to report indicators of stress (e.g., sleep disturbances). Women also reported greater trauma if the length of the predivorce decision period was short.[44]

Very few Soviet data on the economic impact of divorce are available for comparison with American data. One Soviet study reported that divorced persons are in a worse financial condition than married and never-married persons. As in the United States, the economic impact of divorce appears to have the greatest effect on women with children. In both societies, children typically live with their mothers.[45]

Division of property is frequently an important issue in divorce. Although there has been little property to divide in Soviet divorces, the *right* to housing is a very complicated and important issue. Because of the severe housing shortage, former spouses may have to continue living in the same dwelling for a lengthy period of time after the divorce—an almost unheard-of situation in the United States. Many divorced individuals are not eligible for a second apartment; therefore, they may need to move into a "communal flat," sharing the bath and kitchen with other residents. One study reported that about a third of separating couples had to share a dwelling at the time of their divorces. The seriousness of the housing shortage is further reflected in the report of 27% of divorced men and 14% of divorced women that they could not remarry because of the lack of separate housing.[46]

In Soviet studies of adults terminating their marriages, the greatest social impact of divorce appears to be loneliness. Research indicates that divorced mothers more often spend their free time alone. In one study, friends' approval of the divorce was found to reduce the negative impact of separation; conversely, the disapproval of friends was reported to increase the trauma of divorce. Parents' approval of the divorce was found to be important for the emotional status of Soviet women, but not for that of men.[47] As in the United States, the social lives of divorced Soviet adults often decline because friendships were based upon couple activities, and divorced individuals may subsequently be excluded. Furthermore, some studies have found that Soviet spouses, like Americans, sometimes regard their divorced friends as threats to their own marriages. Finally, one Soviet study found that a third of the formerly married men sampled reported believing that their divorces had negative consequences for their careers and work relationships—a result less common for American men. Divorced Soviet women did not report negative career consequences.[48]

In general, then, the consequences of divorce for adults appear to be fairly similar in Soviet and American societies. These consequences are psychological, social, and economic. What is less clear in either society, however, is how many of the negative aspects of being divorced arise from factors that already existed during the marriage, rather than resulting from the divorcing process itself and subsequent postdivorce status.

REMARRIAGE

The rise in Soviet and American divorces has been accompanied by a dramatic increase in remarriages. The overall marriage rate in the United States is higher, with about one-half of all marriages involving a previously married spouse. Furthermore, about 75% of Americans who divorce will probably remarry (nearly all within five years of their divorces). Among divorced women in the United States, the more educated are *less* likely to remarry. Among divorced American males, the higher their education and income levels, the *more* likely they are to remarry. The incidence of redivorce in the United State is projected to be 61% for men and 54% for women.[49]

The interpretation of Soviet data on remarriage is limited by the fact that the few studies undertaken have not distinguished clearly between widowed and divorced individuals who remarry. However, the remarriage rate itself doubled during the 1970s, following the liberalization of divorce policy in the previous decade. During the 1980s, the rate of remarriage leveled off; from 1980 to 1986, the number of remarriages increased only 1%, from 2,725,000 to 2,753,000.[50]

As in the United States, the Soviet remarriage rate for women is related to age, number of children, and level of education. Young divorced women and never-married women have a similar probability of marriage. The probability of remarriage declines sharply with age, approaching zero after age forty. For Soviet women divorced after age thirty who have two or more children, the remarriage rate is greatly reduced. However, if the older woman is well educated, her chance of remarriage increases.[51] Data are not available regarding the influence of education and income on the remarriage rates of divorced Soviet men.

A common myth in Russia holds that second marriages are more stable than first marriages. In reality, however, marriages of divorced persons are more likely to end in divorce than are first marriages. In some Soviet regions, the divorce rate of previously divorced persons is 75% higher than that of first marriages, compared to the American divorce differential of about 10% between first marriages and second marriages. The divorces of remarrieds Soviets are likely to occur in the third to fifth year, and the subsequent interval between remarriage and redivorce is about five years—similar to that in the United States. In both societies, the average length of the first marriage is about two years longer than subsequent marriages.[52]

Soviet scholars have not yet examined the reasons for the higher rate of divorce among remarried couples. However, they assume that many of the reasons given by American scholars will hold true for Soviet society as well—namely, (1) the lack of defined social expectations for remarried couples; (2) a history of previous experience of using divorce as a solution to relationship problems; (3) the complex issues of parenting stepchildren; and (4) financial problems associated with supporting children from two households.[53]

Cross-cultural comparisons of remarriage are quite difficult, because marriage after divorce has not yet been studied extensively in Soviet society. Thus far, the available data indicate significant similarities. However, finding housing and solving economic problems are substantially more difficult for remarried Soviet couples than for most remarried Americans.

CONCLUSION

After comparing divorce and postdivorce family patterns in our two societies, we are struck by the parallels. These include (1) the liberalization of divorce policy, followed by a dramatic increase in the incidence of divorce; (2) the disproportionate economic burdens of divorce for women and children; (3) the reasons couples give for a divorce; (4) the disruption of the father–child relationship following divorce; (5) the increased psychosocial risk for children associated with marital conflict and marital disruption; and (6) the increased incidence of remarriage and redivorce. The primary differences we have observed are the higher divorce rate among American couples and the difficult housing problem faced by divorcing Soviet couples.

Up to the present, the negative aspects of divorce have been emphasized in both societies; however, social acceptance of divorce has increased as it becomes more common. In the next decades, both societies will have to reflect—in social policies and social services—the reality that historically high divorce rates are probably here to stay.

NOTES

1. S. J. Price and P. C. McKenry, *Divorce* (Beverly Hills, CA: Sage, 1988).

2. National Center for Health Statistics, *Vital Statistics of the United States, 1986*, Vol. 3, *Marriage and Divorce*, DHHS Pub. No. (PHS) 90-1103 (Washington, DC: U.S. Government Printing Office, 1986).

3. *Ibid.*; "Population of the USSR in 1987" *Finansi i Statistika*, 7 (1988), 190; *Statisticheskiy*, *1* (1987), 68; A. G. Volkov, *Family as an Object of Demography* (Moscow: Mysl, 1986), 27.

4. A. J. Norton and J. E. Moorman, "Current Trends in Marriage and Divorce among American Women," *Journal of Marriage and the Family*, *49* (1987), 3–14. For USSR estimates, see Volkov, *op. cit.*; L. E. Tolchinsky, "Assessment of the Divorce Level in the USSR," in A. G. Volkov (ed.) *Demographic Development of the Family* (Moscow: Nauka, 1979), 190; A. B. Sinelnikov, *Reproduction of Generations in Our Country* (Moscow: Nauka, 1978), 109.

5. *Population of the USSR in 1987, op. cit.*

6. *Ibid.*, 208.

7. N. D. Glenn and B. S. Shelton, "Regional Differences in Divorce in the United States," *Journal of Marriage and the Family*, 47 (1985), 641–652.

8. For the United States, see Norton and Moorman, *op. cit.* For the former USSR, see A. B. Sinelnikov, "Calculation of Theoretical Probability of Getting Remarried," in L. L. Rybakovsky (ed.), *Problems of Reproduction and Migration of Populations* (Moscow: Nauka, 1981), 110.

9. For the former USSR, see P. Zvidrinsh, "Certain Results of the Study of Divorce Differentials and Causes of Marriage Dissolution in the Latvian SSR," in *Socio-Demographic Studies of the Soviet Family in the Baltic Republics* (Riga, 1980), 113. For the United States, see National Center for Health Statistics, *op. cit.*

10. This discussion of laws in the United States is based on Price and McKenry, *op. cit.*, 91–105; see also G. Riley, *Divorce: The American Tradition* (New York: Oxford University Press, 1991).

11. L. Weitzman, *The Divorce Revolution: The Unexpected Social and Economic Consequences for Women and Children in America* (New York: Free Press, 1985). Deciding to use an attorney has been found to be an important factor in the outcome of economic settlements; see S. Burgess, G. Jackson, and K. Stafford, "Influence of Procedural Decisions on Divorce Outcomes," *Home*

Economics Research Journal, 18 (1990), 211–222. The average award of child support is less than half of what it costs to maintain a child at poverty level. See K. Rettig, D. Christianson, and C. Dahl, "Impact of Child Support Guidelines on the Economic Well-Being of Children," *Family Relations, 40* (1991), 167–179; K. Rettig, L. Yellowthunder, C. Dahl, and S. Keskinen, *Economic Consequences of Divorce in Minnesota: Phase II Research Report* (St. Paul: Family Social Science Department, University of Minnesota, 1991); D. Christiansen, C. Dahl, and K. Rettig, "Noncustodial Mothers and Child Support: Examining the Larger Context," *Family Relations, 39* (1990), 388–394. Studies have examined the possible causal connection between no-fault divorce laws and the rapid rise of divorce rates in the United States. The conclusion has been that this legislation is not directly responsible for higher divorce rates; see Price and McKenry, *op. cit.*, 99–100.

11a. Volkov, *op. cit.*, 129–130.

11b. A. G. Kharchev, *Marriage and the Family in the USSR* (Moscow: Mysl, 1979), 147; E. M. Vorozheikin, *Family Law in the USSR* (Moscow: Juridicheskaja Literatura, 1972).

12. C. Buehler, J. Hogan, B. Robinson, and R. Levy, "The Parental Divorce Transition: Divorce Related Stressors and Well-Being," *Journal of Divorce, 9*(2) (1985–1986), 61–81.

13. D. M. Chechot, *Sociology of Marriage and Divorce* (Moscow: Nanka, 1973), 6–9; A. G. Hkarchev and M. S. Matskovsky, *The Contemporary Family and Its Problems* (Moscow: Nanka, 1978), 113.

14. G. Zaikina, "Divorce Procedures in People's Court: Ways of Improving the Regulation of the Social Sphere in Society," paper presented at the International Seminar of Young Scientists (October 1987); E. A. Chefanova, "Ways of Further Strengthening the Role of the People's Courts in Stabilizing Family Relations," in M. G. Pankratova (ed.), *Family as an Object of Social Policy* (Moscow: Institute of Sociology, Soviet Academy of Sciences, 1986).

15. E. V. Foteeva, "Divorce through Ideas of Workers and Intelligentia," in M. S. Matskovsky, T. A. Gurko, G. A. Zaikina, and E. V. Foteeva (eds.), *Formation of Marriage and Family Relations* (Moscow: Soviet Academy of Sciences, 1989).

16. See review by H. J. Raschke, "Divorce," in M. B. Sussman and S. K. Steinmetz (eds.), *Handbook of Marriage and the Family* (New York: Plenum Press, 1987); A. J. Cherlin, *Marriage, Divorce, Remarriage* (Cambridge, MA: Harvard University Press, 1981).

17. V. A. Sysenko, *Marriage Stability: Problems, Factors, Conditions* (Moscow: Finansi i Statistika, 1981); V. V. Solodnikov, "Conditions and Reasons for Instability in Young Urban Families," in M. S. Matskovsky, T. A. Gurko, G. A. Zaikina, and E. V. Foteeva (eds.), *Formation of Marriage and Family Relations* (Moscow: Soviet Academy of Sciences, 1989).

18. Raschke, *op. cit.;* Price and McKenry, *op. cit.*

19. For Soviet families, see L. R. Kuznetsov, "Divorce Rates: Dynamics, Factors, Tendencies," in *The Methodology of Demographic Prognosis* (Moscow: Nanka, 1988), 85; E. Tyit, "Risk Factors Resulting in Marital Dissolution," in *Sociodemographic Studies of the Family in the Soviet Baltic Republics* (Riga, 1980).

20. A. A. Swsokolov, *Ethnically Heterogeneous Marriages in the USSR* (Moscow: Mysl, 1987), 110.

21. Volkov, *op. cit.*, 86–87.

22. L. V. Chuiko, *Marriages and Divorces* (Moscow: Nauka, 1975).

23. Raschke, *op. cit.*

24. See review by G. C. Kitson, K. B. Babri, and M. J. Roach, "Who Divorces and Why: A Review," *Journal of Family Issues*, 6 (1985), 255–293.

25. See review by Hkarchev and Matskovsky, *op. cit.*

26. P. R. Amato and B. Keith, "Parental Divorce and the Well-Being of Children: A Meta-Analysis," *Psychological Bulletin, 110* (1991a), 26–46.

27. P. R. Amato and B. Keith, "Consequences of Parental Divorce for Adult Well-Being," *Journal of Marriage and the Family, 53* (1991b), 43–58.

28. P. R. Amato, "Children's Adjustment to Divorce: Theories, Hypotheses, and Empirical Support," *Journal of Marriage and the Family, 55* (1993), 23–38.

29. For American studies, see review by P. R. Amato and B. Keith, 1991a, *op. cit.* J. B. Kelly, "Longer-Term Adjustment in Children of Divorce," *Journal of Family Psychology, 2* (1988), 119–140. For national United States data, see D. A. Dawson, "Family Structure and Children's Health and Well-Being: Data from the 1988 National Health Interview Survey of Child Health," *Journal of Marriage and the Family, 53* (1991), 573–584. For Soviet studies, see N. G. Aristova, "Influence of Family Structure on Successful Parenting," in *Family as an Object of Social Policy* (Moscow: Institute of Sociology, Soviet Academy of Sciences, 1986); A. N. Mikrievsky, "The State of Health of Children from One-Parent Families," in *Public Health of the Russian Federation,* No. 6 (1985); G. M. Minkovsky, "An Unhappy Family and the Wrongful Behavior of Adolescents," *Sotsiologicheskie Issledovanija, 2* (1984), 106.

30. Kelly, *op. cit.,* 122.

31. E. M. Hetherington, M. Stanley-Hagan, and E. R. Anderson, "Marital Transitions: A Child's Perspective," *American Psychologist, 44* (1989), 304. For a Soviet study of gender differences, see A. I. Zaharov, *Children's and Adolescent's Neurosis* (Leningrad: Nauka, 1986).

32. For the American experience, see F. A. Furstenberg and C. W. Nord, "Parenting Apart: Patterns of Child-Rearing after Marital Disruption," *Journal of Marriage and the Family, 47* (1985), 893–904. For the Soviet experience, see N. Solovyov, "A Person in a Post-Divorce Situation as a Subject of Sociological Study," in N. Solovjov, V. Ghaidis, V. Titarenko, and S. Papoport (eds.), *A Person after Divorce* (Vilnius: Institute of Philosophy, Sociology and Law, Academy of Science of the Lithuanian Soviet Socialist Republic [SSR], 1985), 5.

33. Kelly, *op. cit.*; D. N. Isaev and V. E. Kagan, *Sexual Socialization and Psychological Health of Children* (Leningrad, 1980); Zaharov, *op. cit.*

34. Hetherington et al., *op. cit.;* Kelly, *op. cit.;* V. Titarenko, "Insufficiency of Upbringing in a One-Parent Family," in N. Solovjov et al. (eds.), *A Person after Divorce* (Vilnius: Institute of Philosophy, Sociology and Law, Academy of Science of the Lithuanian SSR, 1985); A. M. Demidov, "Specific Features of Living in Single-Parent Families," in M. S. Matskovsky, G. A. Zaikina, and E. V. Foteeva (eds.), *Family and Social Structure* (Moscow: Institute of Sociology, Soviet Academy of Sciences, 1987).

35. Hetherington et al., *op. cit.;* Amato and Keith, *op. cit.;* R. A. Muksinov, "A Father's Role in a Post-Divorce Situation," in N. Solovjov et al. (eds.), *A Person after Divorce* (Vilnus: Institute of Philosophy, Sociology and Law, Academy of Science of the Lithuanian SSR, 1985).

36. Hetherington et al., *op. cit.*

37. Longitudinal studies in the United States have begun to examine how preseparation family distress influences children even before the actual marital breakup. These studies are indicating that many of the negative aspects of divorce for children begin to occur while the parents are still living together. See W. J. Doherty and R. H. Neddle, "Psychological Adjustment and Substance Use among Adolescents before and after a Parental Divorce," *Child Development, 62* (1991), 328–327; A. J. Cherlin, F. F. Furstenberg, Jr., P. L. Chase-Lansdale, K. E. Kiernan, P. K. Robins, D. R. Morrison, D. R. Tetler, and J. O. Tetler, "Longitudinal Studies of Effects of Divorce on Children in Great Britain and the United States," *Science, 252* (1991), 1386–1389.

38. See review by L. M. Verbrugge, "Marital Status and Health," *Journal of Marriage and the Family, 41* (1979), 267–285. For similar Soviet findings, see B. D. Karvasarsky, "Neuroses as Personality Diseases," in A. A. Bodaliov (ed.), *Social Psychology of Personality* (Leningrad: Znanije, 1974), 67.

39. S. Kessler, *The American Way of Divorce* (Chicago: Nelson Hall, 1975). For similar Soviet findings, see V. V. Solodinikov, "On the Eve of a Divorce," *Sotsiologicheskie Issledovanija, 1* (1988), 52–58.

40. C. Buehler, J. Hogan, B. Robinson, and R. Levy, "Remarriage Following Divorce: Stressors and Well-Being of Custodial and Noncustodial Parents," *Journal of Family Issues, 7* (1986), 405–420.

41. G. J. Duncan and J. N. Morgan, "Persistence and Change in Economic Status and the Role of Changing Family Composition," in M. Hill, D. Hill, and J. Morgan (eds.), *Five Thousand Families: Patterns of Economic Progress,* Vol. 9. (Ann Arbor, MI: Institute for Social Research, 1981), 1–44.

42. T. Mauldin, N. Rudd, and K. Stafford, "The Effect of Human Capital on the Economic Status of Women Following Marital Disruption," *Home Economics Research Journal, 18* (1990), 202–210.

43. Z. I. Fainburg, "Emotional and Cultural Factors in Family Functioning," *Sotsiologicheskie Issledovanija, 1* (1981), 146.

44. Solodnikov, 1988, *op. cit.*

45. A. Vasilute, "The Financial Status, Household, and Recreation of Divorcees," in N. Solovjov et al. (eds.), *A Person after Divorce* (Vilnius: Institute of Philosophy, Sociology and Law, Academy of Science of the Lithuanian SSR, 1985), 23.

46. V. V. Solodnikov, "Sociological Analysis of the Pre-Divorce Situation of Young Families," unpublished doctoral dissertation, (Moscow: Institute of Sociology, Soviet Academy of Sciences, 1989), 90; I. Zarinsh, "Everyday Life Through the Assessment of Divorced Urban Dwellers in Latvia," in N. Solovjov et al. (eds.), *A Person after Divorce* (Vilnius: Institute of Philosophy, Sociology, and Law, Academy of Science of the Lithuanian SSR, 1985), 132.

47. See Vasilute, *op. cit.;* Demidov, *op. cit.,* 159; Solodnikov, 1989, *op cit.*

For the United States, a classic study of loneliness and isolation after a marital separation is R. S. Weiss, *Marital Separation* (New York: Basic Books, 1975).

48. V. Gaidis, "Specific Features of Human Relations in a Post-Divorce Situation," in *Sociological Studies of Problems of Demography, Family, and Public Health* (Vilnius: Academy of Sciences of Lithuanian SSR, 1987), 166–167. See also Weiss, *op. cit.*

49. L. Bumpass, J. Sweet, and T. C. Martin, "Changing Patterns of Remarriage," *Journal of Marriage and the Family, 52* (1990), 24–27; P. C. Glick, "Marriage, Divorce, and Living Arrangements: Prospective Changes," *Journal of Family Issues, 5* (1984), 7–26.

50. M. S. Toltz, "Certain Summary Characteristics of Marriage Cessation and Duration of Marriage," in A. G. Volkov (ed.), *Demographic Family Development* (Moscow: Nauka, 1988, 101); V. A. Belova and E. M. Moreva, "Women's Remarriages: Situations and Factors," in *The Methodology of Demographic Prognosis* (Moscow: Nanka, 1988). See also *Population of the USSR in 1987, op. cit.,* 204.

51. Belova and Moreva, *op. cit.*

52. Toltz, *op. cit.;* Norton and Moorman, *op. cit.*

53. G. B. Spanier and F. F. Furstenberg, "Remarriage and Reconstituted Families," in M. B. Sussman and S. K. Steinmetz (eds.), *Handbook of Marriage and the Family* (New York: Plenum Press, 1987).

Chapter 4

Sexuality and Family Life

James W. Maddock
Igor S. Kon

INTRODUCTION: THE SEXUAL DIMENSION
OF FAMILY LIFE

In this chapter, sexuality is assumed to be a basic part of human experience, and therefore of family life.[1] "Sex" is a general term used to designate both the reality of biological femaleness and maleness (the *gender* component) and the expression of pleasurable body feelings (the *erotic* component). Although sexuality is rooted in biology and expressed in individual personality, it must be understood within particular sociocultural contexts. Sexuality is constructed by society as well as biology.[2]

Despite some evolutionary variables that are common to all human societies, sexuality as a whole is a social and historical phenomenon. It is mixed with broader cultural patterns, and changes along with these. The sexual attitudes, ideas, and behaviors of different social classes, groups, and strata within a society are also very different; therefore, there exist specific sexual subcultures according to gender, age, ethnicity, socioeconomic status, religion, and sexual orientation.[3]

Several important generalizations regarding the nature of family sexuality should be stated at the outset. They guide the following comparative analysis of sexuality in our two societies:

• *Sex is a basic dimension of family life*—an important motivator of marriage as well as the vehicle for transmitting life to the next generation. Therefore, sexuality is inevitably reflected in the actions of family members.

• *Gender is a key aspect of family organization.* Gender-linked factors powerfully affect patterns of interaction and communication among all family members.

• *Physical embodiment is expressed in family life as well as individual life*. The family shapes and gives meaning to the physical existence of its members. There is an erotic (pleasure-oriented) component to many aspects of family life; the task of finding appropriate physical and psychological distance between members is a necessary part of family development.

  • *Stages of family development are strongly influenced by the sequence of significant events in the psychosexual development of individual family members.* Conversely, patterns of individual psychosexual development are powerfully affected by changing patterns of family interaction at various stages of the family life cycle.

  • *Sexual meanings and behaviors in the family intersect with a variety of elements in the family's historical and cultural environment in mutually influential ways.* Family members' experiences outside the family, as well as circumstantial factors in the broader social and physical environment, inevitably affect their sex-related behavior.

THE SOCIAL CONTEXT OF SEXUALITY IN TWO COUNTRIES

Observations on American Culture

In the family context, many Americans view sexuality as a *problem* rather than a natural part of family *process*. This perspective is probably rooted in a deep cultural ambivalence regarding sex, influenced by a heritage of mind–body dualism and a male-dominated social structure that conflicts with abstract ideals about the rights and freedoms of all individuals. To these can be added the impact of recent technology on reproductive processes, a period of rapid social change, and increasing cultural pluralism. Even if uniformity of opinion about basic values and codes of sexual conduct once existed in America—and very likely it did not—such a consensus is no longer present. Today, Americans have to choose from among a variety of competing value systems, cultural norms, and life style options upon which to base their personal sexual decision making.

The broad cultural context of American society has affected individual and family sexuality in a variety of ways, too numerous and complex to be discussed in detail here.[4] However, a few broad themes can be mentioned and illustrated. The United States is not now—nor, as we now recognize, has it ever been—a homogeneous "melting pot" of cultural ideas and attitudes. Rather, American history is characterized by conflict and by attempts to balance various ideas and influences. Nowhere is this more striking than in relation to sexuality.

Arriving in what was for them the "New World," Europeans often took lands and lives from the native populations, and gave in return new technology to "tame" the land and the people; new religious beliefs and customs that shamed and restricted natives' habits and life styles; and new diseases—including venereal diseases—that decimated local populations. Sexual beliefs and customs were among the first things to be altered by pressure from the European settlers. Clashes between and among groups with European origins also had implications for sexuality. The Judeo-Christian tradition of Western Europe arrived in the Americas in at least three broad forms. One was the Roman Catholic mysticism of the Spanish conquistadores, whose influence combined with native Indian religions and spread through South and Central America into the southern United States. The second was the liberal rationality of the Deists, among whom were many of the earliest political leaders who shaped the original federation of states, and under whom religious freedom was constitutionally established. The third was the pietism ("personal holiness") best represented by the Puritans, who were "separatists" from the Church of England seeking religious freedom in America—but only for themselves. These were the local communities of the New England colonies who publicly tortured citizens and burned witches at the stake for heretical beliefs and "crimes," many of which were distinctly sexual in nature. As the population of the New World grew, these influences were increasingly juxtaposed, sometimes creatively, but often destructively. The tensions that arose have survived to the present day in the United States, mirrored in such controversial social issues as abortion, pornography, gender roles, celibacy of clergy, and individual sexual rights.

A frontier mentality predominated as the United States was settled from east to west. The emphasis was on individual freedom and pragmatic necessity, although these were somewhat tempered by various waves of Protestant revivalism that accompanied the migration across the country. Brothels were common; women were sometimes sold as wives; slaves were used for sexual purposes as well as for hard labor. Yet "sexual purity" was held up as the ideal for all.

As immigration and economic changes brought more and more people into large cities and created the social problems that accompanied the Industrial Revolution of the nineteenth century, a pattern of morality emerged (named for England's Queen Victoria) that dictated strict codes for family values, relations between men and women, and sexual behavior. Narrowly defined moralistic attitudes dominated people's lives. Even those who did not conform knew exactly what rules they were disobeying. Of course, the rules were quite different for males and females. Yet all of American society was dominated by a kind of sexual hysteria. Modesty was emphasized in order to avoid unleashing rampant passions. Masturbation was thought to cause insanity, and extreme measures from chastity belts to surgical cauterization were used to discourage children from touching their genitals. Naturally, some groups opposed the dominant cultural pattern, ranging from celibate New England Shakers to polygamous Mormons to a variety of "free-love" associations. The end of this era produced Sigmund Freud in Austria (with his emphasis on "natural" childhood sexuality) and a post-World War I surge in premarital sex (and venereal disease) that set the stage for the "Roaring Twenties."

Although the hard times of the Great Depression and World War II dampened the personal and sexual freedoms that characterized the collapse of Victorianism, the social control of individual sexual expression continued to lessen steadily over the succeeding decades, more so for males than for females. Freudian notions of sexuality not only influenced clinical work on sexual psychopathology, but filtered into the culture as part of the more general understanding of normal and abnormal sexual expression. The extent of change in sexual behavior patterns in the United States was ultimately reflected in the monumental sociological studies by Alfred Kinsey and his colleagues in 1948 and 1953.[5] These signaled the beginning of more public discussion of sexuality, as well as greater tolerance by many Americans of sexual practices that differed from their own.

Acceptance of diversity in sexual behavior seemed to grow throughout the 1950s and 1960s, considered by some to be a period of "sexual revolution," but actually an extension of the trends begun after World War I. Changes in sexual attitudes were paralled by changes in sexual information, which also served to focus public attention on sexuality. The laboratory studies of human sexual response by William Masters and Virginia Johnson[6] created both curiosity and controversy. What is important to note here are not the findings themselves, but (1) the fact that such studies were conducted at all, and (2) their enormous impact upon the climate of sexual research in the United States, and subsequently upon the sexual attitudes and expectations of American citizens. After the work of Kinsey et al. and of Masters and Johnson, human sexuality could be studied scientifically and talked about publicly (in fact, endlessly in the mass media), and services could be offered to solve sexual problems and improve sexual satisfaction. Eventually, there began to be protests against what some thought to be excess "sexual permissiveness" in American culture. In the past decade, these concerns, along with changes in political ideology and economic con-

ditions, have produced a kind of sexual neoconservatism in some segments of American culture. However, certain liberal trends have also
continued, producing once again a divided society that serves to remind
Americans of their pluralistic cultural roots—and of their sexual ambivalence.[7]

The social boundaries of American families have generally become
more open to cultural influences regarding sex. Various reasons have
been offered for this: increased media impact within the home (especially television); loosening of traditional religious values (though more
conservative values appear to be returning); earlier onset of adolescence
and accompanying peer group influence; heightened awareness of
cultural and ethnic pluralism; and a variety of other cultural and technological factors. Doubtless, each of these has had some influence.
Their overall effect is to confront the American family with the necessity of more frequent and substantial changes in sexual meanings and
behavior patterns than in the past.[8]

Shifts in cultural expectations of gender-linked behaviors have
occurred rapidly but unevenly in American society, meeting with considerable resistance in some quarters. The result is conflict between
competing values—between those wishing to preserve the traditional
traits associated with feminine or masculine images and behavior, and
those wishing to minimize gender differences. The changes to date,
and the controversies that have accompanied them, have produced
considerable confusion about gender roles in American society.[9]

Over the past several decades, lines of interdependence between
the sexes have shifted rather dramatically within the family. The traditional family system in America was based upon gender alliances. In
contrast, today's family depends less upon gender-differentiated role
functions. Instead, generational role alliances have become more prominent—that is, parents on one side, children of either gender on the
other.[10]

Family life in the contemporary United States is characterized more
by diversity than by similarity. The reality of family life is very different from the idealized images traditionally portrayed in the media. Generalizations about "the American family" mask the variety of family
forms, family life styles, and family experiences that actually comprise
life in the United States. Such generalizations can also conceal the
assortment of sexual values, attitudes, and behaviors found among families. Each distinct cultural, socioeconomic, and religious subgroup in
American society exhibits some unique sexual attitudes and behavior
patterns. Even geographic location, and the resulting particularities of
individual and family life style, influence sexual behavior. American
history is actually composed of many histories; similarly, the sexual

histories of individuals and families are complex and varied. The significance of these differences for understanding sexuality in America has increased as sex has moved from the private into the public sphere.[11]

Within this framework of cultural ambiguity, conflicts abound, both between and within individuals. In the 1990s, American society appears to be sharply divided on major sex-related issues. Extremism characterizes much of the debate. There is strong support for both conservative and liberal orientations (with each viewpoint claiming to reflect the "majority" of Americans), while a sizable number of citizens cling to middle ground, either out of apathy or out of preference for moderation. Certain of these divergent views are religiously based—for example, the opposition to free choice about abortion. Other issues are characterized more by subjective opinion and practical arguments—for example, the debate over the connection between pornography and sexual violence.

Observations on Soviet Culture

Conservative Russian historians and theoreticians like to claim that "Holy Russia" has never been troubled by controversies over sex or eroticism. Indeed, this gives credence to the humorous anecdote concerning the visitor who asked a Soviet citizen about the kinds of sexual problems that characterize his country, to which the citizen replied, "What sexual problems? We don't have sex." Actually, historical studies reveal considerable emphasis on the importance of sexuality, although specific knowledge of Russian sexual customs and erotic behavior is limited because of the strict censorship that has taken place for centuries.

A brief historical perspective is helpful in understanding the state of sexology in the Soviet regions today. These remarks are made without special reference to the history of family matters in the former Soviet Union, since that information is recounted in several other chapters of this book.

Ancient Slavic paganism was by no means antisexual; on the contrary, sexuality was believed to be a general cosmic force. Some pagan rites persisted in Russia and the Eastern European countries until the end of the nineteenth century.[12] Among Russian peasants, as among those in other European countries, common-law marriages, illicit sexual liaisons, bawdy songs, erotic tales, and even orgiastic festivals were not uncommon—forming a kind of "sexual underground," despite efforts at prohibition by the church. In these countries, as in Western Europe and the Americas, religious groups attempted to suppress these activities and to exercise strict control over sexual behavior. However, the

Russian Orthodox Church, even in medieval times, appears to have been more lenient than Roman Catholicism and many of the later-emerging Protestant groups.[13] Complete abstinence from sexual relations—even in marriage—was classified as a "holy deed"; however, in everyday life, sexual activity in marriage was fully accepted. Although celibacy was obligatory for the monks from whom the highest church leaders were chosen, ordinary priests were obligated to marry and to have children.

Yet asceticism was especially strong in Russia and Eastern Europe. The canons of the Byzantine Church were particularly strict, inevitably influencing both the art and the culture of these regions. Even before the Renaissance, human flesh was depicted in Western art (always with the genitals covered, of course). By contrast, in Russian icons, the body was completely covered; only the faces were truly "alive." If depicted at all, human bodies were shown as highly emaciated. Nothing similar to the paintings or sculpture of Michelangelo, da Vinci, or Raphael was permitted; even secular paintings of nudes did not appear until the end of the eighteenth century.[14]

The attitudes and actions of the highest classes of Russian society were especially contradictory. Eighteenth-century French "libertines" had particular influence on the Russian imperial court. Although professing to represent genuine "culture" and to set the standards of morality for others, Russian tsars and the nobility took lovers, commissioned frivolous erotic frescos and furniture, and read pornographic literature (mostly imported). Even the revered writer Alexander Pushkin wrote some elegant and witty erotic poetry.

Of course, this kind of prudery and the contradictions and hypocrisy that accompanied it were by no means exclusive to Russia. All of Europe and the Americas were characterized by official puritanical attitudes and public policies that coexisted in tension with the actual erotic behaviors of the populace. Ambivalence regarding sexuality, predicated upon the dualism fostered by religious beliefs, appears to have been a hallmark of Western culture from its earliest inception. In Russia, the antisexual and antisensual mentality was particularly strong because it was supported not only by the moral authority of religious groups, but also by the power of governmental censorship.

In addition, one special set of circumstances has powerfully influenced sexuality in the former Soviet Union: the nineteenth-century "revolutionary–democratic" philosophy. In this view, only broad altruistic social objectives, such as liberation of the poor and oppressed, are morally justified. Everything that is private or personal is considered secondary—and egotistical. Within this framework, internal struggles with one's own sensuality and sexuality are transformed into theoretical principles. These aesthetic and ethical principles are then used as a political ideology to denigrate anything erotic as indecent and vulgar. Thus, until the end of the nineteenth century, erotic imagery, sensual writings, and even lyrical poetry were unacceptable, denounced from both extremes of the political spectrum.

However, by the beginning of the twentieth century, the winds of change were blowing across Europe and Russia. An occasional work of erotic art appeared openly. The problems and contradictions of sexuality were forthrightly described by several popular novelists of the time. The nature of sex and the erotic were seriously discussed by such prominent Russian philosophers as Nikolai Berdjaev, Vladimir Soiovjev, and Vassilij Rozanov. In the early 1900s, the first sexual surveys were conducted among students at Moscow University. Sexual concerns were raised within the disciplines of medicine, history, ethnography, and anthropology. The word "sexology" as a name for a special subdivision of science was suggested by Rosanov in 1909.[15]

For a time following the October Revolution of 1917, these changes continued and even accelerated. No longer was sex a taboo subject. On the contrary, traditional sexual morality, and marriage as a social institution, were themselves suspect. Everywhere there were fierce discussions of "free love" and debates over whether the proletariat needed any sexual restrictions whatsoever. The incidence of premarital and extramarital sexual activity increased dramatically. According to some researchers in the 1920s, 85–95% of men and 45–60% of women in the European republics of the USSR had sexual relations prior to marriage. The rate of unplanned pregnancies was very high, as were the number of abortions and out-of-wedlock births. Anarchistic attitudes and life styles abounded.[16] These were sharply criticized by Lenin, most notably in a well-publicized conversation with Klara Zetkin, in which he strongly opposed the philosophy that likened the sexual drive and its satisfaction to "drinking a glass of water."[17]

By 1930, the sexual anarchy of the postrevolutionary period had receded. The moral orientation toward stable marriage and romantic love had been restored, and new legislation on marriage and the family was established. For an emerging totalitarian society, however, this was not enough. Individual sexual expression was viewed as fundamentally incompatible with unlimited social control. Once again, antisexualism grew to be a political ideology that supported government control at the expense of personal freedom. In the insightful words of British author George Orwell in his novel *1984* (echoing similar thoughts by a banned Soviet writer, Evgenij Zamiatin):

> It was not merely that the sex instinct created a world of its own which was outside the Party's control and which therefore had to be destroyed if possible. What was more important was that sexual privation induced

hysteria, which was desirable because it could be transformed into war fever and leader worship. The way [Julia] put it was:

"When you make love you're using up energy; and afterward you feel happy and don't give a damn for anything. They can't bear you to feel like that. They want you to be bursting with energy all the time. All this marching up and down and cheering and waving flags is simply sex gone sour. If you are happy inside yourself, why should you get excited about Big Brother and the Three-Year Plans and the Two Minutes Hate and all the rest of their bloody rot?"[18]

Initially, the antisexual ideology was simply a natural extension of revolutionary asceticism: The people who were refusing everything for themselves believed they had the right to compel all other people to do the same. The exploitive nature of this thinking was unrecognized. If an individual is primarily a productive force working for the future universal good, then in working hours he/she must produce material goods, and in nonworking hours at home he/she must beget children. Everything else is suspect and needs to be exterminated. This philosophy was quite compatible with both the traditional antisexual attitudes of Russian peasant morality (whatever the peasants' real behavior may have been) and the fanatical left-wing intellectuals' ideas about the necessity of a radical transformation of human nature and social order.

For the half century following 1930, the victims of this totalitarian political orientation included science, art, and education, as well as the citizenry. It was as if the Soviet Union were considered to be without sexuality or even gender. All sex-related research was strictly forbidden, and foreign sexological literature was banned as "pornographic." Sexual surveys, numerous in the 1920s (some of which were known to Alfred Kinsey and his colleagues), completely disappeared, along with the professions of sociology and social psychology. Psychoanalysis, very fashionable in the early 1920s, was sharply criticized on ideological grounds and was virtually forbidden.

Internal moral regulation of personal behavior (conscience) was replaced with direct external social control by the Communist Party and the state, based on repressive intolerance. In 1934, male homosexuality—which had been decriminalized after the October Revolution—was again declared illegal, with even stronger punishment than before. In 1936, abortions became illegal, though no serious efforts were made to develop and make available contraceptive methods; this legislation remained in effect until 1955. Erotic art, and even nonerotic representation of the nude body, were taboo. Sex education was excluded not only from the elementary and secondary schools, but even from medical and educational training and from the research universities. Overt concern about sexual problems was considered "immoral" and "bourgeois."

Virtually no data are available to aid us in chronicling the sexual attitudes and behavior of Soviet people during the traumatic years of World War II and the subsequent years of rebuilding in the 1940s and 1950s. This is the period that has come to be characterized as the Cold War era, whose chill had significant effects on the hearts and minds of the Soviet people, and doubtless also on their sex-related attitudes and behavior. Perhaps new information will come to light in the contemporary efforts toward self-examination that have accompanied *perestroika*.

Gradual changes began in the mid-1960s, though the full implications of these changes were not recognized for nearly two decades; indeed, they are still struggling to manifest themselves today. Until very recently, major sexual research and historical sources could be published only abroad. For example, linguistic research on Russian sexual slang was first published in a two-part article in Hungary.[19] The first and only modern study of *Eroticism in Russian Art* was published by American scholars in London in 1976.[20] The first historical monograph based upon research in Soviet archives—*Sex and Society in the World of the Orthodox Slavs, 900–1700*—was issued by Cornell University Press in 1989.[21] The most comprehensive Russian work on sexuality, Kon's *Introduction to Sexology*, was written in the 1970s; it was published first in Hungary in 1981, then in Germany in 1985, and finally in the Soviet Union in 1988.[22] An English language book, *Sex in Russian Society*, will be published in the United States in 1993.[23]

In the 1960s, several prominent psychiatrists, urologists, and gynecologists initiated seminars and publications on various forms of sexual pathology. A very important integrative role was played by G. S. Vassilchenko, under whose guidance the small Department of Sexopathology of the Moscow Research Institute of Psychiatry received the status of the All-Union Center for Sexopathology in 1973. Vassilchenko believed that "sexopathology" should be an independent clinical discipline, and he published the first Soviet handbooks on general sexopathology and related specialized subjects.[24] Leningrad psychiatrists D. N. Issaev and V. E. Kagan initiated systematic research on child and adolescent sexuality, and subsequently published a handbook.[25] The first two chairs of sexopathology were opened in the Khar'kov and Leningrad Institutes for Higher Medical Education during the 1987–1988 academic year. However, the first comprehensive course on sexuality for medical students is still in preparation, delayed by the chaotic circumstances in Russia. Small, student initiated seminars comprise current efforts to deal with sexual issues in medicine.

Even more problematic is the situation in nonmedical sexology. The first theoretical paper on the sociology of sexual behavior—including a positive evaluation of Kinsey and several other Western research-

ers—was not published until 1966.[26] Researching Soviet sexual behavior has been extremely difficult. In the 1960s, sociologist S. I. Golod
devised several questionnaire surveys on the sexual values and behaviors of Soviet youths.[27] However, when the time came to defend his
doctoral dissertation in 1969, Golod was accused of "ideological sub-
version against Soviet youths," first by the Leningrad Party Committee and then by the Central Committee of the Komsomol. To receive
his doctorate, Golod was forced to prepare another dissertation on
working women in the Soviet Union. Large-scale sexual surveys, like
those of Kinsey and other Western researchers, are still absent from
the former Soviet Union.

Soviet psychology, too, spent fifty years ignoring gender and sexuality. The first review article on Western psychology of sex differences,
which discussed scientific concepts and the measurement of masculinity and femininity, was published only in 1981.[28] Original research on
these topics has just begun, although there are now some reliable
empirical data about sex role stereotypes and gender-linked behaviors
(see Chapter 2).

The general trends in the development of sexual behavior in the
former Soviet Union are similar to those in the United States and other
Western countries. They include earlier sexual maturation and onset
of sexual activity; more tolerance for premarital sexual activity, including open cohabitation; a reduction in attitudinal and behavioral differences between males and females regarding sex; increased importance of sexual satisfaction as a contributor to stability and happiness
in marriage; the growth of public interest in erotica; and sharp differences in amount of sexual information and value orientations between
older and younger generations.[29]

However, ethnic, religious, and regional differences in these matters is vastly greater than in the United States. These differences, along
with the authoritarian styles of social, community, and family life that
have historically characterized the former Soviet Union, keep many of
the most important changes in sex-related attitudes and behaviors
"under cover." Therefore, the incidence of these changes may be considerably underestimated.

SEXUAL ISSUES FOR CONTEMPORARY FAMILIES

Overall "Neglect" of Sexual Health and Hygiene

Many American families may be said to be sexually "neglectful"—characterized by feelings of shame and ambivalence; lacking the language

by which to transmit basic sex information; and intimidated by changing social values. The average American family does not deal openly or adequately even with basic sexual concerns: genital hygiene, personal anxieties about sex, physical affection, body image, sex information, and the like. Although general public communication about sex has increased greatly since midcentury, the ability to communicate meaningfully about personal sexual matters is still extremely limited. More candid discussions about sex take place on national television shows than between individuals in most American households.[30]

As a result of these limitations, Americans are primarily oriented toward solving problems rather than promoting *positive* expressions of sexuality. Therefore, most of their efforts are directed at finding remedies for difficulties that have already developed (e.g., services for pregnant adolescents), rather than at preventing difficulties through efforts to improve sexual health (e.g., devising innovative programs of sex education). An encouraging sign may be found in the contemporary American interest in physical fitness for both females and males of all ages, which enriches a long-standing preoccupation with youth and physical attractiveness.

Like Americans, Russians and other ethnic groups in the western republics are historically rather prudish regarding nudity and bodily functions. The attitudes of Muslims in the eastern republics are even stricter. Twenty-five years ago, there was controversy about wearing any kind of shorts in public, including at beach resorts. Now blue jeans are commonly worn, and walking shorts have begun to appear; however, this is true only in the western regions. Body exposure by Muslim women in the eastern regions is still strictly forbidden, and violating the taboo can lead to severe punishment. In these regions, shorts even on men are considered indecent.

Bodily functions are not openly acknowledged in Soviet culture. Direct reference to the need for a toilet is considered impolite. Soviets will just quietly disappear from a meeting or social gathering, or, at most, will simply refer to their intention to walk in a particular direction. Even young people who are dating and know each other well often make up artificial explanations before excusing themselves to find a toilet. An additional contributor to the avoidance of overt discussion of bodily functions may be the sorry state of contemporary Soviet plumbing. Part of the general breakdown of material goods and services in Soviet society includes the public restroom facilities. Many toilets are cracked and/or missing their flushing mechanisms; most do not have seats or covers. Wash basins may stand idle, or may yield only a dribble of cold water. Toilet tissue is scarce; substitutes for it include newspaper, magazine pages, used office papers, and even cardboard.

Thus, it should not be surprising to learn that standards of Soviet hygiene contrast sharply with those of the United States. Despite the attention paid to cleanliness by many citizens, the combination of bodily inhibitions and inadequate material resources threatens their overall health, makes personal hygiene more difficult, and frustrates their attempts to improve personal appearance through grooming. Even the interest in improving physical fitness through better diet and exercise is only beginning, despite a long history of purported government commitment to the health of all citizens.

All in all, the Soviet ambivalence toward nakedness, bodily functions, intimate hygiene, and sexuality parallels that of Americans. However, the history of heavy censorship and the contemporary lack of material resources combine to make the impact of these factors on everyday life even greater.

Gender Conflicts in Marriage

The social movement known in the United States as "feminism" has raised issues about the value of marriage for women, as well as the impact of traditional family roles and values on the personality development, physical health, and mental health of females in American society.[31] Changes in sex role expectations and behaviors have contributed to changes in marriage, divorce, and postdivorce relationships between men and women. Clearly, patterns of marital interaction are changing, and family life is significantly affected by the social reconstruction of gender currently occurring in North America.[32]

Family scholars now recognize that every marriage is actually two marriages—"his" and "hers"—and that the two often do not coincide. Role-related power struggles and communication difficulties strain the capacity of a couple to maintain an intimate and rewarding relationship over the course of a marriage.[33] What happens outside the family in a society whose gender role patterns are changing can be seen to have a powerful effect on life inside the family. Many of these effects are described elsewhere in this book.

Like the United States, the former Soviet Union is experiencing substantial confusion, change, and controversy regarding sex role expectations within marriage and in the society at large. As in the United States and many other Western countries, the attitudes and values of the Soviet people are ambiguous and contradictory. During the 1940s and 1950s, official government propaganda claimed complete equality of the sexes and professed total disregard for any gender differences. The relationship between the genders was characterized as one of "comrades" in the social struggle. At the same time, the importance of family relationships was minimized; therefore, the normative model of humanity was inevitably the traditional image of masculinity, rooted in extrafamilial social and industrial activities.

In reality, however, the so-called "emancipation" of women was a utopian dream. Certainly women were heavily involved in a variety of industrial and cultural activites outside of the family; however, they were not liberated either from their dependent social status or from traditional household and childrearing tasks. A popular Soviet joke observes that women are capable of doing every kind of work, but only under the supervision of a man.

Hence, from the 1950s on, there has been a growing sense of disappointment in the capacity of the Soviet society to meet the needs and enhance the lives of women. The result has been a kind of backlash against the socialist ideal of emancipation. Although egalitarian on the surface, Soviet society is profoundly sexist at a deeper, and perhaps unconscious, level. Many citizens seem to dream of returning to prerevolutionary, or even preindustrial, models of gender relationships. Much of the scientific—and some pseudoscientific—literature on gender highlights biological differences between the sexes. There are currently numerous public debates on whether it is better to return women to their "natural" functions as wives and mothers or to work toward another new and different social role for women. Thus far, the experiences of Europe and North America are equivocal as guides for Soviet thinking. New roles for women are seen by many as contributing to social problems such as divorce and domestic violence; therefore, some believe they are to be avoided. At the same time, it is interesting to note that former British Prime Minister Margaret Thatcher was one of the public figures most highly regarded by citizens of the former Soviet Union.

The Soviet situation is further complicated by the fact that an entire generation of children was reared following World War II without the significant presence of men. So many males were lost in the war that single-parent families were common (though interaction with extended family members was and still is more substantial than in the United States). Those males who did survive were so vital to the postwar work force that their participation in family life was minimal.

In a sense, this problem is simply an exaggerated version of the global dilemma of men's family role in the industrialized nations. When fathers work outside the home and do little in relation to household work or childrearing, their power is based largely upon general social status, work success, and financial contribution. When women join the work force, but continue to be responsible for managing the family and household, then men's authority and influence inside their families are reduced. A mother becomes the dominant figure for her children, while the father's image becomes more diffuse, stereotyped, even "mystical." Women are burdened with needing to succeed in two different, and sometimes contrasting, social roles. However, men are also burdened by needing to maintain all of their self-esteem in the world of work.

Under the old Soviet regime, the most successful men were those who could be subservient, compromising, and conforming. Independence was not valued; indeed, it was often punished. Therefore, men became passive and sought to avoid responsibility—victimized by a rigid system. This forced women to take more responsibility. They, too, became victims of the society. Women grew bitter, resentful, and cynical about men. Men became disheartened and more dependent within the household, sometimes trying to compensate for their low self-esteem by being tyrannical and even abusive with their wives and children.

In many ways, this remains the state of the Soviet family today. Many citizens are conservative. They want to turn back the clock to a time when women's socially assigned roles were clear and their burdens were lighter—when men had the "superior" position and could be relied upon to be powerful and decisive. The direction in which Soviet society will proceed is still very uncertain.

Sexual Relations in Marriage

American marriages have gradually emerged as companionate arrangements based upon love, rather than as functional arrangements based upon economics—although economic stability has an important influence on marital stability.[34] Aided by research on sexual function and by the technological separation of erotic expression and reproduction, increased attention is now paid to the quality of sexual interaction as a major contributor to marital stability and success. Some of the results are positive: American couples are more sexually active than in the past, and many wives as well as husbands report sexual satisfaction. However, some of the outcomes seem negative: Male sexual dysfunction has increased, and more spouses of both genders report anxiety about living up to high sexual performance standards. The most prominent sexual issues in American marriages today are those of sexual dissatisfaction rather than dysfunction. Primary dynamics relate to differences in level of sexual desire. These, in turn, reflect a variety of influences—ranging from simple fatigue to difficulties in coordinating the schedules of two working spouses to the role-related power struggles previously mentioned.[35] The availability of clinical programs has led to revelations of widespread sexual problems, and a large number of people have sought help. In the past decade, acknowledging sexual problems and seeking help for them have even become somewhat fashionable.

Americans continue to be concerned and confused about nonmarital erotic relationships. The majority of both male and female Americans have sexual intercourse at some time before marriage. Similarly, a substantial number of men and a growing number of women have extramarital affairs, despite a generally disapproving attitude. Americans are somewhat more liberal in their *tolerance* for sexual variety than in their actual behavior.[36] The atmosphere of experimentation in intimate relationships during the 1960s and 1970s appears to have given way to a reaffirmation of monogamy in the 1980s and 1990s, supported both by emerging conservatism in values and by the practicalities of health risks such as herpes and acquired immune deficiency syndrome (AIDS). Future patterns of marital sexuality are unclear. The previous emphasis on the physiological and psychological *similarities* of male and female sexuality, prominent in the research writings of the 1970s and 1980s, has given way to literature emphasizing *differences* in the erotic attitudes and experiences of the genders.

As indicated in the historical summary provided above, Soviet attitudes toward sexual expression have generally tended to be conservative. Nevertheless, the role of sexual relations in marriage has always been important. As in the United States, sexual satisfaction seems to vary in relation to overall satisfaction with the marriage relationship. In surveys of married couples conducted in 1978 and 1981, sexual satisfaction was found to be the third most important contributor to marital satisfaction, following after "just distribution of household work" and "psychological compatibility, including mutual love and esteem." Most happily married couples reported basic sexual compatibility; even among unhappy couples, about 60% still believed that they were sexually compatible. Men are still considered to be the primary initiators of sexual activity, although it is becoming more permissible for younger women to indicate their erotic interests openly. There is some indirect evidence that the frequency of sexual activity in Soviet marriages is rather low. Rather than a sexual problem per se, this is viewed as resulting from lack of time and the pressures of work and daily living.[37]

At least in Russia and the other western republics today, erotic expression is clearly distinguished from plans for marriage or even engagement. Sexual activity with one's future spouse is now statistically normal and is seldom condemned publicly for social or moral reasons. Young couples who are cohabiting have now been nonjudgmentally interviewed on Moscow television. In one study of 1,400 college freshmen, only 17% of the males and 20% of the females declined for themselves the possibility of engaging in premarital, or even extramarital, sexual activity.[38]

The presence of the so-called "double standard" in acceptance of sexual activity for males and females should also be noted. This attitude is particularly prominent in the southern and eastern Soviet regions. Sometimes it can lead to difficult, but interesting, patterns of behavior. For example, in Georgia, women's sexual standards are generally more conservative than those in Russia or the Baltic countries. This includes a strong emphasis upon virginity in young women, to avoid bringing dishonor upon their families when they marry. At the same time, young males are encouraged in their sexual exploits. The result is that young Georgian men frequent the popular summer resorts on the Black Sea, where they encounter young women from other republics who come to "have fun." When sexual activity occurs, stereotypes develop: Georgians view Russian women as "easy," while Russians view Georgian men as "sex-crazy." Neither of these stereotypes is accurate. However, outside of their own cultural context, the behavior of youths and their sense of responsibility for consequences become distorted.

Just as in the United States, Soviet patterns of extramarital sexual activity typically reflect the double standard. Public opinion appears to tolerate infidelity by husbands more readily than infidelity by wives. The actual incidence of extramarital activity is extremely difficult to estimate. Doubtless it has increased over recent decades, along with the rate of divorce. Infidelity (at least by men) is thought by many people to be inevitable. However, its results can be troublesome and even traumatic. In the eastern Islamic republics, the strong double standard permits males to have multiple sexual partners, while severely punishing females who have sex with anyone other than their husbands. In part, this reflects the continuing separation of love and marriage in rural areas, where marriages are still arranged by families.

Atypical practices, such as group sexual contact, are known to occur among certain Soviet youth groups; however, the actual extent of such practices is unknown. So-called "open sex" has always been popular among certain student factions in the western republics. Like other aspects of young people's lives, sexuality is more openly expressed today than in the past.

One particular aspect of youthful frankness in sexual activity contrasts sharply with conditions in the United States. In addition to the growing inclination of young people to be more open and assertive about their beliefs, values, and behavior, in contrast to their elders, certain conditions of Soviet life make this openness a necessity. Specifically, the extremely inadequate housing conditions that exist across the country, particularly in major cities such as Moscow, require youths to be less inhibited (and perhaps less hypocritical) than previous generations. Sexual activity with future spouses, or even with casual dates, must often take place within the family household. Since families are typically crowded into tiny flats and parents seldom leave home to attend recreational functions, young people are often under surveillance by their elders, even though the parents may find this role unpleasant. Scenes like those depicted in the widely acclaimed and controversial 1988 Soviet film *Little Vera*—intergenerational conflict over sexual activity in the family home, and the encroachment on parents' lives by their daughter and her lover—are all too typical of Soviet working-class families.

Changing Patterns of Sex Role Socialization

All cultures have gender-linked social roles, although the content of these roles varies greatly from one society to another. Many different images of masculinity and femininity are currently available to Americans. As a result, ambivalence about gender roles and behavior has become particularly acute. With gender-linked images, attitudes, and behavior apparently in transition, American parents often express concern about childrearing. On the one hand, parents want their children to be individuals; on the other hand, they want them to "fit into" society. Every parent has a particular notion of the best blending of gender-linked characteristics for children—based primarily, of course, on his/her own particular values and life experiences.

Americans have begun to recognize that changes in women's roles and social expectations about female behavior will not occur without some corresponding changes in men's lives and in society's expectations of males.[39] Although many Americans are optimistic about the future, the short-range results of these gender transitions appear to be confusion, anxiety, and frustration, as well as some unique forms of tension between males and females. Concerns about gender-related aspects of childrearing are particularly strong, in light of the fact that a sizable number of children spend significant time during their developmental years in single-parent households (usually with their mothers). Thus, the prevalence of divorce and the increase in out-of-wedlock parenthood contribute to worry about gender socialization. Children without parental role models and direct family influences on their gender learning may well be more responsive to public images and social stereotypes that can increase their confusion and ambivalence.

Since American children spend a great deal of time exposed to communications media (primarily television), cultural images of females and males have a significant impact on their gender development. Despite some nominal changes in the portrayals of females and males in the mass media, gender-linked stereotypes still abound. Several decades may pass before a genuine balance will be achieved, in which both males and females will have a broad range of choices about behaviors and life styles that are not unduly restricted by gender. Here again, Americans' tolerant attitudes toward variety and choice tend to outdistance their actual behaviors.

The issue of sex role socialization has barely begun to receive attention in Soviet society, in connection with controversies over the role of women. Despite official constitutional guarantees of equality and the cultural propaganda that minimized male–female differences for decades, one can still walk into a school or childrearing center (even in the modern industrialized cities) and notice that all of the girls, no matter what the length of their hair, are wearing brightly colored hair ribbons that immediately distinguish them from the boys. Until recently, Soviet psychology had no theoretical basis or research data upon which to challenge the common-sense assumption that the differences observed between boys and girls are in some sense "automatic" and therefore merely an outgrowth of biological necessity—an interesting conclusion in a society that formerly prided itself on shaping human behavior through a variety of mechanisms of social control! Indeed, the behavior of male and female children *has* been shaped in a rather "traditional" direction, most likely in ways that have unconsciously stimulated behavioral differences and thereby put pressure on boys and girls whose behavior does not conform to preconceived notions of masculinity and femininity.

Theoretical discussions of gender socialization patterns are just beginning, and these may eventually have a profound influence on changing the problematic circumstances of women and children in Soviet society.[40] Soviet social scientists recognize that studying women's issues is not enough; the entire subject of gender socialization must be investigated. However, there are many obstacles to these developments, including controversies between progressive and reactionary influences in Soviet society; tremendous barriers of religious resistance to role changes in most of the eastern republics; and even material shortages resulting from the current economic difficulties.

Sex Education and Guidance of Children and Youths

The family is always the primary source of sex education for children. In many ways, sex education occurs even if parents are not aware of providing it. The close nature of everyday family interaction is such that children will inevitably absorb meanings and attitudes regarding both gender and erotic aspects of sexuality. The degree of respect shown to female versus male family members has a significant impact on the emerging gender identities of the children. Similarly, the family's appreciation of embodiment, including positive forms of touch and facilitation of appropriate erotic expression, contributes to the personality development and self-image of its young members.[41]

Sex education is only a particular case of a more general "paternalistic" orientation that characterizes life in most societies of the world. Beneath the problems of providing sex education lies the universal power struggle between parents and children, old and young, teachers and pupils. The general language and tone of every discourse about sexuality convey the message that the wise elders know the "truth" and want to guide their children in avoiding the dangers of life.

Most Americans, both parents and youths, agree that the home ought to be the primary source of information about sex, as well as the place for learning sexual values. Many parents want to provide sex education for their children, but are uncertain of how to go about it. This is understandable, in view of rapid changes in social values and the widespread exposure of young people to contrasting opinions, complex decisions, and options for behavior that their parents never had to face. As a result, most parents do not provide their children with sexual information in a comprehensive and timely way. The primary sources of such information are the peer group and the mass media, with parents ranking further down the list, behind even school programs.[42] As a result, American adults are still woefully ignorant about sex. In a recent national survey conducted by the Kinsey Institute for Sex Research, more than half the respondents "flunked" an eighteen-question test on basic sexual physiology and behavior.[43]

The majority of American parents support sex education in the schools, although it has been a controversial subject in many communities. There is disagreement about what content is appropriate for schools to teach, and at what grade levels. Public school sex education programs have been the source of considerable controversy in many communities. In reponse to pressure from very vocal and well-organized groups (representing a minority of parents), many school systems have omitted sex education from the curriculum or removed courses in order to avoid controversy.[44] Sex education programs are sometimes blamed for various social problems, such as adolescent pregnancy. However, research has shown that such programs actually have *less* effect on sexual behavior than the educators themselves would like. The results they *do* appear to have are as follows: (1) improved sexual knowledge, (2) increased personal comfort with sexual topics, (3) improved communication with peers and parents, and (4) more effective use of contraception when sexual activity does occur.[45]

Well-organized, comprehensive programs of sex education are still lacking across the former Soviet Union, often because of the ignorance, inhibitions, and discomfort of adults themselves. Typically, parents and children do not talk about sex in any but the most general ways. The greater freedom that has emerged recently in Soviet society, along with the willingness of government leaders and public figures to acknowledge mistakes and criticize each other in the spirit of *glasnost*, has highlighted the contrasting attitudes of parents and youths regarding sexuality and a variety of other social issues. At the same time that many parents seem to be longing for a return to "traditional values," young people are openly expressing sexual attitudes and behavior typical of "modern" youths around the world. However, the reduction of social control, coupled with sexual ignorance and poorly articulated values, poses a serious risk to the society.

There is clear evidence that sexual activity is beginning earlier for today's Soviet adolescents. The largest percentage of young people become sexually active between the ages of sixteen and eighteen, with an incidence of intercourse reported in various studies ranging from 22% to 38% of boys and 11% to 35% of girls. "Love" is reported to be the primary motivator for sexual activity by many young people (about 30% of males and 45% of females), followed by "desire for enjoyment" or "pleasure" (approximately 20% of males and 10% of females). Many young people separate sexual motives from those involving marriage or engagement.[46]

The Soviets still have virtually no systematic sex education in schools, not so much because of adverse public opinion as because of the conservatism of the central governments and educational bureaucracies. Some notable efforts have been made, particularly in Moscow, to develop school-based programs. In a recent national public opinion poll,[47] the following answers were given to this question: "What channels of information on sexual life do you believe are the most acceptable and efficient?"

- Special school course—46%
- Special educational literature—43%
- Special educational films or TV—29%
- Consultation with physician—22%
- Conversation with parents—21%
- Discussion with peers—5%
- Personal experience—6%
- No need for sex education—3%

Clearly, a majority of the population favors organized sex education efforts. However, as recently as 1989, a poll in one large city found that adolescents' primary source of sex information was their peers (62%).[48] As this book goes to press, small centers have been opened in Moscow for dealing with sexual issues in the adolescent culture. Several sex education books and pamphlets are being released. These represent a beginning, but much remains to be done. Efforts to develop a large center in Moscow for dealing with adolescent social and sexual problems collapsed in 1992 due to organizational difficulties and lack of funds.

In still another respect, Soviet and American societies are similar. During the height of the Cold War period, organized groups that opposed school sex education programs in the United States charged that sex education was "a dirty Communist conspiracy directed at undermining the morals of American youths." Recently, hard-line Stalinists and Russian chauvinists have claimed that attempts at sex education reflect "a Western imperialist and Zionist conspiracy against the moral standards of Soviet youths." In both countries, these radical right-wing groups have enjoyed considerable success in sabotaging efforts to implement school programs of sex education. Even now, efforts to equip young people with information and assistance in sexual decision making still fall prey to politics resembling those of the Cold War era, as well as to the widespread ambivalence toward eroticism that continues to characterize most of the Western world.

Sex, Disease, and Disability

Even common diseases or temporary disabilities and their medical management can substantially affect sexual desire or the ability to function sexually.[49] Major conditions and disabilities, whether congenital or acquired, will naturally influence the lives of individuals and their families in profound ways. Families in which a member is physically disabled or developmentally impaired face special challenges when dealing with sexuality. Some of these difficulties result from the general attitudes of society toward individuals who are "exceptional" in some way. Negative stereotypes range from the belief that disabled individuals are nonsexual (i.e., that their sexual interest and capacity have disappeared along with their particular physical or sensory impairment) to the view that they are hypersexual (i.e., that they have sexual frustrations or undisciplined sex drives that make them potential rapists or child molesters). Still another concern is a generalized fear of the reproductive potential of physically handicapped, developmentally delayed, or emotionally disturbed individuals—anxiety that more such people will be brought into the world.[50]

The number of disabled individuals in the United States has increased in the past two decades, primarily as a result of advances in medical technology that improve survival rates and make possible greater mobility and higher levels of activity. Along with increase in numbers has come a stronger emphasis on the "rights" of the disabled, including the right to full sexual expression in responsible ways. American technology plays a major role in making possible the repair of physical anomalies and the remedy of a variety of sexual dysfunctions.

Faced with the problems of socialization and/or caretaking, many American families place their exceptional members in institutions, where the problems of dealing with sexuality are likely to be multiplied. Most disturbing of all is the recent recognition that disabled and handicapped individuals are among those most vulnerable to sexual exploitation and abuse—by caretaking staff members in institutions, by both strangers and acquaintances, and even by family members.[51] In the past decade, pressure has increased on health care institutions to provide both medical and psychosocial services that enhance rather than detract from the sexual well-being of individuals who are ill or disabled. However, the necessary changes in attitudes and specialized training of health care personnel will take considerable time and effort.

In the former Soviet Union, physical and mental disabilities in and of themselves were long a taboo topic, very much as sexuality was. The Soviet people's awareness of disabled individuals and the problems they face is still limited, perhaps like that of Americans twenty-five years ago. This may be attributable in part to the ready availability of abortion, permitting termination of pregnancy in which fetal abnormality is detected. However, several important factors have increased social consciousness about disability in the era of *glasnost*, much as the consciousness of Americans was increased in connection with wounded veterans returning from Vietnam. The first is the number of wounded soldiers resulting from the conflict in Afghanistan. The second is the recognition of the terrible long-term effects of the Chernobyl atomic power plant disaster and the devastating earthquake in Armenia. These events, and the media's humanitarian orientation toward them, have alerted Soviet citizens—and government agencies—to the realities of dealing with survivors whose lives have been changed forever by physical disability and long-term illness. However, the sex-related implications of these phenomena have not yet been openly discussed.

In the context of overcrowded and deteriorating conditions in hospitals, institutions, and other care facilities, concern with sexuality appears to be a luxury that society and health professionals cannot afford. In addition, the professionals themselves have little information or training that might make them more aware of sex-related problems and provide them with resources to be helpful to patients. Therefore, just as in the United States, tragic stories of individuals whose loneliness, loss of self-esteem, or sexual frustration as a result of injury or illness characterizes everyday life will continue to be told and largely ignored. Perhaps in the not-too-distant future, physicians and other health professionals will have the motivation and opportunity to consider the positive contribution that "sexual health" might make to a society struggling to create a more humane context for its citizens.

Sexuality and Aging

Sexual capacity and interest are more a function of one's overall state of health than of age per se. Both Soviets and Americans are living longer. One result of this increased longevity is a concern for the intimate relationships of older people—physically, psychologically, and socially. American research has shown that many of the elderly, both males and females, are still sexually interested and active; indeed, sexual interest and activity may contribute to the vigor and well-being of some individuals.[52] However, the effects of aging and some predictable changes in physical health require alterations in expectations and flexibility in behavior that some older individuals find difficult, particularly if they do not have a readily available, interested, and cooperative partner. Since American women outlive men by a number of years, they must often face the prospect of years without the companionship, support, affection, or sexual interest of a partner.[53]

Sexual interest and activity can also complicate the lives of the elderly, as well as the lives of family members and institutional caretakers. Many older Americans (especially women) are single, raising questions about the moral and social appropriateness of sexual activity. Family members are often resistant to the intimacy needs of their aging parents. Retirement and health care facilities are usually ill equipped, both practically and ideologically, for dealing with elderly individuals who wish to cohabit or to engage in short-term sexual liaisons. The result can be sexual frustration and resentment on the part of aging individuals. Many of the sex-related implications of aging in American society have yet to be realized as the population of older Americans increases.[54] The interplay among altered moral values, improved physical health, and changing socioeconomic conditions is likely to lead to a pattern of social life among the elderly that is unlike anything in the past.

The status and care of the aging population are major problems in Soviet society, as in the United States (see Chapter 5). Caregiving by family members or by the state is the most prominent concern; however, questions have also arisen regarding companionship arrangements among the elderly themselves. Some older widows and widowers remarry; most do not, and a few choose to "live together" for companionship, avoiding the loneliness that inevitably arises when family is not available or willing to help. The effects of the rising divorce rate on the life styles and sexual behavior of Soviets as they grow older is difficult to predict. Today's elderly are often guided by religious or social morality that does not sanction sexual activity outside of marriage. Nonmarital sexual expression is more acceptable to middle-aged individuals; however, these liberal sentiments may not follow them into old age. Here, too, economics may be the greatest influence. If physical health and economic survival are not guaranteed, then broader "quality-of-life" issues cannot be addressed. At the same time, it would appear that, in the face of very poor standards of living and few material resources, aging Soviets may discover—as have their American counterparts—the advantages of pairing off and sharing resources, with or without benefit of marriage.

Homosexuality and Families

Research evidence suggests that perhaps 5–10% of American adults are erotically and romantically attracted primarily to members of their own gender.[55] Only recently have a majority of American states repealed laws making consensual adult homosexual behavior a crime. However, antigay sentiments are still very strong among certain groups of Americans; condemnation by religious bodies, and discrimination in living and working conditions, are still common.

No statistical studies of homosexuality are available in the former Soviet Union. Cross-cultural research generally supports estimates of levels similar to those of the United States, though strong social sanctions against homosexuality may reduce the number of individuals willing to acknowledge a same-sex orientation. Until 1988, public discussion of homosexuality did not occur; accurate information was simply unavailable.[56] Homosexual behavior, at least among males, is still a serious criminal offense in Russia and most other Soviet countries. The first "official statistics" ever published revealed that in 1987, 831 men were sentenced to prison for this crime. Since the breakup of the Soviet Union, several countries have decriminalized homosexual behavior, particularly in the Baltic region. Decriminalization of homosexual behavior is now under discussion in Russia; however, the level of homophobia in the population is still very high and is associated with almost every kind of vice and degeneracy in the public mind, not the least of which is the spread of the virus that causes AIDS.

In cultures that judge homosexual orientation to be sinful and/ or sick and/or illegal (such as both the United States and the former Soviet Union), homosexual individuals encounter many obstacles in the course of their own development and in the establishment of a personal identity and life style as adults. Families of homosexuals are also affected by society's antigay/antilesbian stance, in part because they have often been blamed for creating this atypical sexual orientation— even though research evidence does not support such a conclusion.[57] Thus, parents are likely to be both worried and defensive when they confront behavior in one of their children that may lead to questions about homosexuality. Soviet parents must face, in addition, the fear of legal consequences if homosexual behavior is confirmed and becomes publicly known. If an adolescent boy or girl appears to have a "crush" on a classmate or peer of the same gender, his/her parents may consult a physician or psychiatrist, who is almost certain to directly discourage or attempt to eradicate the feelings and to prevent any erotic activity.

If the gay/lesbian individual reaches adulthood without the family's learning of his/her erotic preference, then the family will have to adjust to this revelation or face the separation and alienation that can result when the homosexual refuses to share the secret with family members. At least half of the adult homosexuals in the United States do not disclose their sexual orientation to their parents, even though some of the parents may recognize or infer it.[58] Those individuals who do share their sexual orientation with family members, particularly during adolescence, are likely to experience negative reactions and/or rejection, which can add further to their anxieties and feelings of self-doubt. Recently, books, support groups, and counseling programs have appeared that are designed to help families of gays and lesbians deal with issues that arise from the disclosure and the ensuing relationships.

In Soviet society, virtually *all* gay and lesbian adults attempt to keep their orientation a secret from family, friends, and colleagues in the workplace. The risks of public scandal and humiliation, rejection by family and friends, loss of a job, and even legal complications are simply too great. In addition, a great deal of pressure is likely to be applied for these individuals to seek psychiatric treatment to "change," even though they themselves may have no interest in it.

For a long time, it was thought that the world of gays and lesbians existed totally outside the context of the family. Homosexuals were considered inherently "promiscuous," and their sexual activity was thought to be totally impersonal. Recent research in the United States has revealed that the majority of lesbians are involved in stable, long-term relationships. Similarly, many gay males are in committed, love-oriented relationships, even if some are also engaging in sexual contacts with others outside the primary relationship.[59] Though fear of AIDS has increased homophobia in some quarters, the disease has also had the effect of increasing the level of commitment to monogamy and of coalescing support for homosexual individuals by their family members and friends.[60] In addition, more and more homosexual individuals and couples have taken steps to become parents, either through adoption or through alternative means (artificial insemination from a donor, becoming involved in foster care, etc.).

Finally, we should note that a sizable number of American homosexuals live in heterosexual marriages, with or without the knowledge of their partners. Undoubtedly, a significant number of homosexuals are "hidden" in Soviet marriages as well. This situation is likely to remain the same in the former USSR for the foreseeable future.

Even research efforts will be discouraged in the former Soviet Union as long as legal consequences remain severe and attitudes are so negative. Nevertheless, there are some hopeful signs. Careful initiatives have been made by some "underground" gay and lesbian groups in Moscow and several other major cities to provide a community of support for individuals with a same-sex orientation. For example, in May 1990, Tallinn, Estonia, was host to the first international conference examining the living conditions of sexual minorities in Europe and the USSR. In Moscow, an association of gays and lesbians has been formed, with their own legal newspaper, *Theme*. A similar association has been organized in St. Petersburg. In addition, a handful of psychiatrists and other mental health professionals are sympathetic to the needs of this population and are trying to find some means of helping individuals who must struggle to develop their personal identities amidst circumstances that make "coming out" a negative and even dangerous experience. Recently, sympathetic articles have appeared in the Soviet press, along with open discussions of homosexuality on television. Clearly, the topic is no longer unmentionable.

Sexual Abuse and Violence

Growing evidence of widespread sexual abuse of children has shocked American society in the past decade, particularly the recognition that such abuse occurs primarily at the hands of family members and others who are well known to the children, rather than as molestation by strangers. In the United States, as many as one in three or four girls and one in nine or ten boys have been sexually abused by an adult before the age of eighteen.[61] Much of this adult–child sexual contact is incestuous. The incidence of incest is even higher in selected subgroups of American society, particularly families in which there is serious alcoholism or drug abuse. In light of a number of well-publicized cases, concerns have also been raised about protecting children from sexual abuse by older children or adults in schools, community organizations, and child care centers.

Reports of sexual abuse are extremely uncommon in Soviet society. Under the old Soviet regime, incest was not deemed to exist as a societal problem. Indeed, any kind of child abuse and violence in the family, while thought to be widespread, is only beginning to come to the attention of authorities and the professional community. As in the United States in the past, the number of children who are physically punished is very high; it has not been considered to be a problem. Even children themselves take it to be normal and report that they expect to beat their own children if they misbehave. Very recently, the Soviet press has begun to raise concerns about this treatment of children.

Some health professionals and others have begun to uncover evidence of various kinds of sexual activity between adults and children, as well as between children of different ages in orphanages, youth camps, and even families. Several American professionals attending a 1989 national conference of Soviet psychologists were questioned closely about incest dynamics by the Soviets, who informally acknowledged and were told that adolescents and young adults are beginning to come forward for counseling in the aftermath of sexual abuse by parents and other caretaking adults. At the same time, it seems unlikely that the reporting of sexual abuse will reach the same proportions as in the United States, at least in the foreseeable future. On the one hand, this may reflect a closed society that is less oriented toward the widespread dissemination of family health information, instead leaving such matters to government authorities and health professionals. On the other hand, this reticence may indicate a desire to avoid the hysteria and sensationalism that sometimes characterize media coverage of controversial topics in the United States.

However, the problem of sexual violence, especially among adolescents, is receiving Soviet attention. Though the rape statistics are much lower than those in the United States, their rate of increase is considerably higher. In 1988, the Soviet Union officially registered 17,658 rapes and rape attempts; in 1989, the figure was 21,873.[62] (Given the traditional reluctance of Soviet citizens and authorities to discuss negative information, and particularly sexual topics, these figures are undoubtedly lower than the actual incidence; moreover, they do not include coercive sexual activity within marriages.) There is now also official acknowledgment of large numbers of same-sex rapes in correctional institutions, committed in order to establish and maintain a social hierarchy, just as in American prisons. Coercive sexual activity has been revealed in the context of the Soviet army as well.

At this time, Soviet society is not equipped materially or attitudinally to confront these problems in a creative manner. Rather than examining the built-in sexual contradictions that characterize Soviet culture or the general trends that accompany periods of rapid social transition, many Soviet citizens simply lament the liberalization of traditional morality and blame the influence of "Western" (read "American") capitalism and pornography. Indeed, in desperate economic times, there is a danger that Soviet citizens will be attracted to the worst elements of American sexuality—its commercialization through advertising, and degrading elements of the sex industry such as pornographic videos.

Even if the commitment to deal realistically with these issues were present, the current state of the Soviet economy precludes economic or technical support for remedial services or preventive programs. Telephone hotline services for rape victims are virtually nonexistent, and specialized professional help focusing on sexuality is largely unavailable for sex offenders. However, there is hope that increasing attention to the problems will soon improve efforts toward some solutions.

In the United States, considerable efforts have been made to develop public policies and laws to deal with child sexual abuse and with other kinds of sex-related violence, such as rape. Numerous treatment programs have arisen, and efforts are beginning to be directed toward prevention. Indeed, some contend that an entire "industry" has been created to deal with issues of sex-related violence in American culture. Since research on the long-range outcomes of treatment is limited, questions still exist about various approaches to intervention—their benefits and hazards for victims, for perpetrators, for other family members, and for the family as a unit.[63] Coupled with questions about the reliability of children as witnesses in sexual abuse trials, the definitions of abuse within marriage and the family, and the disputes over the rights of society to intervene in family matters, major controversies continue to exist regarding the "reality" of sexual violence and American society's response to it.

By contrast, Soviet society does not yet have the information base, the professional training, the community awareness, or the public support to confront these sexual issues. Though the organized Soviet system of schools, camps, day care denters, and even orphanages has contributed much to the welfare of children, numerous issues such as abuse remain to be addressed. The formation of the Children's Fund, a charitable foundation designed to fund research and services for children, represents an important step in this direction, as does the continuing development of various centers and clinics designed to deal with "women's problems."

Family Planning and Contraception

Attitudes toward childbearing vary in different cultures and at different times in history, depending upon both demographic trends and social values. Twentieth-century technology has increased the potential for separation between erotic and reproductive motives for sexual activity. As a result, individuals and couples in technologically advanced societies may have choices about whether to have children, and, if so, when and how many. However, many cultures of the world are faced with problems of overpopulation; therefore, social pressures, cultural attitudes, and even government policies may enter into couples' decisions about family size and spacing of births. Other countries are concerned about underpopulation, and may develop policies that encourage couples to have more children. These broader social issues regarding population and their effects on family size are discussed more thoroughly in Chapter 7. Here we deal with their more immediate effects upon family life.

Many Americans worry about controlling unwanted or ill-timed pregnancies. In some cases, these worries seriously interfere with their sexual relationship by creating tension that leads to avoidance of sexual activity. Some couples worry about their ability to support a child economically; others are concerned that having a baby could interfere with the wife's career plans or with personal plans such as travel, putting away money for a house, and the like. Some couples want to space their children in a certain way so as to maximize the time and energy they have available for effective parenting. Others pay little attention to the timing of parenthood, preferring to "let nature take its course" and adjusting their lives as necessary whenever another child is born. For some couples, birth control is dictated largely by religious affiliation—particularly in the case of Roman Catholics, whose beliefs limit family planning to the use of "natural" methods.

The situation is considerably different in Soviet society. Until 1987, the Soviet Ministry of Health conducted a major propaganda campaign against oral contraceptives. Most Soviet citizens are relatively ignorant about the more sophisticated forms of contraception. The former Soviet Union has an extremely high abortion rate. According to official data, there were 115 abortions for every 100 births in 1987. Soviet women have up to ten times more abortions than women in the United States.

According to Soviet demographers, only 15–18% of women in the Russian Federation have never had an abortion. The median number of abortions for the average Russian woman is from two to four over her lifetime, and some women have many more. Financial costs of abortions are evaluated at about 1 billion rubles a year. Officially, about 12% of abortions are done "privately"—that is, outside of government hospitals. However, informal estimates place the figure much higher.[64]

The negative consequences of this situation in general have begun to be officially acknowledged, as well as two problems in particular. The first is the material shortage of modern contraceptives such as birth control pills, intrauterine devices, and even reliable condoms or diaphragms. The second is the lack of information and psychological sophistication regarding sexual and reproductive practices, ranging from inadequate medical sex education to ignorance and superstition regarding sex among much of the population.

As a consequence, the numbers of unplanned pregnancies and unwanted births are growing, despite the prevalence of abortion. According to national statistics, the rate of extramarital births was nearly 9% in 1980 and about 10% in 1987.[65] The rates are even higher in the largest cities of the country. Although still noticeably lower than comparable rates among American adolescents, rates of out-of-wedlock pregnancies are increasing among young Soviets in particular. The rate of premarital conception of first-born children among married couples in Leningrad rose from 27% in 1963 to 38% in 1978.[66] Similarly, one study in the early 1980s found that of 1,000 first pregnancies reported in a large Russian city, 272 were aborted, 140 births occurred out of wedlock, and 271 births took place in the first months of marriage—leaving only 317 children actually conceived within marriage.[67] These rates of nonmarital pregnancies match and even exceed those in the United States, where the out-of-wedlock pregnancy rate is often characterized as "epidemic." In order to raise public awareness of family planning options and to improve the image of contraceptive methods other than abortion, a voluntary association called The Family and Health was organized in 1989 and was soon affiliated with the Planned Parenthood World Federation. In addition, the mass media, particularly television, have begun to deal directly with birth control issues presented in a positive light.

AIDS

AIDS has been identified in the United States for just under ten years, and its effects have begun to be felt across many segments of American society. Over 2 million persons in the United States are infected with the human immunodeficiency virus (HIV); nearly 100,000 people have been diagnosed with AIDS; and thousands of men, women, and children are dying from the disease.[68] Because of its relative social isolation in the past, the former Soviet Union for a number of years was spared the effects of the HIV-related diseases. Even now, the numbers of people infected and ill are much lower than in most Western countries. However, this "lead time" on the HIV epidemic was not well utilized by government authorities and medical professionals. Instead of preparing the country for the inevitable increase in infection rates, the Soviet Ministry of Health and government-sponsored mass media waged an ideological campaign in the early 1980s—even accusing the Pentagon and the CIA of inventing the virus as a form of germ warfare! Next, the blame was put on homosexuals and drug addicts. Hopes for control of the disease were placed on the prisons (for homosexuals) and on moral exhortations in favor of monogamy (for the addicts and the remainder of the population). Unfortunately, this strategy continued even after the disease had claimed its first victims. As late as 1988, an attempt to explore the social and psychological aspects of the AIDS problem—including the dangers of AIDS-induced public hysteria—brought violent attacks in the conservative media.[69] At the present time, both the rate of infection and the amount of "HIV phobia" are rising significantly in Soviet countries.

For a time in both the United States and the former Soviet Union, AIDS was thought of only as a "homosexual disease." Indeed, homosexual and bisexual men still account for the highest numbers of cases reported in the United States. However, additional groups are now strongly represented in the most recent statistics, and the proportions of cases in these categories are increasing rapidly: intravenous drug users, hemophiliacs, transfusion recipients, female sexual partners of high-risk males, and infants born to infected mothers.[70] In the Soviet regions, the primary sources of HIV infection are not sexual partners but medical institutions; this is attributable to acute shortages of disposable syringes and other medical instruments, as well as to the ignorance and negligence of health care personnel. The rate of infection via sexual contact will doubtless also increase, since condoms and other protective materials are not always available. The recent sweeping changes in Soviet society have created a threatening new channel for sexually transmitted diseases, including AIDS: The attraction of Soviet citizens to North Americans has increased the number of young Soviet women willing to trade sexual favors for hard currency, either formally as prostitutes or informally as "dates." The rate of HIV infection in large cities like Moscow is expected to rise rapidly in the near future.

No one can say with certainty what will be the long-range effects of AIDS on families. Although AIDS has not yet had a strong impact on the sexual lives of most young people, some experts have wondered whether a "hidden epidemic" of HIV infections may appear in future families as a result of a partner's exposure through his or her premarital sexual activity.[71] Soviet scientists have predicted that the HIV epidemic will peak there in the year 2006, creating extremely serious social and economic consequences.[72] In March 1990, the administrative council of the Soviet charity foundation Ogonyok–Anti-AIDS published an address to the Supreme Soviet and the government, demanding a program of emergency measures over the next two years. Shortly thereafter, a special AIDS telephone hotline was established, offering help to anyone, including gay men. However, no one knows where the money will come from to support these actions. The former USSR has virtually no hope of creating significant medical and social services for AIDS patients and their families without outside technical and economic assistance.

In the United States, some attention has begun to focus on the demands placed on families with an HIV-infected member, as well as on the social and economic burdens on society of a large population of seriously ill and dying individuals. Families of AIDS patients need social support and practical help in caring for these individuals. Despite limited economic resources, family-oriented programs are being developed to provide information, emotional support, medical and counseling services, and alternative care for persons whose lives are touched by AIDS. These programs are not universally accepted. Some argue that involving AIDS patients with their families can be too stressful for individuals who are already vulnerable because of a life-threatening illness. Others contend that comprehensive services are simply too costly. However, with an epidemic as widespread as AIDS, family involvement in planning and providing care may well be the most cost-effective approach to coordinating and managing a major public health crisis.[73]

Fear of AIDS and ambivalence about sexuality combine to make rational planning and careful implementation of preventive and remedial programs difficult. This struggle is likely to continue in the next several generations of families in both the American and Soviet societies.

CONCLUSION

Family sexuality is just beginning to be thought of as a subject worthy of consideration and study by researchers. Clearly, sexual behavior is diverse in societies as large and heterogeneous as the United States and the former Soviet Union. Although certain values are strong within and between these societies, there is no single standard of "normal" sexuality for family members. Marriage is valued as a primary arena for sexual expression; however, sex-related ideas, attitudes, and activities are extremely diverse. Citizens are exposed to sexual information and images from a variety of public sources; however, their reactions to these differ, and the impact upon their behavior is varied. Parents in both countries seem concerned about the proper sexual development of their children; yet some of these parents respond by suppressing expressions of sexuality in the family, others by obsessively explicating sexual guidelines, and still others by supporting social programs of sex education in schools and community institutions. To develop effective public policies that encourage responsible sexual expression by citizens without reactionary negativism, and to accommodate pluralistic diversity without succumbing to crippling ambivalence—these will be the challenges common to our societies as they enter the twenty-first century.

NOTES

1. For a more complete explanation and discussion of this assumption and related issues, see J. W. Maddock, "Sex in the Family System," in J. W. Maddock, G. Neubeck, and M. Sussman (eds.), *Human Sexuality and the Family* (New York: Haworth Press, 1983), 9–20.

2. I. S. Kon, "A Sociocultural Approach," in J. Geer and W. O'Donohue (eds.), *Theories of Sexuality* (New York: Plenum Press, 1987), 257–286; See also M. Foucault, *The History of Sexuality*, Vol. 1 (London: Allan Lane, 1977), and J. Gagnon and W. Simon, *Sexual Conduct: The Social Sources of Human Sexuality* (Chicago: Aldine, 1973).

3. Kon, 1987, *op. cit.*

4. The material in this section is drawn from the following sources, all of which contain excellent historical information and insights: V. Bullough and B. Bullough, *Sin, Sickness and Sanity: A History of Sexual Attitudes* (New York: New American Library, 1977); J. D'Emilio and E. B. Freedman, *Intimate Matters: A History of Sexuality in America* (New York: Harper & Row, 1988); J. Money, *The Destroying Angel: Sex, Fitness and Food in the Legacy of Degeneracy Theory, Graham Crackers, Kellogg's Corn Flakes and American Health History* (Buffalo, NY: Prometheus Books, 1985); I. Reiss and H. Reiss, *An End to Shame: Shaping Our Next Sexual Revolution* (Buffalo, NY: Prometheus Books, 1990); H. Richardson, *Nun, Witch, Playmate: The Americanization of Sex* (New York: Harper & Row, 1971); and D. Scott and B. Wishy (eds.), *America's Families: A Documentary History* (New York: Harper & Row, 1982).

5. A. Kinsey, W. Pomeroy, and C. Martin, *Sexual Behavior in the Human Male* (Philadelphia: W. B. Saunders, 1948); A. Kinsey, W. Pomeroy, C. Martin,

and P. Gebhard, *Sexual Behavior in the Human Female* (Philadelphia: W. B. Saunders, 1953).

6. Research findings were reported in W. Masters and V. Johnson, *Human Sexual Response* (Boston: Little, Brown, 1966). Clinical applications of these results were reported in W. Masters and V. Johnson, *Human Sexual Inadequacy* (Boston: Little, Brown, 1970).

7. See particularly I. Reiss, *Journey into Sexuality: An Exploratory Voyage* (Englewood Cliffs, NJ: Prentice-Hall, 1986), and Reiss and Reiss, *op. cit.*

8. Maddock, 1983, *op. cit.* See also D'Emilio and Freedman, *op. cit.*, and Reiss and Reiss, *op. cit.*

9. Some excellent discussions can be found in the following: J. Bernard, *The Future of Marriage* (New York: Bantam, 1972); D. Dinnerstein, *The Mermaid and the Minotaur: Sexual Arrangements and Human Malaise* (New York: Harper & Row, 1976); W. Farrell, *Why Men Are the Way They Are* (New York: Berkley, 1988); S. Hite, *Women and Love: A Cultural Revolution in Progress* (New York: Knopf, 1987); H. Lips and N. Colwill, *The Psychology of Sex Differences* (Englewood Cliffs, NJ: Prentice-Hall, 1978); J. Scanzoni, K. Polonke, J. Teachman, and L. Thompson, *The Sexual Bond: Rethinking Families and Close Relationships* (Newbury Park, CA: Sage, 1989); and B. Thorne and M. Yalom (eds.), *Rethinking the Family: Some Feminist Questions* (New York: Longman, 1982).

10. Maddock, 1983, *op. cit.*; Scanzoni et al., *op. cit.*

11. See M. Baca-Zinn and D. S. Eitzen, *Diversity in Families,* 2nd ed. (New York: Harper & Row, 1987); D'Emilio and Freedman, *op. cit.*; B. Ehrenreich, E. Hess, and G. Jacobs, *Re-Making Love: The Feminization of Sex* (Garden City, NY: Doubleday/Anchor, 1986); and A. Francoeur and R. Francoeur (eds.), *Hot and Cool Sex: Cultures in Conflict* (New York: Harcourt Brace Jovanovich, 1974).

12. See a two-part article by B. A. Uspenskij, "Mythological Aspects of Russian Expressive Phraseology," *Studia Slavica Hungaria, No. 20* (1983), and *No. 33* (1987), 37–76. See also T. A. Bernshtam, *Youth in Rituals of the Russian Community of the 19th–Early 20th Century* (Leningrad: Nauka, 1988).

13. E. Levin, *Sex and Society in the World of the Orthodox Slavs, 900–1700* (Ithaca, NY: Cornell University Press, 1989).

14. See A. Flegon, *Eroticism in Russian Art* (London: Flegon Press, 1976).

15. V. Rozanov, *Aphrodite and Hermes* (Moscow: Vesy No. 5, 1909), 5, 47. See also I. S. Kon, *Introduction to Sexology* (Moscow: Meditsina, 1988a).

16. S. I. Golod, "Study of Sexual Morals in the 20's," *Sotsiologhicheskie Issledovania,* 2 (1986), 152–155.

17. K. Zetkin, *Reminiscences of Lenin* (Moscow: Gospolitizdat, 1955).

18. G. Orwell, *1984* (Harmondsworth, England: Penguin Books, 1949), 109.

19. Uspenskij, *op. cit.*

20. Flegon, *op. cit.*

21. Levin, *op. cit.*

22. Kon, 1988a, *op. cit.*

23. I. S. Kon and J. Jordon (eds.), *Sex in Russian Society.* (Bloomington, IN: Indiana University Press, 1993).

24. See G. S. Vassilchenko (ed.), *General Sexopathology* (Moscow: Meditsina, 1977); G. S. Vassilchenko (ed.), *Particular Sexopathology* (Moscow: Meditsina, 1983).

25. D. N. Issaev and V. E. Kagan, *Mental Health Aspects of Sex in Children* (Leningrad: Meditsina, 1986).

26. I. S. Kon, "Sexual Morals in Light of Sociology." *Sovetskaya Pedagoghika, 12* (1966).

27. S. I. Golod, "Sociological Problems of Sexual Morals," unpublished doctoral dissertation, University of Leningrad (Leningrad, 1969).

28. I. S. Kon, "Psychology of Sexual Differences," *Voprosy psikologhii, 2* (1981), 47–57.

29. Kon, 1988a, *op. cit.*

30. A more detailed discussion of these phenomena can be found in J. W. Maddock, "Healthy Family Sexuality: Positive Principles for Educators and Clinicians," *Family Relations, 38* (1990), 130–141. See also Maddock, 1983, *op. cit.*

31. Bernard, *op. cit.*; I. Broverman, S. R. Vogel, M. Braverman, F. Clarkson, and R. Rosencranz, "Sex Role Stereotypes: A Current Appraisal," *Journal of Social Issues, 28* (1972), 59–78; C. Gilligan, *In a Different Voice: Psychological Theory and Women's Development* (Cambridge, MA: Harvard University Press, 1982); A. Rossi (ed.), *Gender and the Life Course* (Hawthorne, NY: Aldine, 1985); Thorne and Yalom, *op. cit.*

32. These changes are detailed by a wide variety of authors, including P. Blumstein and P. Schwartz, *American Couples* (New York: William Morrow, 1983); F. Furstenberg and G. Spanier, *Recycling the Family* (Beverly Hills, CA: Sage, 1984); A. Skolnick and J. Skolnick, *The Family in Transition* (Boston: Little, Brown, 1986); Thorne and Yalom, *op. cit.*; and Baca-Zinn and Eitzen, *op. cit.*

33. Bernard, *op. cit.*; L. Richardson, *The New Other Woman* (New York: Free Press, 1988); L. Rubin, *Intimate Strangers: Men and Women Together* (New York: Harper & Row, 1983).

34. L. Rubin, *Worlds of Pain: Life in the Working-Class Family* (New York: Basic Books, 1976); Baca-Zinn and Eitzen, *op. cit.*

35. For more complete descriptions and discussions, see Blumstein and Schwartz, *op. cit.*; S. Hite, *The Hite Report* (New York: Macmillan, 1976); S. Hite, *The Hite Report on Male Sexuality* (New York: Macmillan, 1981); Masters and Johnson, 1970, *op. cit.*; and L. Rubin, *Erotic Wars* (New York: Farrar, Straus & Giroux, 1990).

36. These issues are more thoroughly discussed in Blumstein and Schwartz, *op. cit.*; J. DeLamater and P. MacCorquodale, *Pre-Marital Sexuality: Attitudes, Relationships, Behavior* (Madison: University of Wisconsin Press, 1979); Reiss, *op. cit.*; and M. Zelnik and J. Kantner, "Sexual and Contraceptive Experience of Young Unmarried Women in the United States—1971 and 1976," *Family Planning Perspectives, 9* (1977), 55–56, 58–63, 67–71.

37. S. I. Golod, *Family Stability: Sociological and Demographic Aspects* (Leningrad: Nauka, 1984).

38. V. I. Ivanov and E. Y. Sychova, "Moral and Sexual Education of College Students," in Proceedings of Republican Scientific Conference, *Pro-*

phylaxis of Sexual Pathology and Marital Disharmonies (Voroshilovgrad: Tezisy Dokladov, 1988).

39. See, e.g., Farrell, *op. cit.*; C. Franklin, *Men and Society* (Chicago: Nelson-Hall, 1988).

40. I. S. Kon, *Child and Society* (Moscow: Nauka, 1988b).

41. For a more complete description of these processes, see H. Harlow, *Learning to Love* (New York: Jason Aronson, 1974); Maddock, 1983, *op. cit.*; J. Money and P. Tucker, *Sexual Signatures: On Being a Man or a Woman* (Boston: Little, Brown, 1975); J. Prescott, "Body Pleasures and the Origins of Violence," *The Futurist, 9* (1975), 64–74.

42. R. Athanasiou, P. Shaver, and C. Tavris, "Sexuality," *Psychology Today* (1970), 39–52; Gagnon and Simon, *op. cit.;* D. Kline, *Sexual Learning and Communication in the Family* (Lexington, MA: Lexington Books, 1981); E. Roberts, *Childhood Sexual Learning: The Unwritten Curriculum* (Cambridge, MA: Ballinger, 1980); H. Thornburg, "Adolescent Sources of Information on Sex," *Journal of School Health, 51* (1981), 272–277.

43. J. Reinisch and M. Beasley, *The Kinsey Institute New Report on Sex: What You Must Know to Be Sexually Literate* (New York: St. Martin's Press, 1990).

44. C. Darling, "Family Life Education," in M. Sussman and S. Steinmetz (eds.), *Handbook of Marriage and the Family* (New York: Plenum Press, 1987); D. DeMauro and D. Haffner, *Sexuality Education and Schools: Issues and Answers* (New York: Sex Information and Education Council of the United States, 1988); M. Orr, "Sex Education and Contraceptive Education in U.S. Public Schools," *Family Planning Perspectives, 14* (1982), 304–313; C. Pollis, "Value Judgments and World Views in Sexuality Education," *Family Relations, 34* (1985), 285–290; P. Scales, "The Changing Context of Sexuality Education: Paradigms and Challenges for Alternative Futures," *Family Relations, 35* (1986), 265–274.

45. S. Green and D. Sollie, "Long-Term Effects of a Church-Based Sex Education Program on Adolescent Communication," *Family Relations, 38* (1989), 152–156; D. Kirby, *Sexuality Education: An Evaluation of Programs and Their Effects (Executive Summary)* (Bethesda, MD: Mathtech, 1984).

46. Golod, 1984, *op. cit.*; A. G. Kharchev and S. I. Golod, "Youth and Marriage," *Chelovek i Obshestvo, 6* (1969); A. Tavit and H. Kadastik, "Beginning Sexual Relationships," in E. Tiit (ed.), *Problems of Marital Stability* (Tartu: State University of Tartu, 1980).

47. *Ogonyok, 3* (1990).

48. *Samarskij Vestnik, 3* (1990).

49. For summaries and illustrations of the impact of physical diseases and disabilities on sexuality, see, e.g., D. Bullard and S. Knight (eds.), *Sexuality and Disability: Personal Perspectives* (St. Louis: C.V. Mosby, 1981); T. Cole and S. Cole, "Rehabilitation of Problems of Sexuality in Physical Disability," in F. Kottke, G. Stillwell and J. Lehman (eds.), *Krusen's Handbook of Physical Medicine and Rehabilitation* (Philadelphia: W. B. Saunders, 1982); and N. Woods, *Human Sexuality in Health and Illness,* 3rd ed., (St. Louis: C. V. Mosby, 1984).

50. S. Gordon and C. Snyder, *Personal Issues in Human Sexuality,* 2nd ed. (New York: Allyn & Bacon, 1989); J. W. Maddock, "Sex Education for the Exceptional Person: A Rationale," *Exceptional Children, 40* (1974), 273–278.

51. S. Cole, "Facing the Challenges of Sexual Abuse in Persons with Disabilities," *Sexuality and Disability*, *1* (1984/1986, 71–89).

52. E. Brecher, *Love, Sex and Aging* (Boston: Little, Brown, 1984); W. Masters, V. Johnson, and R. Kolodny, *Sex and Human Loving* (Boston: Little, Brown, 1986); R. Weg (ed.), *Sexuality in the Later Years* (New York: Academic Press, 1983).

53. Brecher, *op. cit.*

54. Weg, *op. cit.*

55. See, e.g., A. Bell and M. Weinberg, *Homosexualities* (New York: Simon & Schuster, 1978); W. Masters & V. Johnson, *Homosexuality in Perspective* (Boston: Little, Brown, 1979); J. Weinrich, *Sexual Landscapes* (New York: Scribner's, 1987).

56. See Kon, 1988a, *op. cit.*

57. For a discussion of these complex issues, see A. Bell, M. Weinberg, and S. Hammersmith, *Sexual Preference: Its Development in Men and Women* (Bloomington, IN: Indiana University Press, 1981); B. Chapman and J. Brannock, "Proposed Model of Lesbian Identity Development: An Empirical Examination," *Journal of Homosexuality*, *14* (1987), 69–80; E. Coleman, "Developmental Stages of the Coming Out Process," *Journal of Homosexuality*, *7* (1981–1982), 31–43; D. Fuss, *Inside/Out: Lesbian Theories, Gay Theories* (London: Routledge and Kegan Paul, 1991); J. Money, *Gay, Straight, and In-Between* (New York: Oxford University Press, 1988); Weinrich, *op. cit.*

58. D. Clark, *Loving Someone Gay* (New York: New American Library, 1977); G. Weinberg, *Society and the Healthy Homosexual* (Garden City, NY: Doubleday/Anchor, 1972).

59. See, e.g., Bell and Weinberg, *op. cit.*; B. Leigh, "Reasons for Having and Avoiding Sex: Gender, Sexual Orientation and Relationship to Sexual Behavior," *Journal of Sex Research*, *26* (1989), 199–209; and D. McWhirter and A. Mattison, *The Male Couple* (Englewood Cliffs, NJ: Prentice-Hall, 1984).

60. E. Macklin (ed.), *AIDS and Families* (New York: Haworth Press, 1989).

61. D. Finkelhor, *Child Sexual Abuse: New Theory and Research* (New York: Free Press, 1984); D. Finkelhor & Associates, *A Sourcebook on Child Sexual Abuse* (Beverly Hills, CA: Sage, 1986); M. Patton (ed.), *Family Sexual Abuse: Frontline Research and Evaluation* (Newbury Park, CA: Sage, 1991); D. Schetky and A. Green, *Child Sexual Abuse: A Handbook for Health Care and Legal Professionals* (New York: Brunner/Mazel, 1988).

62. *Izvestija* (February 26, 1990).

63. D. Daro, *Confronting Child Abuse: Research for Effective Program Design* (New York: Free Press, 1988); Finkelhor, *op. cit.*; Patton, *op. cit.*; T. Trepper and M. J. Barrett, *Treating Incest: A Multiple Systems Perspective* (New York: Haworth Press, 1986).

64. *Argumenty i Fakty*, *16* (1989), 6; Golod, 1984, *op. cit.*, 108; L. Remennik, "Life Killed in You," *Nedelja*, *38* (1987), 5.

65. "Private Life in Numbers," *Literturnaya Gazeta* (August 3, 1988).

66. Golod, 1984, *op. cit.*

67. M. S. Toltz, L. Y. Oberg, O. A. Shishko, "Initial Stages of Realization of Female Reproductive Function," *Zdravookhranenie Rossijskoj Federatsii*, *7* (1984), 13–15.

68. R. Needle, S. Leach, and R. Graham-Tomasi, "The Human Immuno-deficiency Virus Epidemic: Epidemiological Implications for Family Professionals," in E. Macklin (ed.), *AIDS and Families* (New York: Haworth Press, 1989), 13–37.

69. The study: A. Alova, "Life in the Time of AIDS," *Ogonyok*, *28* (1988), 10.

70. Needle et al., *op. cit.*

71. W. Winkelstein, S. Padian, J. Wylie, W. Lange, and R. Anderson, "The San Francisco Men's Health Study III: Reduction in Human Immune Deficiency Virus Transmission among Homosexual/Bisexual Men, 1982–1986." *American Journal of Public Health*, *77*, 685–689.

72. *Ogonyok*, *12* (1990), 3.

73. K. Tiblier, "Intervening with Families with Young Adults with AIDS," in M. Wright and M. Leahey (eds.), *Families and Life-Threatening Illness.* (St. Louis: Springhouse, 1987); K. Tiblier, G. Walker, and J. Rolland, "Therapeutic Issues When Working with Families of Persons with AIDS," in E. Macklin (ed.), *AIDS and Families* (New York: Haworth Press, 1989).

Chapter 5

Intergenerational Relations
in Families

Daniel F. Detzner
Alexander B. Sinelnikov

Comparing the complex relations between generations in two large, heterogeneous societies is difficult. Our task is even more complex because the *perestroika* of Soviet social, political, and economic institutions and the subsequent breakup of the USSR have created a situation of unprecedented change, while American family life has also been considerably restructured over the past half century. Although some Soviet research literature examines specific populations, such as children, parents, and retirees, studies of the relations between the generations within the various republics and across the spectrum of ethnic groups are still needed. In this chapter, we review important Soviet sociological and demographic studies of different generational groups, with the hope of revealing some patterns and problems confronting Soviet families and comparing these with similar generational phenomena in the United States.

Three major, interrelated phenomena within Soviet and American families have emerged in the past several decades. These provide a framework for understanding the changing relations between generations.

The first phenomenon is the increase in nuclear family households that usually accompanies urbanization and industrialization. A smaller family with one or two generations living in the same urban household is a pragmatic alternative to the large extended, three-generation family living in the same rural household. Large families working together for the common good in agrarian societies are replaced by smaller family units working for the state in Communist nations or for private businesses in capitalist societies. Although family structures and living patterns in American and Soviet societies are diverse, the trend is clearly toward an increase in the absolute number and percentage of nuclear family units. Family dynamics in households where there are only one or two generations are likely to be very different from those where three or four generations may be living in close proximity.

A second phenomenon occurring in both societies is the growing instability of marriages and a resulting increase in the rates of divorce. When marriage partners sever the legal ties that bind them, they often create major rifts not only between themselves, but also between their parents, in-laws, and other relatives. The divisiveness of divorce certainly affects intergenerational relations. When the divorce rate grows rapidly, as it has in both the former USSR and the United States in recent decades, larger numbers of children are separated physically and emotionally from the noncustodial parent and one set of their grandparents. When remarriage and subsequent divorces occur, the family relationships become even more complex, and the relationships with extended family members from previous marriages are likely to become more tenuous still.

A third major phenomenon affecting generational relations in many parts of both societies is the lower birthrate. One- and two-child families have become the norm (though very recent evidence suggests that the birthrate in the United States has begun to rise slightly). Thus, each generation has fewer opportunities for long-term relationships with cousins, aunts, uncles, nieces, nephews, siblings, and other more distant relatives—simply because there are fewer of them. Adding to the dramatically changed demographic profile of both countries is rapid growth in the proportion of the population that is elderly. As a result of better health care, life expectancy has increased well into the seventh decade. More married couples have both sets of parents still living, as well as several grandparents and perhaps even a very old great-grandparent, several of whom may be in need of assistance. Against the background of an overall decrease in size of families stands the fact that there are now more four- and five-generation families living than at any other time in human history.[1]

In both the former Soviet Union and the United States, these demographic changes affect families in diverse ways. This chapter emphasizes the impact of these changes on the structure and household composition of families, the interdependence of the younger and the older generations, and the unique circumstances in each society that are likely to affect future relations between generations.

FAMILY STRUCTURE AND HOUSEHOLD COMPOSITION

Family structure is typically defined in both the former Soviet Union and the United States according to the composition of the household. A family is considered a *nuclear* entity when a single household includes a married couple (with or without children), a single parent with minor children, or an unmarried adult living alone. A married couple (with or without children) living together with one or more parents or other relatives is considered an *extended* family household. The nature of family life and the interactions between the generations is determined to a great extent by who lives together.

When the household composition of the Soviet population is compared to that of the United States, there are both similarities and differences. According to the Soviet census of 1979 and the United States census of 1980, 89% of the populations of both countries lived in private households consisting of two or more persons.[2] The average size of these households in 1985 was 3.52 persons in the USSR and 3.23 persons in the United States.[3] In 1985, 49% of Soviet families with children under eighteen years of age and 41% of similar American families had only one child. In both countries, large families are less common: Only 16% of Soviet and 21% of American households included three or more children. This relatively small average household size also reflects the growth of one-parent families and the number of single elderly adults in both countries. In the United States in the late 1980s, almost 22% of the families with children under eighteen years of age were headed by a single parent, while 15% of Soviet families were in similar circumstances.[4]

However, similarities in household size mask some of the very real differences between the countries in the degree of family nuclearization. According to a Soviet survey in 1985, 77.2% of all households were nuclear family units—that is, one married couple with or without children living in the home; 15.6% of the households were extended families consisting of a married couple and one or more of the parents and/or other unmarried relatives. (Because of the proportionally large number of older women in the Soviet Union who were widowed during World War II, many of these households were composed of a younger married couple and a *babushka*, or grandmother.) Another 7.2% were extended families consisting of two or more married couples. Finally, 13.7% of Soviet households in 1985 were single-parent families, and 3% consisted of other household combinations. According to these data, a total of 19% of all Soviet households in 1985 were extended, non-nuclear families compared with the United States, where only 1.5% of married couples lived in the household of some other family member.[5] However, a number of widowed or never-married elderly persons in the United States lived with their adult children—approximately 6% of older men and 11% of older women.[6]

Although, overall, there are more nuclear families in the United States than in the former Soviet Union, the nuclear family demographics vary greatly from one Soviet republic to another. Some figures for several selected republics[7] are presented in Table 5.1. These Soviet census data clearly indicate that the predominant family structure is nuclear. However, census data reflect the situation only at the time at which the information is gathered, rather than the changes that can occur over the course of a family's development. Thus, these statistics fail to convey the importance of extended households as an ongoing arena for intergenerational relations.

For example, a different picture is created by data from a large-scale 1984 survey of 48,500 young families conducted in all regions of the country by the Central Statistics Office of the USSR. A "young" family was defined as an intact marriage (with or without children) in which both partners were under the age of thirty and married for the first time. Nearly 43% of these young families were living with their parents or other relatives. Furthermore, only 13% of the men and 14% of the women had ever lived separately from their parents before marrying.[8]

TABLE 5.1. Family Composition in the USSR and Selected Republics (in Percentages)

Family type	Years	USSR	Russia	Uzbekistan	Estonia
Married couples with or without children living at home	1970[1]	76.3	77.1	69.3	85.1
	1979[1]	79.0	80.3	68.4	86.6
	1985[2]	77.2	79.4	62.6	83.3
One married couple living with one or more parents or other relatives	1970[1]	19.2	19.1	22.1	13.6
	1979[1]	15.6	15.3	19.4	11.6
	1985[2]	15.6	15.3	17.6	13.3
Two or more married couples	1970[1]	4.5	3.8	8.6	1.4
	1979[1]	5.1	4.2	12.2	1.8
	1985[2]	7.2	5.4	19.8	3.4
Married couples with empty nest (estimate)	1979[1]	17.7	19.1	2.8	20.9

[1]*Source: Size and Composition of the USSR Population* (Moscow, 1984), 242–283, 356.
[2]*Source: World Population: Demographic Reference Book* (Moscow, 1989).

In contrast to young people in the former Soviet Union, most young Americans begin the process of leaving home in their late teens and early twenties. Almost all young married couples in the United States establish their own households after marriage. However, the age at which young adults reach full independence has risen in recent years as the cost of establishing a household has increased. Today, the majority of young people do not leave their parental homes until nearly age twenty-five. And, despite popular notions concerning higher levels of male independence, women are more likely to leave home at younger ages than men.[9]

Differences in household composition between the middle Asian and western republics of the former Soviet Union are most dramatic when the numbers of "empty-nest" families are compared. Although the overall number of nuclear family households in the USSR increased slightly between 1970 and 1985, the percentage of nuclear families in the middle Asian and trans-Caucasian regions declined. In those regions, older sons and daughters typically leave the parental home to begin their own nuclear families sometime after marriage (though not necessarily immediately after the wedding), although it is customary for one of the children—usually the youngest son—to remain with the parents until their deaths. By contrast, in Russia, Ukraine, Byelorussia (now Belarus), Moldavia (now Moldova), and particularly the more "westernized" Baltic republics, almost all children leave the home of their parents after marriage. Thus, older families are much more likely to consist of parents who have launched their children and are now living as couples in their own households. Only because of severe housing shortages is this separation of the generations sometimes delayed, forcing several years of coexistence between the young married and parental couples in a single house or apartment. The numbers of empty-nest families in the former USSR as a whole, and in the populous Russian Republic, are close to those of the Baltics.[10]

Despite the relative independence of the generations in the United States, aging parents often become more dependent on their middle-aged children. Just as there is considerable diversity in household composition across the republics of the Soviet Union, household composition among ethnic groups in the United States also varies. Although not directly comparable to the Soviet data, Table 5.2 reveals variations in the households of elderly persons who were surveyed in a California study in 1982 and 1983.[11] In every group, the very old (those aged eighty and over) were more likely to be living alone, without a spouse, or with one of their adult children than the younger old population (those aged sixty-five to seventy-nine). In addition, those in the nonwhite ethnic groups were more likely than whites to be living in an extended

TABLE 5.2. Household Composition of Elderly from Various Ethnic Groups Living in California

Household type	Age	% Distributions				
		Total	White	Black	Mexican	Chinese
Lives alone	65–79	59	66	61	42	36
	80+	66	71	64	46	48
Lives with spouse	65–79	28	27	21	37	41
	80+	13	14	7	11	14
Lives with child	65–79	16	11	12	35	48
	80+	22	15	24	41	56

Source: Adapted from J. E. Lubben and R. M. Becerra, "Social Support among Black, Mexican, and Chinese Elderly," in D. E. Gelfand and C. M. Barresi (eds.), *Ethnic Dimensions of Aging* (New York: Springer, 1987), 130–144.

family situation with an adult child. Taken together, Tables 5.1 and 5.2 appear to indicate that even if nuclear families are the preferred household form for the majority of both Soviet and American citizens, that ideal may not be possible during certain stages of life. Apparent, too, is the fact that an independent nuclear family is not the ideal of all ethnic groups in either of our heterogeneous societies.

YOUNG ADULTS AND THEIR PARENTS

A strong tradition of individualism in the United States leads to a general consensus about the importance of the independence of generations.[12] The launching of young adult children from the parental home is an important and sometimes stressful stage in the family's developmental cycle.[13] From the perspective of the young people, the psychological separation from parents is a necessary step toward adulthood and a mature identity.[14] Nevertheless, independence from family of origin is neither as abrupt nor as complete as some social stereotypes may suggest. For some American families, an adolescent's leaving home for college is seen as a move toward autonomy; however, many college students continue to be economically dependent on their parents, and quite a few spend their nonschool time living in the family home. In virtually all sectors of American society, getting a "real job" represents an important form of independence, even though many employed young adults will continue to live at home, perhaps paying rent to their parents or contributing in other ways to the family's economic well-being.

Typically, young Americans leave home in stages via higher education, military service, apprenticeships, or marriage. Initially, they may return to their parents' homes for holidays or summer vacation periods; typically, however, they attempt to establish their own households as single individuals, as couples, or as a group of peers sharing living space and expenses. Although most parents who have launched their children do not desire or expect to have them return, the family home is a refuge to which adult children can turn in the event of serious difficulties or crises.[15]

During dating and courtship, an increasing number of young American couples cohabit for a period of time in a type of "trial marriage" before taking formal wedding vows. Although parental permission for marriage is rarely required or formally requested, young Americans hope for approval of their choice by parents. Most young married couples live rather independently of their families of origin; however, parents may provide financial aid early in the marriage and/ or practical help with such matters as home repair, auto maintenance, or child care.[16] These forms of support, particularly financial help and child care, seem to have increased in recent years as a result of greater unemployment and economic stresses in American society.

Like American youths, unmarried Soviet young people seek to leave home in search of higher education, more interesting work, or increased income. Though school-age youths hope to be able to move out of their parents' homes even before marriage, the vast majority continue to live with their parents for a time after completing high school.[17] This contrasts with the situation in the United States, where large numbers of unmarried young adults who are employed live on their own. In general, Americans do not expect the generations to live together once children have reached adulthood. Nevertheless, recent economic trends appear to be prolonging the dependence of young adults on their parents, at least in the form of living in their parents' home while attending school or looking for employment.[18]

A major impediment to young Soviets' leaving home is the severe shortage of housing. Very rarely can one young person, or even several unmarried adults, obtain a separate flat. In most cases, flats are available only after marriage—and perhaps long after the wedding. Several years ago, the award-winning Soviet film *Little Vera* vividly portrayed the clashes between parents and their young adult children as a result of differing value systems and life styles under the conditions of enforced closeness. Great hope currently exists that this situation may be relieved by the newly initiated state program to allow families to own their own flats or houses. A law passed by the Supreme Soviet of the USSR in March 1990 allows every family currently living in a state-owned flat to privatize that apartment by paying a special tax to the state and to use it thereafter as its own private property. As a result, families will be able to buy, sell, and bequeath their apartments in the future. Those suppporting this plan believe that private ownership will stimulate building development, and thereby reduce the acute housing shortage.[19]

MARRIAGE AND INTERGENERATIONAL RELATIONSHIPS

For young people in the United States, marriage is an important rite of passage on the way to adulthood and independence. Although parents frequently continue to provide some kinds of help for their young married offspring, this assistance is most often considered "voluntary" and is not seen as diminishing the autonomy of the young couple. Most newly married couples find their own places to live, perhaps furnished with used items and hand-me-downs from relatives. When separate households are maintained, conflict between the generations is reduced, since the pressures of daily life and numerous opportunities for friction are bypassed.

The autonomous choice of a marriage partner with relatively little regard for the wishes of other family members is perhaps the most obvious symbol of young Americans' independence. In addition to its symbolic value, marriage in the United States today usually facilitates the economic autonomy of the partners, since both are likely to be employed (at least until the first child arrives). After they have children, many young couples grow closer to their parents, sometimes out of economic necessity or practical convenience (e.g., child care), but also because they may have greater empathy for the difficulties of parenthood.[20]

Although most young married couples reside apart from their families, many live in close geographic proximity to parents, and a growing number are remaining in or returning to parental homes in an effort to cope with financial pressures. Divorce, loss of a job, and poor health are all more likely to force young couples into shared living arrangements with parents.[21] Clearly, the relative dependence or independence of the generations is affected by social policies directed toward education, employment, medical care, housing, and other aspects of social and economic assistance in the United States.

Current cultural conditions and government instability across Soviet society make it difficult to generalize about the effects of the housing shortage on typical newly married couples and their relationships with parents and in-laws. More than one-third of young persons who live with parents before marriage are able to secure a separate residence immediately after their wedding. This new freedom for some couples is counterbalanced by the fact that a sizable portion of young people who were living separately from their parents before the wedding—21% of newly married males and 26% of newly married females—move into the flats of their in-laws after marriage. Overall, almost 60% of all couples begin their married life in the cramped living quarters of one spouse's parents. In many cases, this arrangement continues for years. Among those marriages that remain intact after ten years, approximately 20% continue to live in parental households, despite the fact that more than 75% of young couples polled say they would prefer to live independently. Though no data are available on the preferences of the parents, anecdotal evidence suggests that they too would prefer to see their children living separately, because of the inconveniences of crowded living conditions and because of the burdens imposed by the added responsibilities of an extended family (particularly care of grandchildren).[22] Conflict in multigenerational American households has been widely documented,[23] and the situation is presumably similar in the former Soviet Union, though little formal research exists.

Nevertheless, the dependency of young married couples on their parents is not simply a function of the housing shortages in the former Soviet Union. The relatively low incomes of individuals just beginning their work careers are often insufficient to enable them to live separately from parents even if flats were available. A 1980 survey of 350 young couples who were married in Moscow revealed that 51% of the grooms and 59% of the brides wanted to receive financial help from their parents; 31% of the grooms and 22% of the brides did not want this type of assistance; and 18% of the young men and 10% of the young women were unsure about their opinion. Even though a sizable number had negative feelings about receiving this type of parental aid, 85% of the men and 83% of the women expected to receive some assistance after their wedding. Only 3% of the grooms and 2% of the brides did *not* expect any financial help from their parents.[24] Geographic location is often an important factor in the ability of the older generation to give help to their newly married offspring. Parents living in the same city or town as their married children are more likely to provide assistance to the young family. Naturally, the likelihood of assistance is highest when both generations share the same household.

Financial difficulties are particularly critical for young couples with children. A state allowance for maternity leave is provided from the last months of the woman's pregnancy until the baby is eighteen months old. Until recently, the typical maternity allowance was less than 25% of the average monthly wage.[25] This meager allowance, along with the added expenses of a new family member, forces many young couples to ask for financial assistance from their parents. In addition, many grandparents assume major responsibilities for child care, food preparation, and other household tasks, without which most young mothers would have little chance to work outside the home. The variety and importance of services performed by older parents virtually require young couples to continue their dependency for some years after their marriage. In many cases, this dependency creates tensions and strain for both generations.

Beginning on January 1, 1991, the USSR Supreme Soviet increased the size of the maternity allowance to equal the amount of the national minimum wage. More recently, a graduated series of maternity allowances has been put into place, continuing until a child is eighteen months old. Soviet mothers are permitted to stay home from work until their children are three years old, after which they may return to their original positions and receive full credit on the work records for the entire period of leave. The children of both married and single mothers continue to receive an allowance until they are six years old. If the mother remains unmarried, her child receives a "student allowance" until the age of sixteen or eighteen.

Although young adults in the former Soviet Union may continue to be financially dependent upon their parents, they are not necessarily subservient to the wishes of the older generation. One example is found in the area of mate selection. Today, the vast majority of Soviet youths choose their own spouses, even if their parents object. Although parents no longer have veto power over the choice of whom to marry, young people generally feel a continuing obligation to ask for their parents' permission to marry. Surveys carried out by the Institute of Ethnography of the Soviet Academy of Sciences between 1971 and 1982[26] indicate that the attitudes concerning parental involvement in the decision to marry were very different in various regions of the USSR during this period (see Table 5.3).

The table shows that most of the people living in European parts of the USSR (Russians, Estonians, Moldavians) did not believe that parental permission must be requested before marriage, whereas most Georgians and Uzbeks considered it a necessity. Of course, the tradition of requesting parental permission is not the same as the ancient tradition of family-arranged marriages, which were quite prevalent in the Soviet Union prior to World War II and which still occur in some of the eastern republics today. Clearly, there are strong regional and ethnic differences in attitudes toward the role of parents in mate

TABLE 5.3. Belief in the Necessity of Asking Parents' Permission to Marry (in Percentages)

Ethnic group	Republic (urban population)				
	Estonia	Russia	Moldavia	Georgia	Uzbekistan
Native	22	38	41	61	88
Russians	35	38	42	44	55

selection and marriage.[27] Age and urban or rural location also reflect differences in these attitudes, though not as strongly. Older persons in rural areas are more likely to consider it important for parents to give permission to marry than are younger persons in urban areas.[28]

Asking permission for marriage is, in most cases, merely a formality that expresses respect for the parents. However, considering the fact that so many Soviet young people live with their parents for so long after marriage, the investment of the older generation in the "who" and "when" of marriage is certainly understandable. Often parents grant permission even if they have serious reservations about their offspring's choice; they realize that they cannot directly prevent the marriage, and hope to avoid a negative relationship with a future in-law. Unfortunately, however, disapproval of the marriage partner is rather common. In one study of 175 young couples married for three years, 19% of the husbands' parents and 12% of the wifes' parents had expressed negative opinions about their children's prospective partners prior to the wedding.[29]

Just as in the United States, parental attitudes in the former Soviet Union may even have an impact on the marriage itself. In the same study among young spouses who considered their marriages to be "successful," only 13% of the husbands' parents and 9% of the wives' parents had opposed the marriages, while among young spouses who considered their marriages to be "unsuccessful," 36% of the husbands' parents and 30% of the wives' parents disapproved of the marriages.[29a] Of course, we cannot know from such surveys whether the reported marital "failures" are the results of initial good judgment by parents and poor judgment by young people, or results of the effects of continuing opposition and negative attitudes of parents on some marriages—or simply the reflections of disillusioned individuals who have experienced years of marital conflict. Still, a survey conducted in Latvia during the late 1970s is suggestive. Over 4,000 persons of differing marital status were asked several questions about the influence of parents on their marriages. Only 1% of the unmarried men and 3% of the unmarried women (including those who were divorced or widowed) said that the negative opinions of parents had prevented them from marrying the partners of their choice. However, 33% of the divorced men and 17% of the divorced women said that actual parental interference in their marriages was one of the main reasons divorce.[30]

MUTUAL ASSISTANCE BETWEEN THE GENERATIONS

For a large number of families, intergenerational assistance is a mutual process, occurring in different ways and in different directions over the course of the family life cycle. Parent–child relationships in later life have only recently begun to be studied extensively in Western countries.[31] With advancing age, most parents find themselves less able to support their offspring and more in need of assistance themselves. Despite widespread stereotyping of the elderly as sickly and dependent, however, the findings of American researchers indicate that elders *provide* more financial and practical help to the younger generation than they receive. Only when poor health or chronic illness occurs do more resources typically flow from the younger to the older generation.[32] These findings demonstrate that the important and enduring roles and responsibilities associated with parenthood in the United States do not necessarily cease when adult children get married or leave home. Furthermore, a majority of Americans believe that family members should help one another when necessity requires and resources permit.[33]

Even though the overall attitudes toward generational independence are similar in the former Soviet Union and the United States, the realities of intergenerational relationships are considerably different in the two societies. The younger generation of Soviets continues to depend heavily on the older generation for economic help, housing, child care, and domestic assistance. Indications are that these forms of dependence have come to be resented by the older generation. Nevertheless, there is also evidence of more reciprocal forms of exchange between the generations—that is, mutual assistance between parents and children.

In the large 1984 study of 48,500 young Soviet families referred to earlier in this chapter, a majority of the younger generation (60%) reported receiving help of some sort from their parents. But an even higher percentage of these families (68%) indicated that they *provided* assistance to their parents. This assistance was most likely to occur as the parents became elderly; not surprisingly, the most common forms of assistance reported were help with household work and home health care during illness.[34] However, in a sizable minority of Soviet families (31%), assistance did not occur in *either* direction. Overwhelmingly, young families who had not received any kind of help from their parents did not provide any assistance to their parents. This may reflect an absence of need for help, an inability to help because of limited resources or geographic distance, or negative relationships between the generations.

ADULTS AND THEIR AGING PARENTS

For the fifty years from the 1930s to the 1980s, retirement age in the United States was associated with eligibility for full Social Security benefits (age sixty-five for men and age sixty-two for women). With the elimination of mandatory retirement and the spread of antidiscrimination measures that protect the jobs of older Americans, elderly citizens can now choose to work when they reach their seventies, or even their eighties. Recently, however, *voluntary retirements* before *age sixty-five have been increasing.* The tightening economic situation has led more employers to offer financial incentives for retirement as a technique for cutting their costs by eliminating their highest-paid (most senior) employees. In 1984, only 11% of the labor force continued to work beyond the age of sixty-five (16.5% male and 7.4% females), whereas 44% of those ages sixty to sixty-four were still employed.[35]

Over the past two decades, the economic status of older Americans has increased significantly as a consequence of improvements in private and public pension benefits, along with automatic increases based on the annual rate of inflation. In 1983, however, approximately 3.7 million (14%) of the older population (those aged sixty-five and over) had incomes below the poverty level. Poverty is typically highest among widowed women, the very old, and ethnic minority groups. In the United States, relatively few adults provide financial assistance to their elderly parents or grandparents. Estimates are that less than 3% of all income received by the elderly is obtained from family members.[36] Although few young adults or married couples in the United States live with their parents, frequent visits occur between the generations. In one survey, more than half of the older adults reported seeing at least one of their adult children in the previous two days. Only 11% reported that they had not seen any of their children for more than thirty days.[37] The vast majority of older adults have only minor health problems and need little assistance with basic activities of daily living. Of course, the need for assistance increases with advanced age or in the face of a serious health crisis. An older American in need of help is most likely to receive it from a spouse; if no spouse is available to help, adult offspring are most likely to provide assistance. Approximately one-fourth to one-third of all caregivers to frail elderly persons are their adult children, with older women more likely to be cared for by their children than older men.[38]

In the 1970s, a major survey of the Soviet elderly was conducted by Vladimir Shapiro.[39] The study questioned 1,400 men (ages sixty to sixty-three) and women (ages fifty-five to fifty-eight) about their attitudes and behaviors shortly after eligibility for retirement. Approximately 70% of the sample continued to work beyond the minimum retirement age. One portion of the study focused on family issues and on the relations between the generations. Most respondents had adult children and grandchildren. Sixty-four percent of the respondents continued to work, and 26% of those not working continued to provide some financial support for their adult children. In addition, 32% were employed, and 44% of those no longer employed also provided some type of domestic work assistance to the families of their children. And some child care responsibilities were assumed by 29% of the working and 44% of the nonworking retirement-age respondents. When the grandchildren were ill, 20% of the working and 29% of the nonworking grandparents were available to help the parents care for them. Overall, only 6% of the sample reported that they gave no assistance whatsoever to their adult children.

On the other side of the mutual aid ledger, only 5% of the working and 10% of the nonworking older respondents in this study *received* some type of financial assistance from their adult children. Thirty-seven percent of the working and 29% of the nonworking participants received help with domestic chores. When they were ill, 47% of the older adults, regardless of work status, reported receiving assistance from their children. A total of 18% of the older adults reported no help whatsoever from their offspring.

The results of this large study confirm other research findings on mutual aid imbalances in Soviet family relationships. These relatively young older adults were three times more likely to provide help to their children than they were to receive help, with the greatest imbalance in the area of financial support. The discrepancy in intergenerational assistance would have been even greater if the study had not included more intangible types of assistance, such as "moral support." Attitudes of retirement-age adults toward helping their young married children are revealed in their responses to this statement: "It is always the duty of parents to help their children by any means possible in any circumstances." Fifty-three percent of the working and 49% of the nonworking parents agreed fully with the statement, while only 7% of the working and 10% of the nonworking respondents disagreed. The remaining respondents qualified their answers in some way, such as specifying the circumstances under which help would be provided. Approximately one-third attached conditions to their assistance, stipulating that adult children who receive assistance must consider the opinions of their parents and show them respect.[40]

THE FUTURE OF INTERGENERATIONAL RELATIONS

The future of relations between the generations in American families is in flux. However, greater stability in the economic, political, and social systems of the United States makes it somewhat easier to project future scenarios for American families than for Soviet families. Certainly, we can anticipate more complex family relationships as the number of generations living increases and as divorce rates remain high. As many as four generations of family members, perhaps all living in separate households, will share certain responsibilities and will provide different kinds of assistance to one another at different periods of life. These relationships will be even more complicated by the increase in so-called "nontraditional" families—for example, single-parent households, childless couples, serially remarried "blended" families, and homosexual couples—which create a maze of potential patterns of interaction across the generations. Intergenerational bonds may well be loosened by this new family environment; however, there is little to suggest that the "death" of the American family is imminent, as some cynics have predicted.

However, one negative scenario for the future of intergenerational relations has already begun to develop in the United States. Children and the elderly represent two particularly dependent and vulnerable populations, and they are both at risk as economic conditions worsen and poverty increases. Already, there are indications of a public policy confrontation between advocates for the elderly and advocates for children and youths. Demographers and social critics point to a growing disparity in the ratio of middle-aged working people to those who are dependent on them. They also point to the growth in poverty among children who are living in one-parent families headed by women and/or ethnic minorities. Some are concerned about the growing political strength of the elderly, noting that children do not have the same ability to advocate for themselves or to express their views at the polling place. However, this conflict scenario views the generations as unconnected interest groups rather than as family members whose lives are linked by mutual needs and shared resources across the life span.

This intergenerational struggle may indeed be the focus of a growing public policy debate as the American population ages and resources grow more scarce in the future.[41]

The evolution—indeed, the "new revolution"—of the Soviet social, economic, and political environment in recent years has radically transformed the nature of the family and relations between generations. The three-generation family, premised upon marriage as a lifelong commitment and upon the enduring relationships of parents and children, is being replaced by the smaller, less stable nuclear family. Obligations between generations are no longer seen as mutually beneficial when the older generation provides substantial assistance to the younger generation without any guarantees of support in return. With the continuing growth of the older population in the decades ahead, a problem looms ever larger on the horizon: care of a huge population of frail elderly persons. Just as in the United States, Soviet citizens in small nuclear families whose individual members are committed largely to their own self-fulfillment will have difficulty in addressing this problem.

Certainly, the political environment has had a dramatic impact on the relationships between generations in the former Soviet Union. For some time, cultural tradition along with social and economic conditions have, on the one hand, inhibited the natural drive for independence by the young, and, on the other hand, have required parental responsibilities by older adults well into their retirement years. If allowed to run its full course, the current restructuring of Soviet society is likely to encourage young adults to leave their parental homes more quickly, particularly after marriage. The reforms that are now under way in economics, the system of wages, the redistribution of apartments through private ownership, and increases in state aid to families with children should have a positive effect on the independence of both young families and their parents.

In most regions, the future is likely to include a decrease in the number of young families living in extended households. Although conflict with parents and in-laws has been cited as one important reason for the increasing Soviet divorce rate, a decline in divorce as a consequence of a decrease in extended family households is unlikely. Divorce rates are actually higher in the western Soviet regions than in the trans-Caucasian and middle Asian regions, where extended families are more prevalent.[42] Furthermore, both the rate of divorce and the rate of family nuclearization have increased throughout Soviet society over the past several decades. Research suggests that there may be a parallel between the growth of nuclear families and the instabil-

ity of marriages. The full impact of divorce on the youngest generation of Soviets has not been well documented by researchers. American research clearly suggests that there are multiple negative effects
of divorce, not only on young children, but also on the relations
between children and their parents and even grandparents.[43] By contributing to a separation of the generations from one another, divorce
makes long-term relations throughout the multigenerational family considerably more problematic.

A third demographic reality, discussed above and in other chapters of this book, is also part of the complex equation affecting Soviet
families: the continuing decline in birthrates in many regions of the
country. Together, these variables are influencing the future of generational relationships. We have already pointed out that the long
period during which Soviet parents and young married couples reside
together is both necessary and problematic. However, the future decline
of the extended family—and the subsequent loss of in-home child care
so often provided by grandparents—could very well lead to a further
decrease in birthrates. The resulting increase in young married couples
without children could, in turn, produce a further increase in the rate
of divorce—a trend that could even further lower the birthrate![44]

All three of these interrelated processes have a common root in
the gradual growth of individualism in the former Soviet Union—an
emphasis on self-fulfillment and independence that has emerged since
World War II. Within family life, one result of this individualism is a
growing desire for personal autonomy, independent living, and freedom from undue influence by other family members. The data cited
above suggest that this movement toward individual autonomy will be
a prolonged process. However, the current political upheaval in Soviet
society could very well speed the process, with the result that the
younger and older generations will rapidly become more independent
and perhaps also more alienated—divided by loyalties to tradition or
change, to "old" or "new" political systems, to established or emerging cultural institutions.

Although the Soviet experience of change in generational relationships is unique in important ways, comparing it with American family
patterns can be useful. In the United States, an ethic of individualism
has flourished for several centuries, and the separation of nuclear
households by older and younger generations has increased steadily.
Nevertheless, intergenerational family relationships remain relatively
strong. Even though family members are typically self-sufficient economically and live in separate residences, members remain relatively
close, help one another on a regular basis, and assume changing fam-

ily responsibilities over the life span.[45] Clearly, individualism does not automatically lead to a complete isolation of older and younger generations from one another. In fact, smaller nuclear families have considerably more flexibility than larger extended families to adapt to changing cultural and economic conditions, including the development of more adaptive ways of relating and meeting individual needs across the life span.

CONCLUSION

A pessimistic interpretation of the future foresees the destruction of the family as a viable social unit. A more optimistic interpretation suggests the continuing adaptation of the family unit to changing times and circumstances in both Soviet and American societies. Clearly, important challenges confront Soviet society as it undergoes a massive transformation of its political and cultural institutions. Many of the important trends in Soviet society—a growth in individualistic attitudes, the nuclearization of families, a declining birthrate, an increase in divorce—have been in evidence in the United States for many decades. Despite some of the negative results for the overall health of the American family, its capacity to change and adapt in order to serve critical functions for both individuals and society remains apparent. Similarly, the resiliency of the Soviet family, despite its devaluation during the Stalinist period and the accompanying promotion of communal living arrangements, has been amply demonstrated.[46] The changes now ocurring within families and between generations reflect transformations occurring within and between groups in the larger social system. We have every reason to believe that the family unit will continue to survive in both societies well into the next millenium, based in part upon its identity as a bridge between generations and a vehicle for mutual support between parents and children at important stages of the life cycle.

NOTES

1. M. W. Riley, "The Family in an Aging Society: A Matrix of Latent Relationships," *Journal of Family Issues,* 4(3) (1983), 439–454; P. Uhlenberg, "Death and the Family," *Journal of Family History,* 5(3) (1980), 313–320.
2. A. B. Sinelnikov, "Family Structure," in V. A. Borisov (ed.), *World Population: Demographic Reference Book* (Moscow: Nauka, 1989), 165–181; United Nations, *Demographic Yearbook, 1982* (New York: Author, 1984), 980–999.
3. Sinelnikov, *op. cit.*; U.S. Bureau of the Census, *Statistical Abstract of*

the United States (Washington, DC: U.S. Government Printing Office, 1986), 39–45.

4. U.S. Bureau of the Census, *op. cit.; Vestnik Statistiki, No. 8* (1986), 72–74; G. P. Kiseleva and A. B. Sinelnikov, "Marriages, Divorces, and Incomplete Families," in *Population and Social Development,* 2nd ed. (Moscow: USSR Academy of Sciences, 1988), 96–120.

5. Sinelnikov, *op. cit.,* 171; U.S. Bureau of the Census, *op. cit.*

6. H. B. Brotman, *Supplement to the Yearbook on Aging in America* (Washington, DC: White House Conference on Aging, 1981).

7. Sinelnikov, *op. cit.;* "Size and Composition of the USSR Population-1979 Census," *Finansy i Statiska* (1984).

8. A. G. Volkov, *The Family as an Object of Demography* (Moscow: Mysl, 1986), 202.

9. A. Clemens and L. Axelson, "The Not-So-Empty Nest: The Return of the Fledgling Adult," *Family Relations, 34* (1985), 259–264.

10. Sinelnikov, *op. cit.,* 171–176.

11. J. E. Lubben and R. M. Becerra, "Social Support among Black, Mexican, and Chinese Elderly," in D. E. Gelfand and C. M. Barresi (eds.), *Ethnic Dimensions of Aging* (New York: Springer, 1987), 130–144.

12. R. N. Bellah, R. Madsen, W. M. Sullivan, A. Swidler, and S. M. Tipton, *Habits of the Heart: Individualism and Commitment in American Life* (New York: Harper & Row, 1985).

13. E. Duvall, *Family Development* (Philadelphia: J. B. Lippincott, 1971); P. G. McCullough and S. K. Rutenberg, "Launching Children and Moving On," in B. Carter and M. McGoldrick (eds.), *The Changing Family Life Cycle* (New York: Gardner Press, 1988), 285–309; R. C. Aylmer, "The Launching of the Single Young Adult," in B. Carter and M. McGoldrick (eds.), *The Changing Family Life Cycle* (New York: Gardner Press, 1988), 191–208.

14. R. Kegan, *The Evolving Self* (Cambridge, MA: Harvard University Press, 1982).

15. J. Treas and V. L. Bengston, "The Family in Later Years," in M. Sussman and S. Steinmetz (eds.), *Handbook of Marriage and the Family* (New York: Plenum Press, 1987).

16. L. Harris and Associates, *The Myth and Reality of Aging in America* (Washington, DC: National Council on the Aging, 1975).

17. N. G. Aristova, "Images of the Future Family: Internal Conflicts," in M. S. Matskovsky and T. A. Gurko (eds.), *Establishing Marriage–Family Relationships* (USSR Academy of Sciences, 1989), 41–52.

18. Clemens and Axelson, *op. cit.*

19. *Pravda* (March 10, 1990). See also *Izvestia* (August 27, 1993).

20. Duvall, *op. cit.;* McCullough & Rutenberg, *op. cit.;* Carter and McGoldrick, *op. cit.;* Aylmer, *op. cit.*

21. *Ibid.*

22. Volkov, *op cit.,* 198–214.

23. See, e.g., J. Suitor and K. Pillemer, "Explaining Intergenerational Conflict When Adult Children and Elderly Parents Live Together," *Journal of Marriage and the Family, 50* (1988), 1037–1047.

24. L. F. Borusjak, "Study of Newlyweds' Predispositions to Relationships with Parents," in L. L. Rybakovsky (ed.), *Problems of Population Reproduction and Migration* (Moscow: USSR Academy of Sciences, 1981), 58–70.

25. *Pravda* (January 28, 1990).

26. I. A. Grishaev, A. A. Susokulov, and A. P. Novitskaya, "Intergenerational Relations in Soviet Families," in Y. V. Arutunayan and Y. V. Bromley (eds.), *Socio-Cultural Images of Soviet Nations* (Moscow: Nauka, 1986), 151.

27. M. A. Bekaja, "Social Problems of Family in Georgian Industrial Cities," unpublished doctoral dissertation, University of Tbilisi (Tbilisi, 1989), 37.

28. Grishaev et al., *op. cit.*, 151; Y. V. Arutunayan, "On Some Tendencies of Cultural Intermingling of USSR Nations at the Stage of Developed Socialism," *Istoria USSR, 4* (1978), 99–105.

29. T. A. Gurko, "Formation of a Young Family in a Large City: Conditions and Factors of Stability," unpublished doctoral dissertation, Moscow State University (Moscow, 1983), 63–64.

29a. *Ibid.*

30. I. V. Zarinsh, "Creation and Potential Stability of the Family," in I. C. Kirtovsky (ed.), *Factors and Motives of Demographic Behavior* (Riga: Zinatne, 1984), 78, 101.

31. G. O. Hagestad, "Parent–Child Relations in Later Life: Trends and Gaps in Past Research," in J. B. Lancaster, J. Altman, A. Rossi, and L. R. Sherrod (eds.), *Parenting across the Lifespan: Biosocial Dimensions* (New York: Aldine/De Gruyter, 1987), 405–433.

32. D. J. Cheal, "Intergenerational Family Transfers," *Journal of Marriage and the Family, 45* (1983), 805–813.

33. R. Blieszner and J. A. Mancini, "Enduring Ties: Older Adults' Parental Role and Responsibilities," *Family Relations, 36* (1987), 176–180.

34. Volkov, *op. cit.*, 23.

35. F. L. Schick, *Statistical Handbook on Aging Americans* (Phoenix, AZ: Oryx Press, 1986), D1-5.

36. *Ibid.*, E1-1.

37. *Ibid.*, B3-12.

38. *Ibid.*, B3-11.

39. V. D. Shapiro, "Life after Retirement," *Sovetskaya Sociologiya, 22*(1–2) (1983), 3–168.

40. V. D. Shapiro, *Man in Retirement* (Moscow: Nauka, 1980), 125, 129, 135–136.

41. L. Noelker and R. W. Wallace, "The Organization of Family Care for the Impaired Elderly," *Journal of Family Issues, 6*(1) (1985), 23–44. For a discussion of major issues confronting the generations in the United States see E. R. Kingson, B. A. Hirshorn, and L. K. Harootyan, *The Common Stake: The Interdependence of Generations* (Washington, DC: Gerontological Society of America, 1990).

42. G. P. Kiseleva and A. B. Sinelnikov, "Evolution of Family Structure in USSR during the War," in A. Blum, M. Ely, and M. Appreleff (eds.), *Demographic Situation in France and the Soviet Union: Papers of the First Franco-Soviet*

Colloquium, INED, Paris, October, 1984 (Paris: National Institute of Demographic Studies, 1989), 151–165.

43. S. Matthews, "The impact of Divorce on Grandparenthood: An Exploratory Study," *The Gerontologist*, *24*(1) (1984), 41–47.

44. A. B. Sinelnikov, *Marriages and Birthrates in USSR* (Moscow: Nauka, 1989), 47–91.

45. E. Shanas, "The Family as a Social Support System in Old Age," *The Gerontologist*, *19*(2) (1979), 169–174; R. A. Lewis, "The Adult Child and Older Parents," in T. H. Brubaker (ed.), *Family Relationships in Later Life* (Newbury Park, CA: Sage, 1990), 68–85.

46. H. K. Geiger, *The Family in Soviet Russia* (Cambridge, MA: Harvard University Press, 1968).

Chapter 6

Work and Family Life

Sharon M. Danes
Olga N. Doudchenko
Ludmilla V. Yasnaya

Work, paid and unpaid, is central to family life in both the American and Soviet societies. The intersection of outside employment and household work creates many dilemmas for families in the two societies. Labor force participation, motivation for working, gender differences in work patterns, and tensions in family roles are entangled with each society's unique history. Despite differences in economic structure and social ideology, work-related family problems are remarkably similar in these two societies. This chapter focuses on family economic structure and offers comparisons and contrasts between the experiences of Soviet and American families.

Like the authors of other chapters in this book, we must offer some disclaimers. First, recent events in Soviet society are virtually without precedent, and many of the most rapid and far-reaching changes are related to economics. Economics is a historically oriented science; it depends in large part on comparing current and past socioeconomic conditions, and then attempting to forecast the future. In our analysis, we might have chosen to describe well-studied and statistically validated data for their historical value, or to detail emerging patterns of work and family experience resulting from contemporary social and economic changes. Instead, we have tried to *combine* these approaches, since both general research data and descriptions of social change appear to us to be essential to a fuller understanding of the work–family interface. We hope that this has created a more meaningful picture for the reader.

Second, most of our Soviet data comes from Russia, although we have attempted to broaden the data base and to make meaningful comparisons where possible. Generalizations across all areas of the former Soviet Union are difficult, perhaps impossible, to make. Recent events have made clear the large inequities and instabilities of the old Soviet economic system, despite the centralized control of economic planning and the creation of an immense government bureaucracy to implement these plans.

Third, the examination of work and family dynamics in both Soviet and American societies focuses largely on women. The major issue at the intersection of work in the marketplace and work in the household is the overload of women and the minimal involvement of men in family life. (See Chapters 2, 4, and 5 for related discussions.)

HISTORICAL PERSPECTIVES

In the preindustrial economy of the United States, the family was a primary economic unit. Family members were directly dependent upon one another for basic subsistence. With the advent of industrialization in the nineteenth century, many of the products previously made at home by women—for example, clothing—began to be mass-produced in factories. Gradually, women were drawn into the formal labor market. Although World War I accelerated this trend, the Great Depression created the paradox of severe economic hardship coupled with job scarcity. Nevertheless, women continued to seek jobs in growing numbers. The tremendous industrial and personnel needs of World War II assured women a role in the marketplace; never again could it be convincingly argued that their gender alone hampered effective performance in employment roles.

Despite their performance during times of war, however, American women have not been assured equal access to employment opportunities. In more peaceful times, "work" has referred primarily to male occupational status; women are considered to have their major "place" in the home. Nonetheless, economic, demographic, and social forces since World War II have all contributed to a steady increase in the labor force participation of women. The service sector provided work opportunities; birthrates declined; social expectations changed; and many families discovered that they needed two incomes. Growth in labor force participation came first among older married women with children in school, and later among younger women with preschoolers.

Currently, women are highly visible in the paid labor force of the United States, and future labor force increases are expected to occur primarily among women and minorities. Even though well over half of American women are now in the labor force, the responsibility for family provision falls primarily to men. Both women and men continue to be somewhat ambivalent about the role of women as providers.

Until the years after the October Revolution of 1917, Russian family life was very traditional: Husbands were the major wage earners outside the home, and wives were primarily responsible for housekeeping and childrearing. Of course, as in other countries of the world, farm families and those families in home-based trades organized work and family life in overlapping ways. Still, social roles were largely differentiated along gender lines. The postrevolution 1920s brought a need for rapid and extensive development of the national economy. This required a huge increase in the labor force—a demand that could only be met by women. The mass entrance of Soviet women into the sphere of production fulfilled Lenin's call for "full freedom for women." In Marxist–Leninist thought, "freedom" meant more than merely legal rights—it meant equality with men in all spheres of social life, and equal participation in socially useful labor in particular. "Socially useful labor" referred to labor for the state rather than for the family. In fact, a major goal of women's emancipation was supposed to be their liberation from domestic "slavery."

In the ideology of the past seventy-five years, then, Soviet women have been valued primarily as workers and as social activists rather than as homemakers or mothers. As other chapters explain in more detail, theory and reality did not match. Relief from the restrictions of household work was not forthcoming. After all, men, too, were needed for socially useful labor outside the family—all the more so as a result of the war-related devastation of the male population. Thus, Soviet women have retained primary responsibility for managing households and family life. The overload of total work that Soviet women experience has been exacerbated by the even greater shortage of many consumer products in recent times.

LABOR FORCE PARTICIPATION

In the United States, slightly more than half (56%) of all women age sixteen and over were in the labor force in 1987, compared with three-fourths (76%) of all men. Sixty-one percent of married women with children were employed, about the same number as single women in female-headed households. Of all employed women, one in four worked part-time, compared to one in ten employed men. Part-time workers generally work in low-paying and low-status jobs.[1]

Although a large number of employed women is a fairly recent phenomenon in the United States, the Soviet labor force has included large numbers of women for over fifty years. Approximately 90% of Soviet women of working age are employed. (The official "working age" in the former Soviet Union is from sixteen to fifty-five years for women and from sixteen to sixty years for men.) Virtually all Soviet women work full-time, even if they are mothers of small children. In fact, government statistical data do not include part-time work; only small-scale survey data are available. For example, in a Moscow study of 418 women, only 2% worked half-time or less.[2]

In both countries, employed men earn more than women. Despite a growth in average earnings for all working wives in the United States, particularly during the 1980s, wives still earned only 65% of husbands' earnings in 1987. When Soviet industrial specialists were surveyed in 1988, a comparison of male and female income levels indicated that the percentage of women earning a particular income decreased as the income level increased.[3]

REASONS FOR WORKING

We begin with an important reminder that should influence the reader's understanding of this section, and, indeed, of our entire chapter. "Reasons for working," particularly among women, are embedded into the complex network of cultural assumptions that influence gender socialization. In addition, the meaning of "choice," both to females and to males, reflects a society's values and norms regarding the role of the individual within the larger community. The majority of women now employed in the United States report that they "have to" work for financial reasons—and a sizable number report enjoying their work as well. Most working American women are members of households with incomes above the poverty level. Theoretically, at least, these women could choose not to work, although it might dramatically lower their family's level of living.

By contrast, the choice of working in Soviet society is more narrowly defined. The current Soviet economy is in such disarray that most households would literally be unable to obtain basic human necessities if women did not work. However, even more important is the underlying psychosocial dynamic that largely determines Soviet women's experience of employment choices. As indicated above, the still-pervasive socialist ideology dictates that all people must perform socially useful labor in order to have an identity. Work outside the home has been emphasized, while care of children and families has been designated the responsibility of the state. Over time, family work (unpaid) has come to be degraded, while employment (paid) has been exalted.

Little wonder, then, that Soviet women have thought of themselves as not having a choice about employment outside the home, while still carrying the burden of household work without psychological reward or social recognition. However, the reorganization of Soviet society in the wake of *perestroika* and political upheaval includes a strong movement to alter the roles of women, with more emphasis on family issues.

Besides additional income, various factors influence the decision of women in the United States to work outside the home. One factor is the attitude of husbands; a woman is more likely to work if her husband's attitude toward outside employment is positive. Another is education; a woman is more likely to work outside the home after marriage if her job before marriage required special training or a high level of education. Similarly, a woman who continues to work after marriage is likely to work while raising children, although she may work only part-time for a while. Interestingly, studies show that a powerful economic motivator for a working wife in the United States is holding a job that pays enough to raise her family's income to a level comparable to that of families with nonemployed wives in the same age category.[4]

When questioned about their employment, most Soviet women indicate financial motives. In a study done in the early 1980s, 78.9% of Soviet women reported working because the family needed some extra income; 4.9% wanted to be independent from their husbands; 4% wished to be "productive citizens"; and 12.2% wanted to be "a member of a collective group." When these women were asked whether they would give up working if their husbands were paid at a level comparable to their joint incomes, 65% answered "no" and only 22% said "yes." In a similar study done by the Institute of Sociology, Soviet Academy of Sciences, 87% of the women said that they would not stop working if the financial need were eliminated.[5]

The primary explanation for these results would appear to be the continuing influence of socialist ideology, which makes it difficult for Soviet women to imagine a "normal life" unrelated to the labor force. A related factor might be the psychological sense of independence that employment provides—a variable also explored in research on American women. Still another explanation may relate directly to the realities of the Soviet economy. The fact that even the present earnings of husband and wife together cannot supply income adequate for a comfortable level of living probably makes it difficult for contemporary women to contemplate life without employment. This interpretation is supported by the responses of husbands to questions about their wives' employment. In the early 1980s study cited above, only 28% of the men approved of their wives' working, although 61% viewed it as necessary.

FACTORS AFFECTING WORK STATUS

The two factors most frequently cited as influencing women's decision to work in the United States are a woman's level of education and the age of her children. To a considerable extent, young women today acquire their education because they expect to work much of their adult lives. The increases in women's level of education and in their level of participation in the labor force not only are interdependent, but are probably rooted in a third factor—changing attitudes toward gender roles. Women who no longer accept the traditional housewife role are more likely to obtain more education and to work outside the home.

The older her youngest child, the more likely it is that an American woman will choose to be employed. In a study completed in 1980, 62% of all married women with children ages six to seventeen were in the United States labor force, while only 45% of those with a child under age six were working. The age of the children also frequently affects the involvement of the husband in child care duties. When a wife's level of education is higher *and* the children are younger than age twelve, a husband is more likely to care for them than in other circumstances.[6]

The size and structure of the family are also factors that affect the working status of Soviet women. Overall, employed Soviet women are rather well educated; in 1988, 61% of all people with a specialized secondary education or with higher education were women. This trend is expected to continue: Information obtained during the 1988–1989 school year indicated that 54% of the students in higher education programs and 57% of the students in specialized secondary education programs were female. However, the high level of education does not mean that women occupy places of authority and power in the economy. The percentages of women in high-ranking managerial positions at the beginning of 1989 were 9.5% in industry, 9.5% in agriculture, 8.4% in communication enterprises, 0.9% in construction, and 0.6% in transportation. In addition, the overall promotion and advancement of Soviet women are slower than for men.[7]

Although most Soviet women work, some who have "large" families—more than one or two children—may not work for a period of time. (We remind the reader that Soviet women receive an eighteen-month paid parental leave plus an eighteen-month unpaid parental leave after the birth of a child.) In one survey, the percentage of women in larger families who stopped working, at least for a while, varied from 17.4% in Tajik (now Tajikistan) and 19.9% in Turkmen (now Turkmenistan) (regions with a high birthrate) to 45.2% in Estonia and 43.8% in Russia

TABLE 6.1. Labor Market Activity of Moscow Women by Number of
Children Representing Large Families

	Percentage of women having:			
	Three children	Four children	Five children	Six children
Working in labor force	85	83	77	52
Presently on parental leave	5	10	14	28
Not working in labor force	10	7	9	20

Source: E. F. Achildiyeva, "Big Family in Moscow: Living Conditions, Public Opinion, Aid Measures," in *Social Potential of Family* (Moscow, 1988).

(regions with a low birthrate).[7a] Table 6.1 indicates the labor market work activity of Moscow women in larger families.[8]

Family structure influences the distribution of family income in both the United States and the former Soviet Union; however, the influence is particularly strong in Soviet society because of product and service shortages. A large extended family creates an interesting paradox. In large families, the income burden on each working member increases. The greatest burden rests on single parents who have both children and parents living with them. However, large multigenerational families—particularly with more than one working-age adult in the household—have more choices about who will be responsible for generating income. In addition, the members of such families can share some home equipment and consumer services, thereby extending the purchasing power of their collective income.

Employed mothers in large Soviet families often have to choose work that does not match their qualifications. According to research done in Moscow, about 50% of mothers having specialized secondary or higher education work as unskilled labor if they have five or more children.[9]

FAMILY WORK ROLES

Despite the numerous differences between Soviet and American families, one feature of family life is strikingly similar: Many women in both countries suffer from role *overload* as a result of the unresolved gender problem regarding the intersection of work and family life—a theme that recurs throughout the chapters of this book. The "joy of housework" does not appear to exist in either country, if, indeed, such a phenomenon exists at all.

Many observers in the United States have begun to recognize the growing contradiction of dual-income families. As more women work for pay away from home, they achieve greater economic independence. At the same time, the conventional division of family functions still allocates domestic work to women, which in turn slows their achievement of economic independence. Simultaneously, as women assume an increasing share of the collective family labor, they are denied the characterization of their unpaid household efforts as "work."

In both countries, women more than men have experienced changes in family and work roles. In the United States, men are still considered the preferred economic "providers" for the family; full social recognition of the dual-earner family life style lags behind its actual occurrence. Since 1917, the social recognition of women as full and equal members of the Soviet labor force has required that they perform both traditional family roles and a wide variety of additional social roles. Some contemporary Soviet scholars argue that family roles ought to be equal in value to market work, making it possible for women to realize their individual potential within families while making an important contribution to strengthening families.

V. A. Sysenko, a family scholar from Moscow University, believes that the psychosocial consequences of women's double burden at work and at home may be deeper than formerly imagined.[10] The pressure of dual responsibilities sharply decreases women's satisfaction with marriage and has a negative impact on the overall relationship between the spouses, increasing the likelihood of divorce. In addition, some Soviet sociologists and demographers emphasize the indirect influence of traditional role changes on the declining birthrate.

Certainly, conflicts arise in Soviet marriages over the responsibilities of husbands and wives for child care and housework (see Chapters 2, 3, and 8). These conflicts may reflect a deeper disagreement about appropriate roles for women in Soviet society and family life. According to some studies in Byelorussia (now Belarus), an egalitarian division of household responsibilities was reported in 60.8% of "happy/stable" families (those where both spouses were satisfied with their marriages), while only 5.6% of "unstable" families were characterized by a more or less equal division of labor.[11]

Estonian sociologists have drawn similar conclusions: Sharing household duties increases the satisfaction of both spouses with the management of finances, decreases the amount of family conflicts, and produces a greater similarity in spouses' family-related attitudes. Or perhaps a pre-existing similarity in spouses' attitudes makes it more likely that they will share household responsibilities. Regardless of cause and effect, young Soviet wives are increasingly expecting a cooperative and equitable division of household labor, and this expectation is an important factor in the spouses' marital adjustment.[12]

The purchasing of household services by Soviet families (including meals eaten away from home) is uncommon. In a study done in Byelorussia (now Belarus) in 1983, only 20% of the respondents reported purchasing household services, and those services purchased made up only 5% of the total household work.[13] In another survey of women engineers working in a Moscow research institute, only 10% reported regular use of laundry services, and 7% said they bought semiprepared or fully prepared foods.[14] The reasons for the lack of use of such services are rather clear: Many services are geographically remote, have inconvenient hours, and are of low quality. Quality problems are particularly evident in laundries and restaurants. Other major reasons for the large amount of time spent cooking meals in Soviet families include inadequate supplies of kitchen equipment and a lack of convenience foods.

Women's attitudes also enter into the equation. A study completed by the Institute of Sociology, Soviet Academy of Sciences, indicated that the majority of women hold very traditional views about housework. Of the women responding, 74% believed that they should do all of the household work by themselves even if there were the possibility of hired help; 53% replied that all washing should be done at home, since the quality of laundries is so poor. As in the United States, women with higher education were more likely to utilize outside help for household work.[15]

The family-related responsibilities of Soviet women are not confined to household chores. Women are the major caretakers of both children and the elderly; the main links between the family and external institutions, such as schools and health care facilities; and the primary maintainers of kinship ties. Women also make the majority of the family decisions related to such matters as household budgets and leisure time planning. Although these functions are shared somewhat in upper-class families, most women perform these functions alone. Fifty-eight percent of Soviet women are fully responsible for the family budget; 43% solve all the household problems alone; and 34% organize leisure time and vacations.[16]

What about the transmission of work-related roles to children? Although Soviet mothers spend more time with their children than do fathers, the overall time allotment is still rather small, since they are absent from home the greater part of the day. At the same time, small families make it possible for women to "spoil" their children; that is, they attempt to spare their children the effort of household drudgery. As a result, many young people are poorly prepared for their future family roles. And, indirectly, a certain social pattern is perpetuated. Both boys and girls are growing up with the idea that women should view outside employment as primary, but that they must also bear the burden of household responsibility. This may be paving the way for continuing conflicts about work and family roles.

GENDER DIFFERENCES IN FAMILY WORK ROLES

The dual roles of wage worker and family member inevitably reflect gender differences and often produce stress and conflict. "Role strain" occurs when conflicting demands make it difficult to fulfill the requirements of multiple roles, or when the total demands of time and energy are too great to perform the roles adequately or comfortably. Role expectations of males and females can be contradictory, creating considerable interpersonal tension in addition to individual stress. At the same time, having multiple roles can be positive. Claiming several identities provides meaning and guides behavior, thereby contributing to psychological well-being. The relative degree of commitment to each role is the crucial factor. When all roles receive equal commitment, role strain seldom occurs.

Recent research on gender roles in the United States has focused primarily on two aspects of family life. On the one hand, the dual work and domestic roles of women have been highlighted because of the recent influx of women into the labor market. On the other hand, interest in the role of men in family life and household work is increasing. The dual-income family has become a common phenomenon in the United States, and the problem of coordinating the careers of the two spouses is often a source of difficulty. Failure to accommodate both careers can lead to dissatisfaction and even divorce. If both employed spouses were to assume the traditional male model of work—high commitment of time and energy to a job, low commitment of time and effort to the family—the results would almost certainly be detrimental to family life. Thus, a new model of the work–family relationship is needed.[17]

Presently, the bulk of household work in American families is the responsibility of the wife—whether or not she is employed. However, the employed wife spends somewhat less time in household work than the nonemployed wife, and she has much less leisure time. Paradoxically, today's homemaker spends as much time on household tasks as her counterpart did fifty years ago, despite an increase in technological assistance. In the past, Americans assumed that new technologies would virtually free women from housework, and that no one would need to replace them.[18] Today this fantasy can no longer be maintained. The reality is that family life and household management are complex phenomena requiring a substantial commitment of time and energy, regardless of the particular forms they take. If women are to be regularly employed outside the home, then men will inevitably need to become more centrally involved in family life.

Gender-linked values appear to be very influential in determining how much a man will participate in household tasks: The less traditional the values held by a husband and wife, the more likely it is that the husband will share in the housekeeping role. Other sociological factors also influence how much household work a man will undertake. Here are some examples: Higher-income husbands are considerably less likely to do housework than lower-income husbands; as a wife's education increases, her husband is more likely to share housework with her if she works part-time; and African-American couples are more likely to share household tasks than are European-American couples.[19]

Like their American counterparts, Soviet women have been changing their expectations about household work. In one study, 51% thought that household work should be divided equally if both spouses work; 25% believed that housework should be performed according to the paid workload and the preferences of the spouses. Only 10% of the women wished to divide household duties in into specific women's tasks (cooking, washing, cleaning the house) and men's tasks (home and automobile repairs).[20]

As in the United States, what Soviet women want is not what actually happens. In several surveys of urban families, housework was reported to be shared by the couple in only 30–40% of the families, with 45–50% sharing child care. Those men who did share in household work were most likely to shop (55%), clean the apartment (48%), wash dishes (47%), play with the children (38%), cook (31%), and help children with homework (30%). Small repairs were the only sort of household work for which men were reported to be primarily responsible.[21]

These disparities between gender roles within the family have been found in Soviet time studies that have been conducted ever since the 1920s. A comparison of information collected over time from various Soviet regions[22] shows that time allocations on housework and child care have not changed significantly in the twentieth century (Table 6.2). Women consistently spend more than twice as much time on housework than men.

TABLE 6.2. Time Spent on Housework by the Soviet Working Population

	Hours per week	
Year	Men	Women
1923–1924 (big cities in European regions of USSR)	13	34
1936 (big cities in European regions of USSR)	12	34
1965–1968 (big cities in European regions of USSR)	12	27
1967–1970 (big cities in European regions of USSR)	10	27
1980 (Roubtsousk, western Siberia)	16	32
1980, 1982–1983 (small towns of Lithuania)	17	26
1982 (Kerch, southern Ukraine, medium-sized town)	12	28
1986 (Pskov, western Russia, medium-sized town)	15	27

Source: T. M. Karakhanova, "The Amount and the Structure of Time Spent on Meeting the Everyday Life Needs of the Population," in *Time and Its Use* (Moscow, 1988).

Soviet resource management experts have estimated that an optimal time allocation for housework should be no more than twelve and a half hours per week per family. However, the average urban Soviet family currently spends thirty hours per week on housework, while a rural family spends forty to fifty hours per week.[23] For decades, family members have spent many hours each week standing in line for food or other consumer products because of the shortage of goods and poor means of distribution—a situation that has drastically worsened in the past several years. Many small shops sell only one type of product. For each of these individual shops, the buyer has to stand in line to receive a receipt for the desired product, wait in a second line to pay for the product (cashiers often use an abacus for calculations, since there is a shortage of cash registers), and finally return to a third line to actually obtain the purchase. Soviet visitors to the United States (including the Russian authors of this chapter) have reported feeling somewhat overwhelmed by the wide array of products and brands available in American supermarkets, department stores, and specialty stores.

Shopping is frequently reported to be the most distasteful element of Soviet household work—a rather sharp contrast to the attitudes of many American shoppers. In addition to creating extra hours of shopping time, the shortage of Soviet goods increases time spent on household work by limiting the access of citizens to labor-saving devices that Americans tend to take for granted.

Naturally, the presence of children increases the amount of household work, both directly in child care and indirectly in additional maintenance tasks. In families without extra household help (e.g., a relative), the amount of time spent on housework more than doubles when compared to that of families without children. Of course, the expenditure of time is greatest when the children are very young. Ironically, this is the time when Soviet fathers are least likely to be involved with their children.[23a]

The role of the male in Soviet families has been studied very little. Soviet women evidence anger and a sense of powerlessness to change the situation. They feel quite overburdened by their responsibilities, and they resent the unwillingness of men to accept a substantial part of the household workload. Many Soviet men, like American men, view the home as a "refuge" to which they can return after work; as a result, they take a passive family role, leaving women with the burden of more roles to fill.

A Soviet sociologist, Z. A. Yankova, has developed a model of family relationships that contrasts modern family life with the traditional family that has been known throughout Russian history. Four types of family life are identified, based upon gender role values and actual styles of relating. The first type is characterized by an authoritarian role orientation and a corresponding structure of family relationships. Families of the second type retain an authoritarian role orientation, but actually function on a rather egalitarian basis. The third type is characterized by norms of equality in family relationships, but actually behaves in traditional male-dominated authoritarian ways. And the fourth type is characterized by an egalitarian role orientation as well as by actual equality in relationships.[24]

Using this typology, Yankova conducted surveys in a metropolitan area, a medium-sized city, and a small town. He found that families of the first type (consistent authoritarian roles and actual behavior) made up only 5% of the metropolitan sample, 10% in the medium-sized city, and 11% in the small town, while families of the fourth type (consistent egalitarian norms and behavior) made up 65%, 53%, and 50% of the samples, respectively.[25] Despite these findings, many Soviet scholars note that the most detailed studies indicate that males reporting participation in housework are actually only "helping" their wives, reflecting more traditional norms than Yankova's statistics would imply. Furthermore, indications are that the most menial household tasks are still performed almost exclusively by women, without much assistance from men: washing (73%), cooking (72%), everyday cleaning of the house (60%), washing dishes (49%), and shopping (49%).[26]

In a study of 1,600 women working in trades in three small Lithuanian towns, 58% reported that their husbands helped them "seldom" or "never," even though 25% thought that a husband should help with at least the most difficult household tasks and a startling 71% believed that husbands should share *equally* in all household duties.[27] Younger husbands were reported to be more likely to help, as were those with more education. Husbands provided more help in larger families, although the level of their help decreased considerably when children reached school age. Studies in Moscow undertaken in the late 1970s and early 1980s suggest a somewhat more egalitarian gender role division of labor. A sizable number of families (28%) reported that the spouses shared home responsibilities equally; most families indicated at least some participation by husbands; and only 14% of the women and 6% of the men responded that housekeeping was strictly a woman's domain.[28]

FAMILY CHILD CARE ISSUES

Many concerns related to child care are similar in Soviet and American societies, despite the significant differences between government-sponsored Soviet day care and private or corporate-sponsored programs in the United States (see Chapter 7). In each country, women still carry a disproportionate share of the child care responsibilities, even when both spouses earn income. Working Soviet and American mothers share concerns about being available when children return from school, caring for sick children, attending school events, and transporting children to and from day care sites.

Adequate day care is a critical factor in the decision of American mothers to return to work after the birth of a child. The child care industry has not kept up with demand as women have entered the work force in greater numbers. Mothers who cannot find child care may be forced to remain unemployed or may be restricted to part-time jobs with low pay and little opportunity for advancement.[29] Child care problems often hamper the careers of even highly educated professional women. In one study of 5,000 employees in the United States, 45% of the females and 23% of the males with children under age two reported that child care concerns would affect their decision about accepting a promotion. Fifty-one percent of the women and 20% of the men with children between two and five years of age responded in the same way.[30] Child care is also expensive. The average cost of full-time day care in the United States is $3,000 per year per child.[31] Therefore, child care options are particularly limited for low-income families (which are often households headed by single mothers).

Families with employed mothers naturally experience changes in parent–child interaction patterns. On the positive side, mothers' satisfaction with their employment can have beneficial effects on the family system. Employed mothers who are happy with their work often have enhanced self-esteem; they carry over positive attitudes to their roles as mothers, and thereby increase their effectiveness with their children. Other positive effects have been noted, although the results of research have been mixed and interpretation of findings remains controversial.[32]

Women are the primary caretakers not only of children, but also of sick and elderly family members. American women are six times more likely than men to stay home with a sick child. Mothers of children under age eighteen are also interrupted at work twice as often as fathers. And women are much more often than men the primary caregivers for their aging parents. In the United States, nearly 2 million women are caring for both children and parents simultaneously (see Chapter 5).[33]

Women's family role as caregiver reciprocally affects their employment status. Research results to date have been conflicting. Several studies have found that women who juggle parental care, child care, and employment reduce their time spent in leisure and personal activities in order to meet the demands of responsibility to others. However, another study found that 28% of the respondents quit their jobs in order to care for aging parents, and nearly as many were considering quitting or decreasing their work hours. A 1983 study found that nonworking women provided more care of the elderly than working women. Elderly parents were more often assisted by widowed, separated, or divorced women than by married women.[34]

Until recently, very little Soviet research focused on the effects of day care on children, working mothers, and the family unit. Rather, most information was obtained directly from workers at child care centers. Soviet parents are very concerned about the quality of state-run child care institutions (see Chapter 7). Particularly troublesome are overcrowding and the frequency of sickness; these are probably interrelated. Many temporary and poorly managed child care facilities are open during the summer in rural areas, to accommodate families trying to spend a maximum amount of time away from the large cities.[35]

When not in state-run preschool institutions, Soviet children are cared for in a variety of ways that are unique to the circumstances of each family and are often neither reliable nor consistent. In one survey a decade ago, respondents indicated that 44% of the children not in preschool were cared for by their mothers, who were on maternity leave; 21% were in the care of both parents working different employment shifts; 16% were in the care of various other relatives living in the same household; and 14% were in the care of relatives living in other households. In a study in Latvia in the same year, 47.6% of the preschool-age children were reported attending to be government day care centers; of the remainder, 11.4% were cared for by their mothers, 31.8% were cared for by grandparents or by a hired nurse, and 9.2% were cared for by both parents taking turns.[36]

Because child care and socialization have been emphasized to be state concerns in Soviet society, little attention has been paid to the relationship between day care institutions and family life. The primacy of formal aspects of education has simply been taken for granted. This thinking is currently being challenged, and substantial changes are likely to occur in line with the far-reaching effects of *perestroika* and political realignment. In and of itself, the freedom to choose different family life styles, different employment opportunities, and different day care and educational institutions will have an enormous impact on the lives of Soviet family members, particularly women.

THE FAMILY ECONOMIC STRUCTURE

By "family economic structure," we refer to the cash flow of income and expenses within a household. Naturally, the economic structure of families reflects the overall economic organization of the broader society. It also reflects the ways in which the society influences the life styles and decision-making patterns of family units. This section includes information on income sources, family expenditure patterns, and family saving patterns. (The use of tables helps us to present some technical economic data in a more concise and, we hope, clearer way.) Direct economic comparisons between our two countries are difficult to make.[37] In addition to the extreme diversity of each culture, the nature of our respective economic systems highlights the great divergence in financial choices available to citizens. Americans have many more options than Soviets for obtaining and expending income. As this book goes to press, the society that was the Soviet Union is in the midst of another great revolution, once again involving massive changes in economic organization that have far-reaching implications for the lives of the people.

Income Sources

Table 6.3 outlines the average income sources of Soviet families.[38] Although the figures indicate that incomes rose steadily in the 1980s,

TABLE 6.3. The Total Family Income of Industrial and Office Workers and Collective Farmers in the Soviet Union

	1980		1985		1988	
	Industrial and office workers	Collective farmers	Industrial and office workers	Collective farmers	Industrial and office workers	Collective farmers
Monthly total income per head (rubles)	121	91	135	110	153	121
Percentage derived from:						
Wages of the family members	80.4	10.5	79.2	10.0	79.1	9.8
Income from a collective farm	–	47.9	–	50.2	–	52.0
Pensions, grants, allowances, subsidies for rubles to sanatoriums, rest homes, pioneer camps, kindergartens	9.1	9.7	9.6	9.7	8.9	9.4
Income from subsiduary smallholding	3.5	27.5	3.3	26.3	3.3	24.5
Other sources of income	7.0	4.4	7.9	3.9	8.7	4.3

Sources: The data are from "Public Education and Culture in USSR," *Finansi i Statistika* (1989); *Semya, 38* (September 18–24, 1989); *Argumenti i Facti, 14* (April 1990); and "Public Economy of USSR in 1988 (1989).

the severe socioeconomic changes of this period greatly eroded Soviet family incomes. Income from private farming of personal parcels of land added substantially to the overall income of those who farmed in large collectives—for which they were paid only a stipend. When private income and collective income were combined, farmers' total income more nearly approximated the incomes of urban industrial and office workers.

The sources of American family income vary much more than those of Soviet families. Table 6.4 outlines these sources.[39] The table is similar to Table 6.3, except that the American figures are aggre-gated rather than averaged. The largest sources of income for Americans during the 1980s were of course, wages and salaries, followed by transfer payments, proprietors' income, and personal interest income. Note that income from labor sources decreased somewhat over the years; however, personal interest income and transfer payments increased slightly during those same years. Table 6.5 reflects the distribution of average family incomes in 1986 by source and household type.[40] Except

TABLE 6.4. Distribution of Aggregate Personal Income Sources in the United States

	1980		1985		1988	
Source of income	Billions of dollars	Percent	Billions of dollars	Percent	Billions of dollars	Percent
Wage and salary disbursements	1,372.0	60.7	1,975.4	59.4	2,429.9	59.8
Other labor income	138.4	6.1	187.6	5.6	228.9	5.6
Proprietors' income	180.7	8.0	255.9	7.7	327.8	8.1
Rental income of persons	6.6	0.3	9.2	0.3	15.7	0.4
Personal dividend income	52.9	2.3	78.7	2.4	102.2	2.5
Personal interest income	271.9	12.0	478.0	14.4	571.1	14.1
Transfer payments	324.7	14.4	489.8	14.7	584.7	14.4
Less: Personal contributions for social insurance	88.6	-3.9	149.3	-4.5	194.9	-4.8

Source: U.S. Bureau of the Census, Statistical Abstract of the United States: 1990, 110th ed. (Washington, DC: U.S. Government Printing Office, 1990).

TABLE 6.5. Distribution of Average Family Income in 1986 by Source and Household Type in the United States

	Amount in thousands of dollars	
Source of income	Male-headed household	Female-headed household
Wage or salary income	34,843	20,983
Nonfarm self-employment income	16,197	13,307
Farm self-employment income	7,077	3,630
Property income	3,430	2,790
Interest income	2,273	1,861
Transfer payments and all other income	8,644	5,720
Public assistance and welfare income	3,250	3,588

Source: U.S. Bureau of the Census, *Current Population Reports*, Series P-60, No. 159, *Money Income of Households, Families, and Persons in the United States*, 1986 (Washington, DC: U.S. Government Printing Office, 1988).

for public assistance and welfare income, male-headed households received more income than female-headed households.

Family Expenditures

Approximately 65% of the income of Soviet citizens during the 1980s was paid to the government as taxes, while the remaining 35% was "take-home pay" used for living expenses. Many of the services that Americans must pay for directly were subsidized in Soviet society. For example, health care and housing were provided as government services. As a result, many of the living costs that most Americans worry about were taken for granted by Soviets.

Table 6.6 indicates the percentage of income that families in the United States spent on major family budget categories in the 1980s.[41] The data come from the Consumer Expenditure Interview Survey, which provides a continuous and comprehensive flow of data on the buying habits of consumers. The figures represent average annual expenditures for the total population. An individual family might spend

TABLE 6.6. Percentage Distribution of Total Household Expenditures in the United States

	1980	1985	1988
Food	19.2	15.2	15.6
Food at home	13.2	10.3	11.3
Food away from home	5.9	4.9	4.3
Housing	28.7	30.7	31.8
Shelter	15.6	17.9	18.7
Utilities, fuels, and public service	7.3	7.3	7.0
Household operations	1.4	1.6	1.5
House furnishings and equipment	4.4	3.9	4.6
Apparel and services	5.2	5.4	7.1
Transportation	21.1	19.3	17.6
Vehicle purchases	7.3	8.4	7.2
Gasoline and motor oil	7.4	4.4	3.7
Other transportation expenses	6.4	6.5	6.7
Health care	4.5	4.4	4.6
Entertainment	4.4	4.9	5.6
All other expenses	16.9	20.1	17.6

Source: U.S. Department of Labor, *Consumer Expenditure Interview Survey: Quarterly Data, 1984–1987*, Bulletin No. 2332 (Washington, DC: U.S. Government Printing Office, August 1989).

more or less than the average, depending on particular characteristics, tastes, and preferences.

Overall, expenditures on housing consumed the largest share of the American household budget in 1988 (approximately 32%). According to the 1989 *Statistical Abstract of the United States*, 64% of American households owned their own dwellings. The second largest expenditure category was transportation (17.6%). On average, there were 1.8 vehicles per household in the United States.[42] Food expenditures ranked third in the family budget (15.6%), followed by expenditures on apparel/services and entertainment, respectively. Although health care costs were rising sharply, less than 5% of the average family budget was spent on health care at this time, since many American workers had a portion of their health insurance costs paid by their employers. However, as people age and as costs rise ever more steeply, expenditures on health care can be expected to comprise a higher proportion of the family budget.

Expenditures differ in those American families in which the wife works outside the home, compared with households in which the wife is not employed. When income and other variables were held constant, expenditures in the 1970s and 1980s for households in which wives were employed full-time or part-time were greater for food away from home, child care, women's apparel, and auto maintenance. Predictably, families with working wives bought more prepared foods and ate at restaurants more frequently (working women were more likely to indicate a distaste for grocery shopping and cooking that stemmed from time constraints). Families with two full-time earners owned more vehicles than one-earner families, although expenditures for vehicles did not differ significantly.[43]

Home ownership rate in the United States in the 1970s and 1980s was about the same for one-earner and two-earner families; however, families with two full-time workers were only half as likely to own their home *mortgage-free*. Despite the higher incomes of two-earner families, their average house value was slightly lower than the average value for one-earner families—no doubt reflecting the fact that the majority of employed women in the United States were and are working because their income is needed for family support. As a wife works more hours in the labor market, a family gains financial security that enables it to make the decision to change from renter status to owner status, while maintaining their preownership level of living. A major contribution of employed wives is reducing the burden of housing costs, either by contributing to savings for home purchase or by augmenting home equity over time.[44] Researchers in the United States have generally concluded that wives' participation in the labor force does not, by itself, have a major influence on family purchasing decisions. Rather, *total family income* plays the biggest role in determining expenditures, probably because two-earner families are more likely to reflect joint responsibility for money management tasks than are one-earner families.[45]

Examining the budget structures and expenditure patterns of Soviet families requires an orientation that is largely unfamiliar to most Americans, although some of the problems are easily recognized. In a large heterogeneous society, it can be meaningless to identify the economic situation of an "average" Soviet family. Furthermore, family economic structure is particularly susceptible to extreme fluctuation, in light of the vast socioeconomic changes sweeping through what used to be a more uniform Soviet economy. Until recently, however, Soviets thought about a family's "standard of living" in ways very different from that in the United States. The American notion of living standard is more abstract and subjective, reflecting individual perceptions, goals, and choices. The Soviet tradition involved a more rational computation by scholars that established norms, or estimates of what a standard of living *ought to be*. On this basis, the central government *legislated* a standard of living. Thus, when actual consumption figures were compiled, they were compared against these specific rational standards in order to draw conclusions, which in turn were used for further central planning.

Here is an example: In 1988, the average income of Soviet industrial and office workers was 220 rubles per month, and the average consumption requirement in their families was 153 rubles per member. According to Russian economic scholar V. Rogovin, the "rational," or normative, consumption budget in the 1980s was 250 to 300 rubles per capita. Thus, the actual standard of living for these Soviet citizens was considerably less than what it was intended to be. This already significant discrepancy has grown rapidly in the past several years as the effects of social change have spread economic chaos.[46]

Table 6.7 delineates household expenditure patterns in the Soviet Union during the 1980s.[47] Food and clothing costs were higher for Soviets than for Americans, partly because of the difference in availability of such items (those long lines again!). Choices among goods with differential prices were and still are virtually unknown, thus minimizing differences in expenditure categories over time. Regular restaurants were so scarce that a budget category for "food eaten away from home" could not be constructed.

Housing and transportation costs were dramatically lower than costs in the same categories in the United States. Soviet housing has been heavily state-subsidized. An average apartment, or "flat," is only two or three rooms, plus a tiny kitchen and bath—though many fami-

TABLE 6.7. Expenditure Patterns by Percentage of Total Income for Industrial and Office Workers and Collective Farmers in the Soviet Union

	1980		1985		1988	
	Industrial and office workers	Collective farmers	Industrial and office workers	Collective farmers	Industrial and office workers	Collective farmers
Foodstuffs	35.9	39.1	33.7	36.3	32.2	35.4
Manufactured goods	30.3	31.1	31.0	31.0	31.3	29.9
Cloth, clothes, footwear	18.5	18.0	18.1	17.2	17.1	15.6
Furniture; cultural and welfare goods	6.5	4.6	7.1	5.0	7.7	5.5
Cars, motorcycles, bicycles, etc.	1.7	2.7	1.6	2.7	1.9	2.6
Alcohol	3.6	4.9	3.0	4.2	2.8	3.5
Cultural and welfare services	10.3	4.9	10.0	5.0	10.1	5.5
Rent, public utilities, house maintenance costs	3.0	2.0	3.0	2.1	2.9	2.2
Family savings (cash, deposits)	5.6	8.0	7.8	11.2	8.8	14.3

Source: "Public Economy of USSR in 1988" (1989).

lies share common bathrooms located in corridors outside their living quarters. Most rooms serve several purposes; for example, a living room and/or study during the day contains a sofa used for sleeping at night. In major cities, such flats are usually located in high-rise complexes. In Moscow in the late 1980s, families typically paid only 15–25 rubles per month for these accommodations.

Waiting lists for urban flats may be years long. Divorced spouses are often forced to continue living with each other because of lack of available space. Young adults live with in-laws while they wait for their own accommodations. Some unfortunate individuals even lose their places on the housing lists and are forced to share cramped quarters with strangers, as many as two or three families in a flat.

Understandably, there has been little geographic mobility in the Soviet Union. Particularly in large cities, housing is so scarce that individuals dare not move and risk loss of access to living quarters. At age sixteen, citizens of the former Soviet Union were given identification "passports" to use for various purposes. A special stamp was required in order to work in most major cities, proving that the individual had obtained housing there. Until this occurred, the individual was forbidden to accept a job offer.

While virtually all American households own at least one automobile, most Soviets used and continue to use the public transportation system—like citizens of most European countries. For those few Soviets who do own cars, the risks are high. Autos may be stolen or vandalized; if repairs are needed, parts are seldom available. Cars are an extremely expensive luxury in Soviet society, and for many people they are "not worth the bother."

One of the most dramatic differences in budget delineation between Soviet and American families is the lack of a Soviet category for health care. Like housing and transportation, health services were almost exclusively provided by the central government. Health services, while somewhat primitive by American standards, were presumed to be the equal right of all Soviet citizens. At the same time, certain hospitals were identified as being for "the privileged," and growing numbers of private or semiprivate medical services have appeared since the early days of *perestroika*. Like other European countries, the former Soviet Union provided more readily accessible everyday care for virtually all families than has the private health care system of the United States (in which millions of family members are uninsured and underserved). Nevertheless, with few exceptions, the Soviet health care system has not made the technological advances that would permit seriously ill individuals to receive treatments that could cure them or prolong life without suffering.

Family Savings

The average savings rate of American families in 1987 was 3.2% of disposable personal income. That rate represented a steady decline from 8.1% in 1970 (except for a slight increase in 1984). Both in absolute dollars and in proportion of total income, two-earner families saved less than one-earner families. However, "savings" can be defined in two ways: as an increase in liquid assets or as an increase in net worth. In terms of an increase in liquid assets, the propensity to save was higher for one-earner than for two-earner families. By contrast, two-earner families were more likely than one-earner families to increase their net worth.[48]

In the United States, higher rates of savings often do not reflect wives' wages in two-earner families, in part because their earnings are likely to be directed toward a specific purchase or used to defray the cost of her employment (e.g., child care or a second car). Many working wives use their earnings for the education of their children or contribute to the down payment on a house.[49] In addition, the presence of a second income earner in a family encourages family members to rely on the second income for contingencies, thereby reducing the need for a savings plan.

One of the most noteworthy paradoxes of the contemporary Soviet economic situation is the relatively large amount of money that has been saved by many families while their actual family budgets have fallen far behind the normative consumption budgets projected by economic planners. This is attributable primarily to the lack of goods and services available to Soviet citizens, because of the failure of the larger economic system. The exact scale of this accumulation is difficult to specify, since available statistics record only the savings kept in banks and not the rubles tucked away in homes or pooled among members of a community. During the 1980s, even official figures increased substantially (Table 6.8). At the end of 1988, the level of savings in the banks of the Soviet Union was listed at almost 297 million rubles, based upon a population of 208 million workers (males and females over age 16).[50]

Despite the ethic of economic equality that characterized the official policies of the former Soviet regime, savings (like consumer goods) were not distributed evenly in the population. At the end of the 1980s, approximately one-third of Soviet savers had 300 rubles or less; 20% had saved 300–1,000 rubles; and another third had 1,000–5,000 rubles. Fewer than 2% of Soviet citizens had accumulated a considerable savings of more than 5,000 rubles.[51]

Like Americans, a sample of Soviets surveyed in 1988 saved for various reasons (Table 6.9).[52] The wish to aid their children was an important motivation, since the life situations of young families were economically hazardous because of low wages and the near-impossibility of credit or loans. However, economic uncertainty was the major factor in Soviets' hoarding of rubles. And now their worst fears are coming true. Despite their general insecurity, few Soviets could have predicted what citizens of many countries of the world, including the

TABLE 6.8. Savings Kept in the Banks of the Soviet Union

	1980	1985	1988
Total savings (millions of rubles)	156.5	220.8	296.7
An average amount of savings (rubles)	1,102	1,293	1,514

Source: "Public Economy of USSR in 1988" (1989).

TABLE 6.9. Reasons Given by Soviets for Saving, 1988

	Percentage	
Purpose of savings	Industrial and office workers	Collective farmers
Anticipated large expenses	28.9	24.5
Aid children	41.4	48.2
Preservation of life style after retirement	20.0	27.9
Unexpected expenses	55.4	51.2
Miscellaneous or "no purpose"	9.1	6.7

Source: "Public Economy of USSR in 1988" (1989).

United States, have come to expect: The economic forces of free enterprise and capitalism periodically produce serious inflation that devalues currency at a rapid rate. Thus, the "unexpected expenses" for which Soviets saved during the 1980s have turned out to be the escalating costs for staples such as food and fuel. As the transition to a "hard-currency" economy continues, Soviet family savings may very well be wiped out in the struggle to survive.

CONCLUSION

Both marketplace (paid) and family (unpaid) work are integral to the dynamics of family life. The general themes of conflict about work and family roles are similar in American and Soviet societies. However, as we have tried to show, the specifics of life have been quite different as a result of our differing ideologies, histories, and economic systems— at least until now. In most of this century, Soviet women as well as men have been valued primarily as workers rather than as homemakers or parents (roles that were taken for granted). The loss of so many males in war and political repression, along with their lack of involvement in family life, has had a significant impact on the individual socialization of many children, as well as on overall cultural norms and expectations. Even more than Americans, Soviet people have many obstacles to overcome in the attempt to better integrate work and family life.

Americans find it difficult to fully understand the pervasive lack of choice experienced by Soviet citizens prior to *perestroika*. Even more difficult to absorb is the impact of the sudden contradiction between theoretical freedom and practical lack of opportunity or choice brought about by the tumultuous events of the past several years. The resulting economic insecurity has had an enormous impact on family life—a largely negative impact thus far. In addition to the regular burdens of everyday life, feelings of frustration are growing with the recognition that the general level of economic equity across individual workers and among families in the same community is disappearing. Rapid changes in work roles, which are likely to continue for the foreseeable future, are certain to have a major impact upon gender relationships and family life. The economic structure of Soviet families will inevitably change as a result. Many of these changes will mirror trends that have taken place or are taking place in the United States; however, some may take very different directions. The comparison of Soviet and American families we have undertaken here may help provide a baseline for analyzing future patterns in work–family relationships in each country, as well as helping us better understand the complex interaction of economic structures and family life.

NOTES

1. The data on labor force participation in the United States come primarily from three sources: Commission on the Economic Status of Women, *U.S. Population Profile: 1986–1988*, Newsletter No. 142 (St. Paul, MN: Author, September 1989); E. Jacobs, S. Schipps, and G. Brown, "Families of Working Wives Spending More on Services and Nondurables," *Monthly Labor Review*, *112*(2) (1989), 15–23; and U.S. Department of Commerce, *Earnings by Married-Couple Families*, Series P-60, No. 165 (Washington, DC: U.S. Government Printing Office, 1987).

2. The data on labor force participation in the former USSR come primarily from three sources: L. V. Yasnaya, "The Analysis of Employment for Women Having Many Children," paper presented at the Conference on Forecasting Social Development and Demographic Processes (Yerevan, 1988); M. S. Matskovsky (ed.), *Family and Social Structure* (Moscow: Institute of Sociology, Soviet Academy of Sciences, 1987); and A. I. Antonov and V. M. Medkov, *Second Child* (Moscow: Mysl, 1987).

3. *Vestnik Statistiki, 1* (1990).

4. Most of the studies about why women work were done in the 1960s and 1970s, when the number of women entering the labor force in the United States began to rise. Here are a few of the primary ones: R. Bartos, "What Every Marketer Should Know about Women," *Harvard Business Review, 56*(3) (1978), 78–85; M. G. Sobol, "A Dynamic Analysis of Labor Force Participation of Married Women of Childbearing Age," *Journal of Human Resources, 8*(4) (1973), 497–505; J. A. Sweet, "Family Composition and the Labor Force Activity of American Wives," *Demography, 7*(2) (1970), 195–209; M. W. Weil, "An Analysis of the Factors Influencing Married Women's Actual or Planned Work Participation," *American Sociological Review, 26*(1) (1961), 91–102.

5. B. M. Levin and M. V. Petrovich, *Economic Function of Family* (Moscow: Nauka, 1984); L. V. Yasnaya, "On Combining Family and Professional Roles of Women," in *Social Potential of Family* (Moscow: Nauka, 1988).

6. The data on the factors affecting work status in the United States come from three sources: J. A. Ericksen, W. L. Yancey, and E. P. Ericksen, "The Division of Family Roles." *Journal of Marriage and the Family, 41*(2) (1979), 301–313; C. Hefferan, "Workload of Married Women," *Family Economics Review, 3* (1982), 10–15; and J. M. Sampson, M. M. Dunsing, and J. L. Hafstrom, "Employment Status of the Wife–Mother: Psychological, Social, and Socioeconomic Influences," *Home Economics Research Journal, 3*(4) (1975), 266–279.

7. *Vestnik Statistiki, op. cit.*

7a. Antonov and Medkov, *op. cit.*

8. E. F. Achildiyeva, "Big Family in Moscow: Living Conditions, Public Opinion, Aid Measures," in A. I. Antonov (ed.), *Social Potential of Family* (Moscow: Soviet Academy of Sciences, 1988).

9. *Ibid.*

10. V. A. Sysenko, *Marriage Stability: Problems, Factors, Conditions* (Moscow: Mysl, 1981).

11. N. G. Yurkevich, *Soviet Family* (Minsk: BGU, 1970), 190.

12. A. V. Keerberg, "Women's Load and Household Work Distribution in Young Estonian Families," in *Family Stability and Quality* (Tartu: Tartu University Publishing House, 1982); S. I. Golod, *Family Stability: Sociological and Demographic Aspects* (Leningrad: Nauka, 1984); N. S. Minayeva, "The Influence of Young Family Micro-Climate on Its Stability," in B. S. Pavlor and V. A. Orchinnikov (eds.), *Development and Stabilization of the Young Family* (Sverdlovsk: Urals Scientific Center, Soviet Academy of Sciences, 1986), 37–46.

13. M. G. Pankratova, "Women–Employment–Family," in *Family as an Object of Social Policy* (Moscow: Nauka, 1986).

14. E. F. Safro and G. V. Subbotina, "On the Problems of Relations between Women's Work and Family Roles among Engineers," in M. G. Pankratova (ed.), *Social Problems of Women, Work and Family Roles* (Moscow: Soviet Academy of Sciences, 1980).

15. L. V. Yasnaya, "Women at Work and at Home," in M. S. Matskovsky (ed.), *Family and Social Structure* (Moscow: Institute of Sociology, Academy of Sciences, 1987).

16. *Ibid.*, 34–37.

17. G. Spitze and S. J. South, "Women's Employment, Time Expenditure, and Divorce," *Journal of Family Issues, 6*(3) (1985), 307–329.

18. G. Spitze and S. J. South, "Women's Employment, Time Expenditure and Divorce," *Journal of Family Issues, 6* (1985), 307–329; J. Vanek, "Time Spent in Housework," *Scientific American, 231* (1974), 116–120; P. Voydanoff, "Work Role Characteristics, Family Structure Demands, and Work–Family Conflict," *Journal of Marriage and the Family, 50* (1988), 749–761; K. E. Walker and M. E. Woods, *Time Use: A Measure of Household Production of Family Goods and Services* (Washington, DC: American Home Economics Association, 1976).

19. Ericksen et al., *op. cit.*

20. Yasnaya, 1987, *op. cit.*

21. Safro and Subbotina, *op. cit.*; Z. A. Yankova, *The Urban Family* (Moscow: Nauka, 1979).

22. T. M. Karakhanova, "The Amount and the Structure of Time Spent on Meeting the Everyday Life Needs of the Population," in V. D. Patrushev (ed.), *Time and Its Use* (Moscow: Soviet Academy of Sciences, 1988).

23. I. Raig, "What Can the Household Economy Do," *Sociological Research Journal, 1* (1986), 35.

23a. Z. A. Gosha, "On Combining By Women of Two Functions: Motherhood and Work," in P. A. Gulyan, et al. (eds.), *Socio-Demographic Studies of the Family in the Soviet Baltic Republic* (Riga: Zinatne, 1980), 17.

24. Yankova, *op. cit.*

25. *Ibid.*

26. K. A. Akopdganyan, "Household Activities of Different Generations in the Family," in Z. A. Yankova and V. D. Shapiro (eds.), *Intergenerational Relations in the Family* (Moscow: Institute of Sociology, Soviet Academy of Sciences, 1977), 131–137.

27. V. Kanopene, "On Work and Everyday Life of Women Employed in the Service Sphere," in P. A. Gulyan, et al. (eds.), *Socio-Demographic Studies of the Family in the Soviet Baltic Republics* (Riga: Zinatne, 1980), 24–31.

28. Yasnaya, 1987, *op. cit.*

29. P. Voydanoff, *Work and Family Life* (Beverly Hills, CA: Sage, 1987).

30. B. Olmsted and S. Smith, "Time to Balance Work and Family Responsibilities," in Bureau of National Affairs, *Work and Family: A Changing Dynamic* (Washington, DC: Bureau of National Affairs, 1986).

31. *Ibid.*

32. D. King and C. E. Mackinnon, "Making Difficult Choices Easier: A Review of Research on Day Care and Children's Development," *Family Relations, 37* (1988), 392–398; K. A. Moore and S. L. Hofferth, "Women and Their Children," in R. E. Smith (ed.), *The Subtle Revolution: Women at Work* (Washington, DC: Urban Institute, 1979), 125–158.

33. J. A. Birnbaum, "Life Patterns and Self-Esteem in Gifted Family Oriented and Career Committed Women," in M. S. Mednick, S. S. Tangri, and L. W. Hoffman (eds.), *Women and Achievement* (Washington, DC: Hemisphere, 1975), 396–419; A. N. Farel, "Effects of Preferred Maternal Roles, Maternal Employment, and Sociographic Status on School Adjustment and Competence," *Child Development, 50* (1980), 1179–1186; N. Gerstel and H. E. Gross, *Families and Work* (Philadelphia: Temple University Press, 1985); D. Gold and D. Adres, "Developmental Comparisons between Adolescent Children with Employed and Nonemployed Mothers," *Merrill–Palmer Quarterly, 24* (1978), 243–254; D. Gold, D. Andres, and J. Glorieux, "The Development of Francophone Nursery School Children with Employed and Nonemployed Mothers," *Canadian Journal of Behavioral Science, 11* (1979), 169–173; E. Hock, "Working and Nonworking Mothers and Their Infants: A Comparative Study of Maternal Caregiving Characteristics and Infant Social Behavior," *Merrill–Palmer Quarterly, 26* (1980), 79–101; M. B. Woods, "The Supervised Child of the Working Mother," *Developmental Psychology, 6* (1972), 14–25; M. R. Yarrow, P. S. Scott, L. M. DeLeeuw, and C. S. Heinig, "Childrearing in Families of Working

and Nonworking Mothers," *Sociometry*, 25 (1962), 122–140; M. J. Zaslow, F. A. Pedersen, J. Suwalsky, T. D. Cain, L. Richard, and M. Fivel, "The Early Resumption of Employment by Mothers: Implications for Parent–Infant Interaction," *Journal of Applied Developmental Psychology*, 6 (1985), 1–16.

34. E. M. Brody, "'Women in the Middle' and Family Help to Older People," *The Gerontologist*, 21(5) (1981), 471–480; A. Lang and E. M. Brody, "Characteristics of Middle-Aged Daughters and Help to Their Elderly Mothers," *Journal of Marriage and the Family*, 45 (1983), 193–202; E. P. Stoller, "Parental Caregiving by Adult Children," *Journal of Marriage and the Family*, 45 (1983), 851–858; U.S. House of Representatives, Select Committee on Aging, Subcommittee on Human Services, *Exploring the Myths: Caregiving in America* (Washington, DC: U.S. Government Printing Office, 1987).

35. M. M. Zhuravleva, "Development of Preschool Educational Network in the Whole Country during the 10th Five-Year Plan Period," in *Public Preschool Education at the Current Stage* (Moscow: Proveshcheniye, 1981).

36. T. V. Ryaboushkin, et al. (eds.), *Incapacitated Population: Sociodemographic Aspects* (Moscow: Nauka, 1985); I. H. Kirtovsky (ed.), *Factors and Motives of Demographic Behavior* (Riga: Zinatne, 1984).

37. Although some readers may want to know the value of rubles compared to dollars, such comparisons are not very feasible. During 1991 alone, the exchange value changed four times, and four different values existed: (1) black market, (2) tourist, (3) official, and (4) trade. Whenever possible, percentages are given to provide a relative measure of comparison between the former Soviet Union and the United States.

38. "Public Education and Culture in USSR," *Finansi i Statistika* (1989); *Semya*, 38 (September 18–24, 1989); *Argumenti i Facti*, 14 (April 1990); "Public Economy of USSR in 1988," *Finansi i Statistika* (1989).

39. U.S. Bureau of the Census, *Statistical Abstract of the United States: 1990*, 110th ed. (Washington, DC: U.S. Government Printing Office, 1990).

40. U.S. Bureau of the Census, *Current Population Reports*, Series P-60, No. 159, *Money Income of Households, Families, and Persons in the United States, 1986* (Washington, DC: U.S. Government Printing Office, 1988).

41. U.S. Department of Labor, *Consumer Expenditure Interview Survey: Quarterly Data, 1984–1987*, Bulletin No. 2332 (Washington, DC: U.S. Government Printing Office, August 1989).

42. U.S. Bureau of the Census, *Statistical Abstract of the United States: 1989*, 109th ed. (Washington, DC: U.S. Government Printing Office, 1989).

43. D. Bellante and A. C. Foster, "Working Wives and Expenditure on Services," *Journal of Consumer Research*, 11(2) (1984), 700–707; E. H. Hacklander, "Do Working Wives Shop Differently for Food?", *National Food Review*, 2 (1978), 20–23; B. Oriz, M. MacDonald, N. Ackerman, and K. Goebel, "The Effect of Homemaker's Employment on Meal Preparation Time, Meals at Home, and Meals Away from Home," *American Journal of Agricultural Economics*, 62(2) (1980), 234–237; R. L. Rizek and B. B. Peterkin, "Food Costs and Practices of Households with Working Women and Elderly Persons, Spring–Summer 1977," *Family Economics Review* (Winter 1980), 13–17.

44. E. A. Roistacher and J. S. Young, "Two-Earner Families in the Hous-

ing Market," *Policy Studies Journal, 8* (1979), 227–240; S. M. Danes, "The Impact of the Wife's Employment on the Acquisition of Home Ownership and the Accumulation of Home Equity," unpublished doctoral dissertation, Iowa State University (Ames, IA, 1986); S. M. Danes and M. Winter, "The Impact of the Employment of the Wife on the Achievement of Home Ownership," *Journal of Consumer Affairs, 24*(1) (1990), 115–131; B. J. Frieden and A. P. Solomon, *The Nation's Housing: 1975–1985* (Cambridge, MA: Joint Center for Urban Studies, 1977); M. Griffin-Wulff, "The Two-Income Household: Relative Contribution of Earners to Housing Costs," *Urban Studies, 19* (1982), 343–350.

45. V. S. Fizsimmons, "Family Money Management: How One-Earner and Two-Earner Families Handle Money," in V. Hampton (ed.), *Proceedings of the 34th Annual Conference of the American Council of Consumer Interests* (Chicago, 1988); A. C. Foster, "Wife's Earnings as a Factor in Family Net Worth Accumulation," *Monthly Labor Review, 104*(1) (1981), 53–57; A. C. Foster, M. Abdel-Ghany, and C. E. Ferguson, "Wife's Employment: Its Influence on Major Family Expenditures," *Journal of Consumer Studies and Home Economics, 5*(2) (1981), 115–124; A. C. Foster and E. J. Metzen, "The Impact of Wife's Employment and Earnings on Family Net Worth Accumulation," *Journal of Consumer Studies and Home Economics, 5*(1) (1981), 23–36; J. Kinsey, "Working Wives and the Marginal Propensity to Consume Food Away from Home," *American Journal of Agricultural Economics, 65*(1) (1983), 10–19; M. H. Strober and C. B. Weinberg, "Working Wives and Major Family Expenditures," *Journal of Consumer Research, 4*(3) (1977), 141–147; C. B. Weinberg and R. S. Winer, "Working Wives and Major Family Expenditures: Replication and Extension," *Journal of Consumer Research, 10*(2) (1983), 259–263.

46. *Argumenti i Facti, 3* (1988); "Public Economy of USSR in 1988," *op. cit.*

47. "Public Economy of USSR in 1988," *op. cit.*

48. C. Hefferan, "Saving Behavior in Multiple Earner Families," in N. M. Ackerman (ed.), *Proceedings of the 25th Annual Conference of the American Council of Consumer Interests* (Columbia, MO: American Council on Consumer Interests, 1979), 177–178; C. Hefferan, "Determinants and Patterns of Family Saving," *Home Economics Research Journal, 11* (1982), 47–55; U.S. Bureau of the Census, 1989, *op. cit.*

49. M. S. Carroll, "The Working Wife and Her Family's Economic Position," *Monthly Labor Review, 85*(4) (1962), 366–374; A. H. Caudle, "Financial Management Practices of Employed and Nonemployed Wives," *Journal of Home Economics, 56*(10) (1964), 723–727; Danes and Winter, *op. cit.*; Griffin-Wulff, *op. cit.*

50. "Public Economy of USSR in 1988," *op. cit.*

51. *Ibid.*

52. *Ibid.*

Chapter 7

Social Policy and Families

Shirley L. Zimmerman
Anatolyi I. Antonov
Marlene Johnson
Vladimir A. Borisov

Comparing family-related social policies of the United States and the former Soviet Union creates complexity and even confusion, given our divergent histories and differing political and economic systems, not to mention the rapid pace of social change in both societies. Despite these differences, however, Soviet and American families experience many of the same problems, as earlier chapters have illustrated. These similarities invite comparisons regarding policy approaches toward families. After defining the realm of family policy and examining the values that have helped shape policies in Soviet and American societies, two of us (Antonov and Zimmerman) engage in a dialogue about the definitions of "family" in our societies and about the goals of family policy. This discussion is useful, we believe, in highlighting cultural and personal differences in viewpoints on these complex issues. The chapter concludes with an extended analysis of social policies and programs related to a family problem common to both societies: the care of young children in families with working parents.

DEFINING THE POLICY REALM

The term "policy" can be defined in a variety of ways. In this chapter, we define it as a *temporarily* settled course of action in pursuit of some agreed-upon goals and values—for example, universal health care in order to improve the overall health of a country's population. The values that have dominated policy debates in the United States are those associated with democracy and capitalism: freedom and individualism, involving personal rights, private property, and minimal government.

By contrast, the values that have most influenced twentieth-century Soviet policy are those associated with socialism: equality, economic security, and social justice, involving economic cooperation and centralized planning. Because values lie on a continuum, their overlap is reflected in the social policies of each country—for example, efficiency and productivity under Soviet *perestroika,* or fairness in United States tax laws. However, certain value *themes* come to predominate in every culture, in contrast to the topical issues that arise during a particular era. At the same time, value priorities change along with changes in policy objectives. For example, the Soviet transition to a market economy has heightened the value of efficiency, productivity, and competition, whereas in the United States, intensifying demands for equality and social justice have begun to affect the implementation of social policies associated with capitalism.

Social policy emphasizes the "social" aspects of policy choices and the implications of these choices for individuals, groups, and intergroup relations—whether pertaining to the development, allocation, and distribution of resources or to the regulation of social status, roles, and entitlements.[1] Social policy is also concerned with the social costs and consequences of public and private actions, and with how these costs and consequences are distributed in the population. In a capitalist society, social policy often serves to support the free market through government actions to meet needs that the market cannot or will not meet for large segments of the population.[2] Examples include tax subsidies for child care and housing, unemployment insurance, social security, education benefits, sponsored health care programs, and the like. "Need" can be defined as some basic minimium that is indispensable to the performance of a person's primary social roles (as citizen, worker, spouse, or parent).[3] Zimmerman has previously noted that governmental support for services to meet basic human needs has eroded in the United States over recent years, as free-market principles were allowed full rein.[4]

Although the cultural context is very different, Soviet social policy has also addressed needs considered essential to the performance of primary social roles. The central government of the former Soviet Union provided such things as old age and survivor pensions, medical and maternity care, disability benefits, universal family allowances (e.g., birth grants), and direct financial assistance for lower-income families with children. In addition, the state supplied subsidized housing and free day care for children of working parents.

The radical changes originally undertaken in connection with *perestroika* had an impact on all areas of social policy; therefore, the patterns of benefit distribution and the provision of social services slowly began to shift. The 1990 decision to convert the Soviet economy to a market orientation was clearly the major influence on the revolutionary transformations that are currently taking place in Soviet society. These transformations have had a powerful impact on families and promise to have far-reaching implications for the entire social structure, including the formation of family-related social policies. In the short term, at least, the costs of the transition from a centrally planned to a free-market economy have been high for Soviet society, both literally and figuratively. Of course, we are unable to specify just what will happen in the long run. It appears as this book goes to press that the governments of independent nation-states will be the sole shapers of social policy, but many questions remain unanswered. For instance, what roles will trade unions or political parties play in effecting these changes? Only time will supply definitive answers to these questions.

In the short term, sharp increases in the prices of food and consumer goods have drastically lowered the living standard of most Soviet citizens, creating great psychological and economic burdens and fueling political upheaval—even a reactionary longing for the past. The health care system is collapsing. Environmental contamination is rampant. The incoming flow of essential goods and supplies has nearly stopped. Food prices have risen dramatically, and nutritional standards have fallen. A carefully controlled, gradual transition to a "regulated market economy" in Soviet society was only a fantasy. Some economic plans have advocated compensation for consumers hurt by inflation; others have called for centralized distribution of consumer goods according to need and income. Job guarantees or subsidies for the unemployed have been suggested, somewhat reminiscent of the Works Progress Administration (WPA) program of President Franklin Roosevelt to deal with the post-Depression unemployment in the United States. Although reliable statistics are scarce in the former Soviet republics, estimated job losses from a too-rapid economic transition to a market economy approach 40 million out of a current Soviet labor force of 125 million; this translates into an unemployment rate of 32%.[5] Clearly, the incrementalism that characterizes most policy developments in the United States is virtually impossible at this time in Soviet society, where issues of national identity and governmental stability remain stubbornly unresolved.

FAMILY POLICY IN THE AMERICAN CONTEXT

Just as the problems of individuals and groups are central to the concerns of social policy, so the problems of families in relation to society are central to the domain of family policy. Just as the well-being of individuals and groups is a core goal of social policy, so the well-being of families can be regarded as a core goal of family policy. However, the traditions that have generally guided social policy in the United States—individualism, private property, and minimum government—have done much to create the perception that families, government, and the economy are separate, even incompatible, spheres of life. The result has been difficulty in recognizing the many ways in which families, government, and the economy intersect—and the implications of these intersections for individual and family well-being. Although some authors limit the definition of "family policy" to those policies that have specifically stated family objectives, the American authors of this chapter prefer to recognize the broader use of the term, since almost all social policies affect families in some manner, directly or indirectly. Yet, as readers will see in the following pages, the distinction between explicit and implicit family policy has implications for understanding Soviet family policy and comparing it to that of the United States.

"Well-being" has been defined as a composite of satisfaction with major life domains, such as marriage, family, job, leisure, and housing.[6] *The New Lexicon Webster's Dictionary of the English Language* defines "well-being" more succinctly as "*the state of being healthy, happy, and free from want.*" Although these definitions are rooted in subjective experience, they also have an objective component. For example, certain groups—women, African-Americans, and those with lower incomes—tend to respond more negatively when questioned in surveys about their sense of well-being. Because this sense of well-being is differentially distributed in the population, it merits attention by social policy makers. Although marriage and family life are primarily individual and private matters, they also have a more public, social aspect. Laws and customs reflect society's interest in the well-being of individuals and families when, for example, they regulate marriage and divorce, require school attendance, prohibit child abuse, or encourage wise management of family financial resources.

We agree that contemporary family policy in both American and Soviet societies falls far short of meeting a reasonable standard of well-being for all families. Early in 1992, the satisfaction level of individual Americans dropped to a ten-year low. Fewer people reported being satisfied with their lives than ten years earlier, with most of the changes occurring in households with annual incomes of $30,000 or less.[7] According to some economists, financial inequality in the United States is now greater than at any time since World War II. One recent analysis found that the top 1% of the population reaped about 60% of the gains during the economic growth of the 1980s; this group is now collectively wealthier than the bottom 90% of the population.[8] In the United States over the past decade, major social policies related to health care, education, income assistance, housing, employment, and social services have had a more and more negative impact on families. Despite the fact that "family" became a political buzzword during the same decade—implying that candidates for political office were all concerned about strengthening the American family—governmental policies and programs have had the effect of putting more pressure on families to perform more functions with fewer resources to help them.

In the 1970s, some critics faulted the United States government's policy approach to families for its lack of coherence. More recently, critics charge that cutbacks in both state and federal programs have created a policy of exclusion and have failed to address important family needs, particularly among the poor. In the 1980s and early 1990s, federal support for active intervention on behalf of families has been minimal. For example, during his administration, President Bush vetoed two congressional attempts to enact a family and medical leave bill for working parents. Instead of government sponsorship, policies to promote family well-being were initiated by a variety of special-interest groups competing with one another for scarce dollars. Although many are deserving of support, their programs often address only the interests of a particular group of families on whose behalf they are lobbying; Mothers Against Drunk Driving and the Association for Retarded Citizens are two examples. At this point in history, perhaps the most comprehensive proposals for promoting a coherent set of family policies have been made by women's organizations on both sides of the political spectrum. This is true even though some of the values underlying these policies appear unalterably opposed, such as the "pro-life" versus "pro-choice" dichotomy upon which much of the policy debate over abortion has been based.

Despite the election in 1992 of a federal administration more favorably disposed to governmental efforts to promote the well-being of families, the extent of change in the near future remains uncertain. On the hopeful side we note that early in 1993 the Family and Medical Leave Act was passed by the U.S. Congress and signed by President Clinton. Nonetheless, the tax cuts of the 1980s, coupled with an economic recession and significant political opposition to social spending, seriously limit the capacity of the federal government to undertake bold new initiatives on behalf of the nation's families, at least in the short term.

FAMILY POLICY IN THE SOVIET CONTEXT

Whereas the well-being of family members can be identified as the major goal of family policy in the United States, the official goal of family policy in the Soviet society to this point has been the successful functioning of the family as a social institution that supports the welfare of the larger society. As a social institution, the "family" refers not only to a particular structure of roles, but also to the orientation of individuals toward certain domestic values. The type of family institution that prevails in Soviet society can be considered an indication of the extent to which the society is family-oriented. Based on this assumption, Soviet family policy can be thought of as an effort to preserve a family-oriented life style and to neutralize trends opposing it.

Social policy that aims to strengthen families has acquired increased significance only recently in Soviet society. In March 1990, President Gorbachev was successful in urging the Supreme Soviet to pass a resolution improving the position of women within the society, protecting mothers and children, and supporting families. "This is not just a pressing socioeconomic problem," he said. "This is a core issue of our society, its present and future. However critical the situation might be in other spheres, care for mothers and children should be above all [else]."[9] This action was related in part to the dislocations resulting from the country's transition to a market economy, particularly affecting poor families with three or more children, who make up a disproportionate share of poor Soviet families.

However, policy aiming to improve the living standard of poor families has not actually been part of family policy in Soviet society, any more than the protection of maternal and child health. Instead, these have been part of larger economic and health care policies, such as the regulation of employment and leisure time for working mothers or pregnant women. Thus, family policy is easily subsumed under the broader rubric of social policy.

Assessing the impact of social policies on Soviet families requires information on social trends and processes that has traditionally been difficult to obtain, for a variety of cultural and historical reasons. In addition, modern methods of analysis are not easily available, particularly under current conditions of social upheaval. Furthermore, although we can offer our interpretation that the trends found in Soviet society reflect generally accepted values, the tremendous cultural diversity of Soviet regions makes such an assertion extremely problematic. Recent events have amply demonstrated that the Soviet peoples (like Americans) often hold competing values. In a 1990 speech outlining his plan for a transition to a market economy, President Gorbachev claimed that the Soviet Union was not rejecting socialism. Rather, "People value socialist ideals not because socialism is a nice word, but because of its fundamental social fairness, equality, freedom and democracy." Achieving these goals, he asserted, can be "done only through the market as the country strives for a genuine socialism."[10] However, events subsequent to Gorbachev's speech indicate a growing conviction on the part of many that "market" and "socialism" may well be incompatible concepts.

Students of American history will recognize similar justification for free-market principles in relation to democratic ideals in the United States. Soviet society has been confronted, from the opposite side, with the same value conflicts that plague the United States: A free-market economy leads inevitably to certain inequalities, and government intervention to reduce such inequalities inevitably reduces certain individual freedoms. Of course, these issues have been explored from many different standpoints in the dialogues between Marxists and capitalists.[11] What have not been very thoroughly examined are the implications of these issues for families in our respective societies.

WHAT IS A "FAMILY"?
SOME COMPARISONS AND CONTRASTS

How one views family policy depends to a considerable degree on how one views the family. In the United States, the family has gradually begun to be redefined to some extent, largely because older definitions are inconsistent with the current family life experience of many people. Customarily, a "family" was defined as a group of individuals descended from a common ancestry (*The New Lexicon Webster's Dictionary of the English Language*), or as two or more persons related by blood, marriage, or adoption (U.S. Bureau of the Census). Recent surveys show that other definitions are taking hold: For example, the family can be identified as a group whose members love and care for one another,[12] or as persons related by mutual expectations of emotional and material support regardless of their living arrangements, their behaviors conveying mutual responsibility, intimacy, and care on a continuing basis.[13]

These latter definitions are in keeping with recent court rulings in several United States cities. At stake are important health, housing, and other socioeconomic benefits that heretofore have been reserved for those meeting the standard definition of "family"—mainly married, cohabiting heterosexual couples and their children (if any). Advocates for an expanded definition argue that many nontraditional households have been formed out of economic and social necessity—not only among the poor and elderly, but among the mentally ill or retarded, as well as cohabiting homosexual and heterosexual partners who love and care for each other on a long-term basis. In 1989, "family" households constituted 71% of all households in the United States; the remainder were "nonfamily" households, slightly over half of which were headed by females. Of the "family" households, only 52% contained children under age eighteen.[14]

An apparent deterioration of Soviet family functioning over the past century engendered the need for the central government to become involved in so-called "family policy." The analysis of historical changes and current trends has suggested to some the need for strategic targets for family policy, in order to contribute to maintaining the traditional structure and functions of the family. In this regard, Russian sociologist A. Kharchev's definition of the family is relevant:

> A family is a historically determined system of relationships between the spouses, parents, and children; a small group whose members are connected by marital or kin relationships, a common household, and mutual responsibility, which is necessitated by society's need for physical and intellectual/cultural reproduction of the population.[15]

This functional definition can be extended to incorporate the family's economic role, in which parents and children engage in common activity connected with production *outside* the household as well.

These definitions reflect the general concept of a unity of people based in a common household, performing the functions of reproduction, socialization, and the maintenance of individual family members, as well as contributing to the economic welfare and stability of the larger society. According to the 1979 census, 84% of all families in the Soviet Union met the criteria above—full nuclear and extended families, two-thirds having children under eighteen years of age.[16]

Just as any normally functioning system undergoes change for a variety of physiological, social, or ecological reasons, the family is involved in a continual process of restructuring throughout its life cycle. Calamities, epidemics, ecological catastrophes, wars, and the like—all lead to changes in family composition and equilibrium. The potential disorganization associated with such extraordinary events has been the object of the Soviet government's *general* social policy, whereas the disruption of individual families in the course of everyday life (unrelated to extraordinary circumstances) is the object of *family* policy. The latter includes such things as the care of orphaned children, aid to single parents, and services to families with disabled or seriously ill children. In 1985, such families constituted 16.7% of the Soviet population, the largest share in Latvia and Estonia (21.3%) and the smallest in Tajik (now Tajikistan) (10.9%).[17]

THE FUNCTIONS OF THE FAMILY:
A SOVIET-AMERICAN DIALOGUE

At the face-to-face meetings that led to the writing of this book, we often had to spend time clarifying our individual understandings of family concepts and our views of society. Substantial differences existed in the kinds of family data we had available to us in our respective societies, as well as in our interpretations of that data. Of course, there were also differences in perspective among colleagues in each society, particularly when it came to understanding and implementing social policy. The material in this section is based upon a dialogue between one of the American and one of the Soviet authors of this chapter. The dialogue began in a casual conversation during one of the meetings and continued in written comments sent back and forth between Moscow and St. Paul.

ANTONOV: It seems to me that the family as an institution exists not only because it performs functions necessary for society, but because marriage, childbearing, and the upbringing of children meet very deep personal needs of millions of people. The predicament of the family as an institution—and thus the predicament of society—come from diminishing such personal needs and wishes. In my view, the widespread uninterest of contemporary Soviet couples in having more than one child is itself a demonstration of the crisis of the family as a social institution.

ZIMMERMAN: To my knowledge, small families are not viewed as a problem in the United States. In fact, women receiving public assistance are discouraged from having more children, and in some states are penalized if they do. In general, there is the view that people should not have more children than they can financially support and emotionally nurture. What has come to be viewed as a problem by many in this country is the increasing number of single-parent families, largely because of the hardships they experience and what this means for the successful performance of their functions. Yet even the relative merits of the single-parent family are viewed differently by various cultural groups within the United States. It is interesting to note that over 50% of all families in the United States had no children in the household in 1988. Even the average family size, 3.17 persons per household, was down (from 3.58 in 1970), a trend reflected in African-American and Hispanic families as well.[18] At the same time, it appears that the birthrate in the United States has very recently begun to rise again.

ANTONOV: The most important aspects of family policy are those that oppose family disorganization by controlling its primary functions—childbearing and socialization—in order to support the family's existence as an institution. The family's responsibility for the economic support of children is perhaps its most easily identified function. Admittedly, determining the degree to which families are failing to adequately perform other child socialization functions is considerably more difficult. For example, deviant behavior or delinquency of children can be interpreted very differently by parents and by the larger society. In Soviet society, the trend toward socialization of children in institutions outside the family may reflect the family's failure to perform its social functions, although theoretical work and research on child development are only beginning to be done. Regardless of its causes, antisocial behavior by young people is a widely recognized problem in Soviet society.

ZIMMERMAN: In the United States, deviant child behaviors and delinquency are also viewed as resulting from the failure of families to adequately perform their socialization and social control functions. These deviant behaviors include truancy, teenage out-of-wedlock births, drug addiction, and the like. In 1985, there were 42.3 reported cases of delinquency per 1,000 youths ages ten to seventeen—an 8% increase over the previous year, and up from 33.8 cases per 1,000 in 1975. The failure of families to perform their social functions can also be extended to observations of child abuse and violence; over three times as many cases of maltreatment were reported in 1986 (328 cases per 10,000 children) as in 1976, when the officially organized reporting of those statistics first began.[19]

ANTONOV: I think that the criteria for effective child socialization should reflect the views of *both* parents *and* the larger society. The potential for conflict between personality and society makes the synthesis of these interests extremely complicated, particularly in the sphere of marriage and family, where people have a tendency to choose on the basis of individual wishes rather than on the basis of what might be best for the larger society. Therefore, if the performance of family functions is successful, individuals acting on the basis of their own selfish interests must also find something valuable for themselves in family life.

The essence of the family as a social institution is its mediation of the conflicting interests of the individual personality and society. As American sociologist William Goode said, "The fundamental significance of the family lies in its mediation function," connecting each individual to the larger social structure.[20] A society cannot exist if, in addition to the socialization of new generations, it does not meet the practical needs of children, the elderly, the sick, and others who must be cared for. A society will survive only if individuals themselves are motivated to act in ways that meet social needs.

ZIMMERMAN: To this I would want to add the observation that only as a society is motivated to address the needs of *families* will individuals and the society survive. Today 20% of all American children are living in poverty, primarily in female-headed households. Study after study has documented the stress and hardship that poverty creates for these families, as well as the difficulties they experience in coping with daily life. The consequences of such hardship is reflected in the statistics on high adolescent birthrates and low school completion rates— both of which, in turn, are predictive of high poverty rates.[21] In the United States, the prevalence and severity of family problems have increased to the point where agencies, under severe budgetary constraints as a result of cutbacks in federal and state funding, are unable to respond effectively. Perhaps this signals a breakdown in the performance of the mediating function at *both* family and governmental levels. Families are unable to meet the requirements of the larger society, and society, via its agencies, is unable to meet the needs of families. I believe that these relationships have changed significantly over the past decade, as American culture has once again become more extreme in its ethic of individualism.[22]

Although I certainly agree that the continuation of a society depends on the ability and willingness of families to perform their different functions, we should also recognize that families must have the requisite resources and means to do so. Just as the well-being of society depends on the families that comprise it, the well-being of families depends on the society of which they are a part—each reinforcing the other. However, before such mutuality of interests can evidence itself, some sort of consensus has to emerge as to what ought to be government's role in mediating connections between and among individuals, families, and other social groups. Therein lies the problem.[23]

ANTONOV: Of course, the actual forms by which the mediation function of the family is realized are different at different stages of history. The aim of social organization in encouraging the reproduction of the population through high birthrates is demonstrated by thousands of years of history in which families have been encouraged to produce many children. The question is this: In what way does this aim manifest itself in the motives of individuals with respect to different family forms at different historical stages? I believe that this question has not been sufficiently addressed from a historical perspective in either of our countries.

The entity we call "society" does not need children as people per se; it needs children as potential workers, as resources for labor, and for the performance of social roles. Herein lies the contradiction—the possibility of a dialectical noncoincidence between the interests of society and the interests of the individual, their interaction determining the fate of the population. In other words, there is no specific entity within a society that has the need for "population reproduction" per se and strives to meet this need. Rather, the *family* is the element that harmoniously transforms those needs, which appear to be incompatible—the human personality's need for children and the society's economic need for workers.

It seems to me that this circumstance is of basic significance for understanding the role of the family as a mediator between the reproductive interests of the personality and the society. The family is a social institution ensuring both demographic and social reproduction. This implies that the elimination of what I am calling "the family's reproductive function," for whatever reason, eliminates the family's critical mediating role between the personality and the society.

ZIMMERMAN: You must admit that many professional colleagues, both in your society and in mine, do not place primary emphasis upon the family's reproductive function as a cornerstone of family policy. That notion may have some logic from a demographic point of view; however, it is difficult to support from either a feminist or an environmental perspective. Given the differing histories of our respective societies, it is curious that in our dialogue, you emphasize individual motives while I emphasize social justice—an interesting switch from the traditional stereotypes of Soviet communism and American capitalism. The following consideration of a specific family policy will help concretize the abstract principles we have been discussing and will highlight the practical implications of differing approaches to policy implementation. We remind readers that this is intended as an illustration of the nature and implications of family policy in two societies, rather than as a comprehensive review of child care in each society. Considerable selectivity was required to make comparisons and contrasts more meaningful, because of the complexities of differing historical conditions and differing approaches to data gathering.

A FAMILY POLICY ILLUSTRATION: SOVIET AND AMERICAN CHILD CARE

"Child care" as a public institution is widespread in Soviet society; however, the meaning of the term in Russian is rather ambiguous. Although used in the sense of "preschool upbringing," "child care" can refer to child socialization, early childhood education, or simply "babysitting" children of younger ages (the age range is also ambiguous). Of course, similar definitional confusion exists in the United States. "Day care" or "child care" can refer to the arrangements that parents make for the care of their children while they work, or it can involve the regular or occasional supplemental care that children receive from adults other than their parents. In the United States, the term "day care" typically refers to care provided outside the family home—in centers under public or private auspices, or in the homes of other families (known as "family day care"). The term "organized child care" usually refers to day/group care centers and nursery schools/preschools.[24] An American child care center may be operated by an individual at home, a government agency, a business corporation, or a charitable or religious organization. If not registered as a business enterprise, child care in a private home is referred to as "family day care." "Nursery schools" or "preschools" are terms used to describe formal organizations that provide an educational experience for children before they are old enough to attend kindergarten in the public school system. Here, the term "child care" refers primarily to the regularly scheduled care of preschool children whose parents work outside the home, although it can apply to all children regardless of the employment status of their parents.

The Historical Development of Soviet Day Care

Community-based child care is not at all new in the Soviet world. As in many regions of Europe and Asia, various kinds of "professionals" have provided care for children since ancient times. Depending upon their financial means and other circumstances, families often invited teachers and governesses into their homes to care for and to educate their children. Many families sent their children to monastaries, boarding schools, or other educational institutions, sometimes far from home.

In contrast to the close association between support of child care and a certain political attitude in the United States, organized forms of child care are unrelated to any specific Soviet social structure, political ideology, or geographic area. Nonfamily forms of child care began to be a problem only with the development of capitalism and the mass entry of women into the labor force in the nineteenth century. The first creches and kindergartens appeared in Russia in the middle of that century.[25] At first, these were mainly private, available to families on a fee-paying basis. Later, free (called "people's") kindergartens and creches were established, mainly by voluntary or charitable organizations. After the October Revolution of 1917, the issue of rearing preschool children became part of the Communist Party's policy in the spheres of education, women's employment, and family. The notion of "women's liberation" was viewed mainly in terms of their participation in political activity and nonfamily economic production. In Marxist thought, household activities were associated with "private property"; therefore, they stood in opposition to "social production," which was regarded as more progressive. The term "social" was synonymous with the concept of the "state"—state ownership, the state sector of the national economy, and the like. Today, the concepts of government and society are more clearly distinguished from each other.

As far back as 1884, Engels wrote in *The Origins of the Family, Private Property and the State*:

> With the transition of the means of production into social ownership, an individual family stops being an economic unit of society. Private households will become a branch of social production. Child care and upbringing will become a social concern.[26]

In an important article, "Beginning the Great Undertaking" (1919), Lenin linked this idea to the reorganization of society:

> A woman still remains a *home* slave, in spite of all the liberation laws, since everyday *household duties* suppress and suffocate her, make her torpid, rivet her to a kitchen and a child's nursery, make her do non-productive dull drudgery work. The genuine women's liberation, the genuine communism, will start only there and then, where and when the mass struggle against household drudgery begins—led by the proletariat holding state power, or, to be more exact, its mass restructuring (*perestroika*) into a large socialist economy.[27] (italics in original)

In the same article, Lenin called public kindergartens and creches "the sprouts of communism."

The concepts of women's liberation from household duties and of society's role in childrearing have been prevalent in Soviet society for decades. They were the foundation for the development of government-run creches and preschool institutions, which were originally expected to care for *all* preschool children.[28] In reality, however, the construction of child care institutions has always lagged far behind the need for them, right up to the present day. Even by the end of 1940, these institutions could accept only about 6% of all preschool children, even though the actual number of children receiving care (about 2 million) made the effort seem more substantial. To complicate matters further, women made up nearly 45% of the employed population prior to the outbreak of World War II.[29] Thus, a growing number of children were left without supervision (a situation not unlike that of the United States today), the social consequences of which can only be imagined, since no studies were ever conducted.

The Development of Child Care in the United States

Unlike the evolution of child care in Soviet society during this century, no consistent goal or vision has guided the development of child care policy in the United States. Rather, differing interests have converged for a variety of reasons. Day nurseries were first established in the United States in the early 1800s to serve working mothers, widows of seamen, and others deemed "worthy."[30] The federal government first sponsored a day nursery in Philadelphia during the Civil War. Private and charitable organizations became involved in day care in the later years of the nineteenth century, responding to the large influx of European immigrants. Recognizing that children of immigrant families often lived in conditions harmful to their development, these organizations established day care program in order to prevent the institutional placement of children, thereby helping, they believed, to "preserve family life." However, this perspective came under attack by representatives of the Charity Organization Societies, who thought that day care should become part of comprehensive family services for the poor—a view that persisted well into the twentieth century.

Since 1900, government involvement in day care has been cyclical. During the Great Depression, day nurseries for children of the unemployed were financed for the first time by state and federal governments through the WPA.[31] Following this effort, government interest declined. With the advent of World War II, however, the nation faced a labor shortage that could be eased through maternal employment; federal funding for day care again increased. When the war ended, these funds were withdrawn, and few state programs survived (a notable exception being California's network of child care centers).

Amendments to the Social Security Act during the 1960s revived interest once again. As a strategy to reduce costs of public assistance, additional federal funds for child care were allocated to encourage mothers receiving public assistance to become financially independent. Simultaneously, federal day care funds were appropriated to provide compensatory education for disadvantaged children. The most successful and popular of these programs was Head Start.

During the 1970s, the politics of day care reached a stalemate between a liberal constituency in which the women's movement played a significant role (advocating for subsidized day care as a right) and a conservative movement that opposed day care.[32] The concept of comprehensive day care emphasizing development, health, and education, rather than just custodial aspects of day care, was reflected in the Comprehensive Child Development Act of 1971. Although supported by both houses of Congress, the act was vetoed by President Nixon, who declared that he would not commit the "vast moral authority of the National Government to the side of communal [read 'communist'?] approaches to child rearing."[33] Despite this opposition by the executive branch, the 1970s saw modest increases in federal funding for day care programs, income tax deductions for child care for working parents, and the development of federal day care standards.

Child care in the 1980s reflected the conservative trend of the decade, as initiatives were shifted to the private sector and states or local communities were given greater responsibility for setting standards and regulating day care services. Employer-supported child care programs increased, as did the use of federal and state child care income tax credits. Private, profit-oriented centers, especially national chains, arose to capture a large share of the child care market. Information and referral child care services were also developed to increase the accessibility of child care to families who needed it.

In 1990, the United States Congress passed the first major piece of child care legislation since 1971. Projected to cost as much as $12 billion over the next five years, funds were allocated for grants to states to help pay for child care, including the training of child care workers and the subsidization of state-regulated child care centers.[34] In addition, the maximum tax credit was increased for low-income working families with children; families with more children would be able to get larger tax credits (the most costly part of the legislation).

Comparing Soviet and American Day Care Efforts

The Scope of Child Care

There are some notable differences in Soviet and American day care efforts up to the present time. According to Soviet data, in 1988 there were more than 147,000 full-time creches, kindergartens, and combined creche–kindergartens. These were attended by 17.4 million children, or 58% of all children ages one to seven.[35] However, if we include the number of children ages two months to one year who were eligible to attend creches but remained at home, then the percentage of children using Soviet preschool institutions would drop to about 49%. Most of these institutions (70%) were located in urban communities, the remainder in rural areas. However, virtually all day care expansion in the 1980s occurred in these rural areas.

The number of children attending preschool institutions varies greatly in the various Soviet regions. Table 7.1 presents the percentages of eligible children in child care institutions in the various republics of the Soviet Union in 1988. The figures range from a maximum of 71% in Russia and Byelorussia (now Belarus) to a minimum of 16% in Tajik (now Tajikistan) and 20% in Azerbaijan. In urban communities, this coverage varied from 81% in Moldavia (now Moldova) to 47% in Armenia, and in rural areas from 62% in Moldavia to 5% in Tajik.[36]

These statistics alone do not directly reflect the degree to which the population's need for child care institutions is satisfied. Despite quality and/or availability of space, there are always some parents who prefer home care to institutional care, as well as some children who are unable to attend preschool institutions for individual reasons (e.g., poor health). Thus, the normative goals for attendance are always less than 100% of all eligible children. According to the government guidelines most recently in effect, facilities are supposed to exist for 75% of all children. In some areas, coverage meets or exceeds this goal, especially in urban communities. However, some experts have argued that the 75% guideline is not valid, since higher rates of day care use have been demonstrated in other countries. For example, in the former German Democratic Republic (East Germany), a late 1980s census showed that 89% of all preschool children attended child care institutions; 95% of all children of kindergarten age attended kindergartens;

TABLE 7.1. Preschool Children in Child Care Institutions in the Soviet Republics in 1988 (Percentage of Total Population of Preschool Age Children)

	Total population	Urban locations	Rural locations
USSR	58	69	40
RSFSR	71	76	59
Ukranian SSR	61	68	45
Byelorussian SSR	71	79	51
Uzbek SSR	36	56	25
Kasakh SSR	53	60	45
Georgian SSR	44	56	30
Azerbaijanian SSR	20	31	8
Lithuanian SSR	61	71	39
Moldavian SSR	70	81	62
Latvian SSR	63	72	42
Kirgiz SSR	30	51	20
Tadjik SSR	16	48	5
Armenian SSR	39	47	25
Turkmenian SSR	31	50	18
Estonian SSR	68	73	53

TABLE 7.2. Comparisons of Need and Provision of Preschool Care in the Soviet Republics in 1988

	The number of children in preschool institutions	The number of children waiting for a place in these institutions	Percent of need met
USSR	17,354,000	1,875,000	84.3
RSFSR	9,766,000	910,000	86.3
Ukranian SSR	2,684,000	205,000	88.4
Byelorussian SSR	662,000	112,000	80.7
Uzbek SSR	1,263,000	204,000	76.2
Kasakh SSR	1,085,000	184,000	77.7
Georgian SSR	213,000	2,000	90.2
Azerbaijanian SSR	183,000	3,000	100.5
Lithuanian SSR	205,000	17,000	98.2
Moldavian SSR	351,000	38,000	73.3
Latvian SSR	143,000	41,000	77.7
Kirgiz SSR	206,000	49,000	63.1
Tadjik SSR	153,000	54,000	63.3
Armenian SSR	163,000	2,000	95.8
Turkmenian SSR	188,000	50,000	69.7
Estonian SSR	89,000	4,000	103.2

and 85% of all children from birth to one year of age attended creches, of which there was still a shortage.[37] Table 7.2 compares the need and provision of child care in the Soviet republics in 1988.

Although certainly growing, the exact numbers of children in day care in the United States are difficult to determine. However, the relative size of the American day care effort appears to contrast sharply with that of the former Soviet Union. Counts vary from report to report, depending on the procedures and categories used for counting. According to a report issued by the National Center for Health Statistics in 1990, over 13.3 million children under age five were in some type of regular child care arrangement in 1988. Thirty-one percent were enrolled in a nursery school or day care center program; another 32% were cared for outside their homes by relatives or nonrelatives. Approximately 83% of all children in day care were children in families in which the mothers worked.[38]

These counts differ from a Current Population Report issued by the U. S. Bureau of the Census in July 1990, which reported that only one-fourth of the children of employed mothers in the United States were involved in a day care or nursery school program in 1987, up from 13% in 1977. The percentage of children cared for in their own homes was about the same as the National Center for Health Statistics report based on 1988 data, 30%—half of whom were cared for by their fathers, slightly more than a quarter by other relatives, and approximately a fifth by "nannies" and other nonrelatives. However, during this period (1977 to 1987), the number of children cared for by relatives in their own or the relatives' homes declined, as did the proportion of children cared for by their mothers while at work. This occurred at the same time that the percentage of children enrolled in formal day care centers or nursery schools increased, almost double the number enrolled in 1977.

The Adequacy of Child Care

On the average, there are about 107 children for every 100 available spaces in preschool institutions in the Russian Republic. This overcrowding has been a chronic problem in Soviet society since World War II. From 1970 to 1988, the severity of the problem actually increased in some Soviet republics. Except for Azerbaijan, Lithuania, and Estonia, the situation is most acute in large cities; however, some rural areas are affected as well. By the end of 1988, there were about 1.9 million Soviet children waiting for places in preschool institutions, representing an increased need of almost 12%.[39]

In 1988, for the USSR as a whole, 84% of the need for preschool institutions was satisfied—up from 79% at the beginning of the 1980s. There are no direct urban and rural comparisons; however, other trends suggest that most of the increase occurred in rural areas. Patterns of child care availability do not correspond strictly to the birthrates in the various Soviet regions. Although there is a higher level of day care provided in Azerbaijan (where the fertility rate is higher) and a lower level in Latvia (where the fertility rate is lower), some regions with high birthrates (such as central Asia) have rather low percentages of children attending day care institutions.[40] Despite an increase in the number of day care institutions in all of these regions, the provision of child care services has still lagged noticeably behind the actual need for them, even before the social upheavals of the past several years. No doubt this has reflected a governmental tendency to consider child care among the "nonessential" social programs, for which funds are not available under difficult economic circumstances.

Recently, Communist Party and central government documents proclaimed the importance of meeting the population's need for child care. The number of places in preschool institutions was first projected to grow by 3 million between 1986 and 1990; later, the number was increased to 4 million, which would have provided child care facilities for 73% of all Soviet children. If this plan had been achieved, the problem would have been completely resolved within four to five years. Of course, this has not happened and will not happen. Even in 1988 and 1989, institutional programs were available to only 55% of Soviet children. The target increases for 1989 were achieved in only four republics: Ukraine, Byelorussia (now Belarus), Kirghiz (now Kyrgyzstan), and Turkmen (now Turkmenistan).[41] The political and economic events of 1991 have cast doubt upon the ability of various Soviet regions to maintain even levels of child care services from the late 1980s, let alone expand them, in the face of increasing poverty and widespread unemployment.

Since the United States has no official target for child care coverage, no absolute shortage of child care resources exists. However, geographic accessibility, quality of care, and the ability of families to pay for services constitute serious problems. Families must select from among a range of child care options, which may be extremely scarce in one geographic area and bewilderingly abundant in another. Relative to the the number of children, the supply of center care is more concentrated in the South (41% of all centers are in the South, where 35% of all young children in the country live), and less concentrated in the West (18%, where 23% of all young children live). Approximately three-fourths of all child care programs (centers and family day care) are located in urban and suburban areas, which also is where most children and their parents live (75%).[42]

In the United States, the government does not directly provide day care services; in fact, both federal and state governments have sometimes *opposed* attempts to subsidize such programs, arguing that such programs undermine family values. Most private employers do not typically offer child care services, though some are experimenting with innovative programs. Therefore, parents are left to locate their own resources from among whatever options are available to them. Some quality guidelines were devised in the 1970s; however, they have never been consistently fostered or enforced at the federal level.

More than anything else, the question of the "adequacy" of day care for American children hinges on economics. The largest commitment ever made by the federal government at the time of this writing occurred in 1990. The promise was to help low- and middle-income families find "decent and affordable" child care by administering block grants and matching funds to states for child care services. However, critics have charged the federal administration with sabotaging the program by designating that it be administered by Aid to Families with Dependent Children (AFDC) rather than by the Administration for Children, Youth and Families. They contended that administering it as a welfare program would lower quality standards, limit the number of beneficiaries, and stigmatize the program.[43] Clearly, day care for children is still a debatable issue in the United States. Most Americans probably agree that something should be done to improve the situation, even if they cannot agree on what that something should be.

Sources of Child Care

Most family day care providers in the United States operate independently. However, they are regulated in a variety of ways, and many are sponsored by community groups or run as businesses. Of the children who are cared for in their own homes while mothers work, most are cared for by fathers; 8% are cared for by unrelated providers, 6% by grandparents, and 3% by other relatives. Care by family members is more common among ethnic minorities, such as African-Americans and Hispanic-Americans, than among the European-American majority.[44]

In addition to the large percentage of children receiving group care in nurseries or preschools, 8% attend day care centers, including kindergarten/extended day care programs and day camps. Thus, about one-third of all children are cared for in group settings, another third in their own homes, and the remainder in others' homes. Nearly 30% of children in child care are involved with multiple sources of care, and about one-quarter of the children involved in care will experience a change in the provider of that care within a twelve-month period.

According to the 1990 National Child Care Survey, two-thirds of all early education and care centers serving preschool children are nonprofit organizations; the remaining one-third are for-profit centers. For-profit centers tend to be located in the South more than in other regions of the country. They also are more likely to be found in rural and suburban areas than in urban areas. Most for-profit centers are independent and autonomous, and constitute 29% of all centers; for-profit chain centers constitute only 6%. A small number of business firms sponsor day care programs for children of their employees (2%). Nonprofit centers constitute 61% of all child care programs; these are sponsored primarily by religious organizations, public schools, or Head Start. Independent nonprofit centers constitute 26% of all formal day care centers. Finally, important in the growing child care network in the United States are federal, state, and local agencies that, together with national professional associations, provide leadership to the child care field.[45]

Center enrollments average sixty-two children per program but vary considerably with sponsorship. Head Start and public school programs average fifty to fifty-eight children per program, respectively—

fewer than other programs. Independent for-profit programs average sixty-seven children per program, whereas for-profit chains have a much higher average of ninety-one children per program.

The sources of care for American children vary with the age of the child. Most one- and two-year-old children of working parents (74%) are cared for by a non-relative, in either their own homes or the providers' homes. For children ages two to five, the most common source of care is a nursery or preschool. Four- and five-year-old children who are enrolled in some kind of school often attend a day care center as well, although home care before and after school is also common. In general, the proportion of children cared for in their own homes decreases with the children's age regardless of their mothers' employment status.[46]

Sources of child care also differ somewhat for children of employed and unemployed mothers. Unemployed mothers strongly prefer nursery schools or preschools, which together account for 63% of all day care for this group. The emphasis in these institutions is on the developmental and school-related aspects of child care. Employed mothers use more varied child care resources, partly because their motivations are more diverse. About 5% of preschool children are cared for by their own mothers in the mothers' work setting. Nearly two-thirds of the children of employed mothers receive care outside their own homes; 38% are cared for by relatives.[47]

In contrast to Americans, Soviets have long had access to an extensive public network of child care institutions. This network consists of creches for children from two months to three years of age; kindergartens for children from three to seven years of age; and creche–kindergartens, which combine the functions of the other two. This last type of institution, first created in the late 1950s, has now become the predominant form. In 1960, creches made up 38% of all permanent preschool institutions; kindergartens, 53%; and creche–kindergartens, only 9%. By the end of 1985, the structure of the preschool network had shifted: creches, 7%; kindergartens, 21%; and creche–kindergartens, 72% of all child care institutions.[48]

Of the total number of Soviet children attending permanent preschool institutions in 1960, about 30% were in creches, 62% in kindergartens, and 8% in creche–kindergartens. In 1985, comparable figures were 4% in creches, 12% in kindergartens, and 84% in creche–kindergartens. Experts expect even further development of these institutions in both rural and urban communities. Although concentrating children of various ages in one institution has some administrative advantages, it has exacerbated the existing problems of teacher overload and stresses on children associated with overcrowding.

Soviet day care has been administered in a variety of ways. Early in the 1980s, 76% of the preschools (enrolling two-thirds of all preschool children) were under the jurisdiction of—and financed by—approximately 120 different ministries of either the USSR or the individual republics. The remaining 24% of preschools were directly subordinate to national educational administrative bodies.[49] Until recently, however, the education and health of young children have been the responsibility of the central Soviet government's planning bodies.

Soviet child care institutions have differing hours: 33% are open nine to ten hours per day, 58% stay open twelve to fourteen hours, and 9% are open around the clock.[50] Seventy-four percent of preschool institutions in urban areas are open five days a week, while only 26% stay open for six days. In rural communities, this pattern is reversed: Eighty-two percent of the child care facilities stay open six days a week, and only 18% restrict themselves to five days.[51]

Numerous Soviet schools offer after-school or extended day programs for younger school children, supervised by regular or special teachers. In these programs, children can have lunch in the school cafeteria, do their homework with help from adults, or just spend leisure time in groups. These programs were first established in 1959. By 1985, 37% of all school children ages seven to fourteen attended them; then the percentage began to decrease. The exact cause of this decrease is not known. Possibly it was related to a 1986 decision to lower the age at which Soviet children could begin school (from seven to six years). This change resulted in an overloading of school programs, as more and more six-year-olds began attending regular classes. Strain on the schools appears to have lowered both the quality and availability of extended day care programs.[52]

Qualitative Aspects of Child Care

In theory, specialized institutions staffed by professionally trained personnel should result in high-quality child care. Not every family, especially poor families or those with little education, can supply what such facilities can provide for children: good nutrition, medical care, a stimulating social environment, and educational opportunities. Indeed, some surveys in the United States have demonstrated that children attending preschools are often better prepared for school and more sociable that those brought up alone at home. Given the low birthrates in both our societies, day care experiences may help compensate for social relationships that only children might otherwise lack. The contribution of Head Start and similar programs to the development of low-income children in the United States has been documented.[53]

The 1990 National Child Care Survey in the United States underscored the importance of high-quality day care for children's emotional and cognitive development.[54] In that same year, the benefits of high-quality child care for children and their working parents were similarly reaffirmed by a panel of the National Academy of Sciences. However, the panel issued a cautionary note with regard to infant day care, referring to research suggesting that infants in full-time day care are less likely to develop secure attachments to their mothers.[55] The exact relationship of child care services to care within the family cannot be firmly established, making it difficult to draw specific conclusions about the benefits of high-quality care outside the home.

Generally, "quality" in child care is a multidimensional phenomenon consisting of attention to the individual needs of the child, promotion of the child's intellectual and social development, and recognition of the child's unique personality. Operationally, the quality of American child care has been defined in terms of such things as curriculum; age-graded child–staff ratios; nutritious meals; the provision of health or social service referrals and developmental assessments; and health and safety training for staff members. Adequate toys and equipment, a warm and caring atmosphere, ample time for play, proper supervision, and discipline that builds self-esteem are additional components of quality child care. Although high- and low-quality care can be found under all types of sponsorship, for-profit centers in the United States consistently spend a smaller share of their budgets on wages and have more children per staff member than nonprofit centers.[56]

The ratio of children to providers in a given location is a commonly agreed-upon measure of child care quality in both Soviet and American societies. Not only does this directly measure the level of supervision available; it also indicates indirectly some of the conditions that may affect a particular child, such as the number of children with communicable diseases to whom he/she may be exposed. Because the majority of Soviet day care facilities are overcrowded and understaffed, the quality of child care falls far short of the ideal. Many excellent teachers and workers are simply overwhelmed. By the end of 1988, the overall Soviet average was one adult teacher for every twenty-six children (one teacher per twenty-five children in urban facilities and one per twenty-nine in rural areas). Some institutions in middle Asian regions had thirty-eight or more children per adult. This kind of overcrowding has been cited as one of the major factors explaining high sickness rates (particularly respiratory diseases) among children attending Soviet preschool institutions.[57]

Existing Soviet guidelines specify that creches and creche-kindergarten groups should be limited to fifteen to twenty children per adult, and kindergarten groups should be no larger than twenty-five. Even these figures seem high. A recently drafted set of regulations for preschool institutions recommends limits of one staff member to every six children younger than one year; one staffer to every ten children from one to three years of age; one staffer to every thirteen four- and five-year-olds; and one staffer to every fifteen children ages six and seven. These regulations have not yet been officially adopted.[58]

In the United States, federal guidelines once called for a ratio of three infants or toddlers per provider and a five-to-one ratio for older children. However, these standards no longer apply, and enforcement is left to the states, whose rules about child–staff ratios vary widely. Most family day care and in-home child care are unlicensed, and therefore largely unregulated. Generally speaking, the child-to-provider ratio in the United States is lowest in nursery schools and day care centers, and it increases with the age of the child. In one 1988 study of child care in the United States, 23% of the children were cared for on a one-to-one basis by a single provider; 35% were in a situation where the ratio was two or three children per adult; and 20% were in homes or centers where the ratio was one adult for every four to six children. Only 12% of the children were cared for in groups of seven to twelve per supervising adult.[59] According to the 1990 National Child Care Survey, the average child–staff ratio has risen by 25% since the mid-1970s, and the average group size has increased by 16%.[60]

Comparative Costs of Child Care to Parents

According to 1988 data, the estimated annual aggregate cost of child care in America was $15.5 billion (averaging about $49 per week per child). The average weekly cost rose $8.20 between 1985 and 1988. Child care costs vary significantly in different geographic areas; in 1988, for example, comparable child care cost $43 weekly in the South and $57 in the Northeast.[61]

Child care costs represent a large portion of the cost of living for poor American families—about one-fourth of their total income. Geographic proximity and cost greatly restrict the child care choices of many families. Availability and type of child care arrangements are closely associated with overall family income, and particularly with the income level of working mothers. Thus American children from families whose annual incomes are $40,000 or greater are more likely to attend child care (78%) than children from families with annual incomes of $10,000 or less (48%). Extent of day care participation is similarly associated with mothers' levels of education: In one study, 78% of the mothers who attended college utilized some sort of day care arrangement, whereas child care was used by only 47% of the women who did not complete high school.[62]

Although it might be assumed that child care cost to parents would not have been a major factor in the former Soviet Union, this was not the case. Even before the financial crisis that began in 1990, both the quantity and quality of Soviet child care were decreasing because of lack of adequate funding. The average annual cost per child in government-run preschool institutions was 439 rubles in 1970 and 571 rubles in 1988. Fees paid by parents covered about 20% of the total cost. Certain Soviet politicians, and some citizens, alleged that these costs were very high. However, dividing the amount by the average number of days that a child attended a preschool facility (231) would yield a per-day cost of 2.47 rubles—a modest amount even by Soviet standards.[63]

Until recently, parents paid for child care on the basis of their family income, ranging from 11 to 17 rubles per month for creche and from 12.5 to 20 rubles per month for kindergarten. Families with per capita income under 60 rubles a month paid nothing for kindergarten, and parents with four or more children paid only half the required fee, regardless of income. In January 1990, the USSR Council of Ministers decided to establish uniform payment rates, regardless of the type of preschool institution or the jurisdiction under which it was administered. Fees for facilities open twelve hours a day were set at 50 kopeks per day per child; those open more than twelve hours were set at 60 kopeks. Low-income families and families with several children were permitted to pay at the former lower rate. These figures represented a modest increase that could be managed by the average Soviet family. However, current economic instability has left the future of child care, and its cost, very much in doubt. In fact, the closing of a number of centers for financial reasons could precipitate a major crisis in the Soviet work force.[64]

The Wages of Child Care Workers

The issue of wages for child care workers is problematic in both Soviet and American societies. Of all the major Soviet occupational groups, the average wages of preschool teachers have ranked lowest. In 1988, their average monthly wage was only 128.2 rubles, whereas the average for all workers in the Soviet Union was 219.8 rubles. Industrial workers averaged 240.8 rubles, construction workers 288.9 rubles, and teachers in comprehensive schools 188.9 rubles, making clear why it was and still is difficult to find highly qualified teachers in creches and kindergartens.

In 1988, only 15% of all Soviet preschool teachers had attended college (and some of these 15% had received no formal training in education). A sizable number (60%) had taken some education courses at the high school level. By comparison, in 1988–1989, 77% of all comprehensive (elementary and secondary) school teachers were college-educated. In some Soviet regions, the percentage of preschool teachers with formal training in education is even lower. Despite widespread recognition of the importance of early childhood socialization and education, Soviet society has failed to develop high-quality preschool programs in any part of the network of public child care institutions.[65]

The overall picture is much the same in the United States, where child care workers earn less than others with comparable education. According to the 1990 National Child Care Survey, the average hourly wage for all child care staff was $7.49, or $5.35 in 1988 constant dollars. However, child care wages vary with center sponsorship: $9.67 per hour for teachers in Head Start, $8.10 for teachers in centers sponsored by religious institutions, $7.40 in independent nonprofit centers, and $5.43 in for-profit centers. By comparison, average hourly wages for public school teachers in 1990 were $14.40.[66] Whereas average hourly earnings for all American workers increased 88% between 1975 and 1985, hourly wages for child care providers increased only 34%. In addition to low wages, most child care workers receive no health insurance, life insurance, retirement benefits, or paid vacations.

These wage discrepancies persist despite the fact that professional child-care workers (ranging from teacher aides to center directors) are generally well educated. Certification standards for head teachers require educational qualifications similar to those of public school teachers (whose annual salaries in 1986 ranged from $16,355 to $36,659.[67] According to the 1990 National Child Care Survey, almost one-half of the teachers in child care organizations have a college degree.[68]

The number of persons classified as child care workers in the United States is projected to increase by nearly one-third by the year 2000.[69] In 1987, almost 800,000 people were employed as child care workers; their average job tenure was less than three years. Low pay, poor working conditions, and high staff turnover are serious issues to be faced in order to assure high-quality care that is professional, stable, and well organized.[70] Both Soviet and American societies face major challenges in this regard, and failure to address these issues adequately could create a social crisis seriously affecting family life.

Parent Choice of and Participation in Day Care

In the United States, the choice of child care arrangements is largely up to parents. Though availability and geographic proximity play a role, the largest single influence on this choice is probably cost, consistent with the free-market principles that underlie American institutions. Of course, the degree to which child care *should* depend upon economics is a matter of continuing debate in American society.

Beyond the selection of a provider or program, American parents have relatively little involvement in most child care furnished outside the home. However, more day care centers, nursery schools, and preschools are attempting to integrate parents into their programs, in an effort to work more closely with families to meet the individual needs of their children. Some centers use parent volunteers on a regular basis. Others recruit part-time paraprofessional workers as aides. A few innovative programs are even located in companies, community centers, or senior citizen residences, where they attempt to integrate child care into the life of the larger community and to facilitate intergenerational contact that can benefit all parties.

One of the greatest shortcomings of Soviet child care institutions is the *lack* of parental choice about the location or nature of their children's preschool experience. Only rarely can parents place their children in a creche or a kindergarten connected with one parent's workplace or close to the family residence. Parents virtually never influence the nature of their children's education in preschool institutions, despite the fact that many parents are better educated than many preschool teachers. Of course, since *perestroika* parental complaints have increased, and more parents are demanding to have a voice in the child care programs they are offered. At the same time, the Soviet economic crisis is so severe that both families and child care institutions are currently fighting for financial survival, which leaves little time and energy for improving the quality of child care programs.

On a brighter note, the future development of Soviet preschool institutions may be positively influenced by the ongoing processes of democratization and a broadening scope of child care choices for parents. Cooperative community programs and private institutions have begun to appear, though they are still few in number and rather expensive (in 1989, 130 rubles per month for eleven hours of day care). Nevertheless, there are promising signs that Soviet families are taking seriously the need to invest in the future of their children by actively working to improve the conditions of child care throughout the society.

The Status of Home Child Care

How are Soviet children who do not attend preschool institutions cared for? Information on this question is minimal and scattered. For example, in a survey conducted in Taganrog in 1979, 44% of these children were cared for by mothers who had temporarily left their jobs, 21% by both parents working different shifts, 16% by relatives living in the same household, and 14% by other relatives living outside the household.[71] In another survey of Latvian towns conducted in 1979, 47.6% of the children ages one to three attended preschool institutions. Of the remainder, most were cared for by their mothers; a sizable number by hired babysitters; and the rest by grandparents, fathers, or some combination of relatives.[72]

With most American men and more than 70% of American women working outside the home, the lack of a coherent medical leave policy for family members has created substantial problems. Emergency child care is difficult to locate and very expensive, making it hard for working parents (particularly single mothers) whose children become ill. Until 1993 the United States was virtually the only major industrial country without such a policy. Very few workers receive paid maternity or paternity leave; in 1989, the figure for employees in medium and large firms was only 4%.[73] This issue is a matter of considerable social debate. The Family and Medical Leave Act authored by the United States Congress in 1990 was vetoed by President Bush, on the grounds that it constituted unwarranted government intrusion into the affairs of business, and might have the unintended effect of discouraging employers from hiring women of childbearing age as well as men with family obligations. It was passed and signed into law by President Clinton. A number of states have already adopted some form of job protection for workers who need time off from work to attend to family matters, and most of the remaining states are considering similar legislation. However, coverage and the length of leave vary widely from state to state.

In contrast, the Soviet central government in 1990 granted partially paid maternity leave to all families with newborn children and extended unpaid child care leave until the children are three years old. This additional leave is available to a child's mother or, depending on the family's decision, to the father, grandmother, or other relatives who actually care for the child.[74] Other measures have been planned to promote more favorable conditions for child care at home, in an effort to increase the choices for parents who would prefer to care for their children themselves rather than relying on preschool institutions.

In part, this action was an attempt to counter the traditional Soviet ideology that public care of children is somehow superior to that of the family. Some social scientists have gone further and begun to claim that not even the best teacher can substitute for a child's own mother. They have proposed reducing funds for preschool institutions and shifting them to encourage in-home child care. Just as in the United

States, this issue is far from settled. Nevertheless, some steps have already been taken. Beginning July 1, 1990, the duration of partially paid maternity leave was increased to eighteen months, and the allowance for mothers was doubled from 35 to 70 rubles per month. In 1991, the amount was raised to equal the minimum wage. Payments to unemployed women who care for a child up to eighteen months are equal to half the minimum wage.[75] The challenge facing both our societies is to simultaneously develop policies supporting home care and institutional care of young children.

CONCLUSION

As an example of explicit family policy, child care aims to meet the needs of working parents and their children. In both countries, child care issues clearly illustrate the role that values play in shaping the relationship between government policies and families. Soviet child care reflects centralized planning; American child care reflects market forces and individual interests. Despite differing ideologies, however, the substantive problems faced by Soviet and American societies regarding child care are remarkably similar: accessibility and quality of child care, and the relationship of child care institutions to families.

In both countries, child care suffers from financial neglect. In most Soviet regions, this has resulted in severe overcrowding of facilities. In many areas of the United States, this has translated into frequently fruitless searches for facilities and/or long waiting lists for accessible, low-cost services. Child care workers in both countries are still underpaid. The child care problem illustrates the often conflicting interests involved in policy choices that affect the family. Clearly, adequate child care resources contribute to family well-being. However, the exact nature of these resources, and the means to attain them, remain controversial and elusive in both societies.

During the writing of this book, many events and policy changes have occurred in both the United States and the former Soviet Union. We are reminded that policy is shaped not only by general cultural forces, but by particular social and political events as well. Policies, and the programs that implement them, can only be *temporarily* settled courses of action; they are in continuous flux, and our analysis of them is inevitably several steps behind. By the time this book has been published, perhaps the governments of the United States and of the former Soviet Union will be acting more decisively to support families. Perhaps there will be a greater recognition that as government seeks to enhance the well-being of families, it also contributes to the stability and order of the larger society.

NOTES

1. D. G. Gil, *Unravelling Social Policy: Theory, Analysis and Political Action Towards Social Equality* (Cambridge, MA: Schenkman, 1973); E. C. Baumheier and A. L. Schorr, "Social Policy," in J. B. Turner, R. Morris, M. N. Ozawa, B. Phillips, B. Schreiber, and B. K. Simon (eds.), *Encyclopedia of Social Work* (Washington, DC: National Association of Social Workers, 1977), 1453–1463.

2. R. Titmuss, *Commitment to Welfare* (New York: Pantheon, 1968).

3. D. Braybrooke, *Meeting Needs* (Princeton, NJ: Princeton University Press, 1988).

4. S. L. Zimmerman, *Family Policies and Family Well-Being: The Role of Political Culture* (Newbury Park, CA: Sage, 1992).

5. In 1990, the head of the national trade union council expected Soviet unemployment to at least triple or quadruple, which meant that as many as 8 million people could be out of work. See C. Bohlen, "Mandate Is Sought: Soviet Economic Reform Will Be Put to the Voters in First Policy Referendum," *New York Times* (May 24, 1990), A1.

6. For comparative definitions and fuller explanation of this concept, see A. Campbell, P. E. Converse, and W. L. Rodgers, *The Quality of American Life: Perception, Evaluations, and Satisfactions* (New York: Russell Sage Foundation, 1976); F. M. Andrews and S. B. Withey, *Social Indicators of Well-Being: America's Perception of Life Quality* (New York: Plenum Press, 1976); K. Rettig and M. Bubolz, "Perceptual Indicators of Family Well-Being," *Social Indicators Research, 12* (1983), 417–438; C. Buehler, J. Hogan, B. Robinson, and R. Levy, "The Parental Divorce Transition: Divorce-Related Stressors and Well-Being," *Journal of Divorce, 9*(2) (1985), 61–81; S. L. O'Bryant, "Sibling Support of Older Widows' Well-Being," *Journal of Marriage and the Family, 50*(1) (1988), 173–183.

7. "Satisfaction with State of Nation at 10 Year Low," *Star Tribune* (March 12, 1992), A18.

8. S. Nasar, "However You Slice the Data, the Richest Did Get Richer," *New York Times* (May 11, 1992), C1.

9. President's Address to the USSR Supreme Soviet (Moscow, March 1990).

10. President's Address to the USSR Supreme Soviet (Moscow, October 1990).

11. For example, see A. Okun, *Equality and Efficiency: The Big Trade-Off* (Washington, DC: The Brookings Institution, 1975).

12. R. Footlick, "Redefining the Family," *New York Times* (April 22, 1989), Y18.

13. R. Burant, "The Families' Focus of Families in Society," *Social Casework, 70*(9) (1989), 523–524.

14. U.S. Bureau of the Census, *Statistical Abstract of the United States: 1990,* 110th ed. (Washington, DC: U.S. Government Printing Office, 1990a).

15. A. G. Kharchev, *Marriage and Family in the USSR* (Moscow: Mysl, 1979), 75.

16. V. A. Borisov, A. B. Sinelnikov, and G. P. Kislyova, *Population, Reproduction and Demographic Policy in the USSR* (Moscow: Nauka, 1987), 203.

17. *Ibid.*

18. U.S. Bureau of the Census, 1990a, *op. cit.*

19. U.S. Bureau of the Census, 1990a, *op. cit.*

20. W. Goode, *The Family* (Englewood Cliffs, NJ: Prentice-Hall, 1964), 2.

21. S. L. Zimmerman, "State Level Policy Choices as Predictors of State Teenage Birthrates," *Family Relations, 37*(3) (1988), 315–321.

22. S. L. Zimmerman, "The Welfare State and the Family Breakup: The Mythical Connection," *Family Relations, 40*(2) (1991), 139–154.

23. Zimmerman, 1992, *op. cit.*; D. MacRae, *Policy Indicators: Links between Social Sciences and Policy Debates* (Chapel Hill: Universtiy of North Carolina Press, 1985).

24. U.S. Bureau of the Census, 1990a, *op. cit.*

25. "Creche" is a term used to refer to nursery care for infants. See L. L. Litvin (ed.), *History of Soviet Preschools and Pedagogic Institutions* (Moscow: Prosveschenije, 1988, 121–138).

26. F. Engels, "The Origins of the Family, Private Property and the State," in K. Marx and F. Engels, *Writings,* Vol. 36 (Moscow: Politizdat), 293–294.

27. V. I. Lenin, "Beginning the Great Undertaking," in *Complete Collection of Writings,* 5th ed., Vol. 39 (Moscow: Politizdat), 23–25.

28. The first Soviet Congress on Early Childrearing (April 25–May 4, 1919) passed a resolution proclaiming the goal of organizing compulsory preschool education that would be accessible to all children. See Litvin, *op. cit.,* 131. In 1931, a Soviet Central Committee ordered the building of enough kindergartens to care for all children of production (i.e. industrial and farm) workers. By the mid-1930s, plans were advanced for creches for all Soviet children from birth to age 3. See V. P. Lebedjeva, *Protection of Mothers and Children in the Soviet World* (Leningrad: Gosmedizdat, 1934), 159.

29. "Labor in USSR," *Finansi i Statistika,* (1988), 107–108.

30. E. S. Beer, *Working Mothers and the Day Nursery* (New York: Whiteside, 1957).

31. M. O. Steinfels, *Who's Minding the Children? The History and Politics of Daycare in America* (New York: Simon & Schuster, 1973).

32. P. Roby, *Child Care–Who Cares?* (New York: Basic Books, 1973).

33. *Ibid.*

34. "Congress Passes Child Care Legislation and Expands Earned Income Tax Cuts," *Washington Social Legislation Bulletin* (November 12, 1990), 177–180.

35. "Public Education and Culture in the USSR," *Finansi i Statistika,* (1989), 411. This figure is minus the number of six-year-old children attending school.

36. "National Education and Culture in USSR," *Finansi i Statistika,* (1989), 38–39.

37. 1989 CEC Secretariat, "Statistics Yearbook of Member-States of Council of Economic Cooperation," *Finansi i Statistika* (1989), 425; N. Ivanova, "Why Do German Mothers Love Kindergarten So Much?", *Semya, 25* (June 19-25, 1989), 12.

38. U.S. Bureau of the Census, "Who's Minding the Kids? Child Care Arrangements 1986-1987." *Current Population Reports*, Series p-70, No. 20 (Washington, DC: U.S. Government Printing Office, 1990b).

39. "National Education and Culture in USSR," *op. cit.*, 29-32; "USSR National Economy in 1988," *Finansi i Statistika*, (1989), 59.

40. According to the data of the survey conducted by the State Committee on Statistics of the USSR, as of January, 1, 1988, almost three-fourths of the rural communities of the country with one-third of the population in the USSR did not have any permanent preschool facilities. Ninety-two percent of the rural communities in Lithuania, 90% in Estonia, 89% in Tadzhikistan, and 86% in Byelorussia lacked permanent preschool institutions. Only 3% of the rural communities had seasonal or temporary preschool institutions. *Social Development of USSR* (Moscow: Statistical Collection, Office of Finances and Statistics, 1990), 189-190.

41. *Proceedings of XXVII Congress of the Communist Party of the Soviet Union* (Moscow: Politizdat, 1986), 154, 312; *Doshkolnoye Vospitaniye, 1* (1990), 3; *Izvestiya* (January 28, 1990), 2.

42. G. Willer, S. Hofferth, E. Kisker, F. E. Divine-Hawkins, and F. Glantz, *The Demand and Supply of Child Care in 1990: Joint Findings from the National Child Care Survey 1990 and a Profile of Child Care Settings* (Washington, DC: National Association for the Education of Young Children, 1990).

43. K. DeWitt, "U. S. Plan on Child Care is Reported to Be Stalled," *New York Times* (January 27, 1991), A-13.

44. U.S. Bureau of the Census, 1990b, *op. cit.*

45. Willer et al. *op. cit.*

46. U. S. Bureau of the Census, 1990b, *op. cit.*

47. This information is summarized in a 1988 research report by D. A. Dawson and V. S. Cain, "Child Care Arrangements: Health of Our Nation's Children," *Advance Data from Vital and Health Statistics*, No. 198 (Hyattsville, MD: National Center for Health Statistics, 1990).

48. M. M. Zhuravleva, "Development of Preschool Educational Network in the Whole Country During the 10th Five-Year Plan Period," in M. M. Zhuravleva (ed.), *Public School Education at the Current Stage* (Moscow: Prosveshcheniye, 1981), 9.

49. *Ibid.*

50. *Ibid.*

51. "Public Education and Culture in the USSR," *op. cit.*, 40.

52. *Ibid.*, 77; *Vestnik Statistiki, 3* (1988), 6.

53. "Head Start Prepares for a New Decade," *Washington Social Legislation Bulletin 34*, (May 28, 1990), 133-136.

54. Willer et al. *op. cit.*

55. C. D. Hayes, J. Palmer, and M. J. Zaslow (eds.), *Who Cares for America's*

Children? Child Care Policy for the 1990s (Washington, DC: National Research Council, National Academy Press).

56. Willer et al. *op. cit.*

57. "Public Education and Culture in the USSR," *op. cit.*, 29–32, 43–44; G. A. Ostrovskaya, "Clinical and Immunological Grounds for Measures Aimed at Reducing Morbidity among Young Children Attending Preschool Institutions," unpublished doctoral dissertation (Institute of Ivanova, 1988), 1; M. I. Talalay, "Preschool Institutions and Children's Health: Number of Children Per Family," in *Yesterday, Today, Tomorrow*, (Moscow: Mysl', 1986), 171–177; "State of Health Screening of Young Children," in *Berlin, People and Health* (Moscow: Medizina, 1987), 40, 62, 215.

58. *Doshkolnoye Vospitaniye*, 2 (1990), 42.

59. Willer et al., *op. cit.*

60. *Ibid.*

61. *Ibid.*

62. Dawson and Cain, *op. cit.*

63. "Public Education and Culture in the USSR," *op. cit.*, 11.

64. *Semya*, 38 (September 18–24, 1989), 10; "Aid for Agitators and Propagandists," *Finansi i Statistika*, (1989), 250; *Argumenti i Facti*, 14 (April 1990), 8.

65. "Public Education and Culture in the USSR," *op. cit.*

66. Willer et al., *op. cit.*

67. *Ibid.*

68. Willer et al., *op. cit.*

69. U.S. Bureau of the Census, 1990a, *op. cit.*

70. Willer et al., *op. cit.*

71. V. G. Kopnina, "About Combining Family and Public Forms of Upbringing of Preschool Children," in T. V. Ryaboushkin (ed.), *An Incapacitated Population: Social and Demographic Aspects* (Moscow: Nauka, 1985), 40.

72. Z. Gosha, "Actual and Desirable Combination of Family and Public Upbringing of Children," in I. H. Kirtovsky (ed.), *Factors and Motives of Demographic Behavior* (Riga: Zinatne, 1984), 165.

73. U.S. Bureau of the Census, *Statistical Abstract of the United States: 1991*, 111th ed. (Washington, DC: U.S. Government Printing Office, 1991).

74. *Government Newsletter*, 4(30), (January 1990), 12; Decree by USSR Supreme Soviet, "On Urgent Measures for Improvement of Conditions of Women, Protection of Motherhood and Childhood, Strengthening the Family," *Pravda* (April 14, 1990), 2.

75. E. Rybinsky, "How Should the USSR Law on Children's Rights Look?", *Semya*, 35(87) (August 28–September 3, 1989), 4; *Government Newsletter*, January 1990, *op. cit.*, 12; *Government Newsletter*, 4(36), (March 1990), 1.

Chapter 8

The Futures of Families

M. Janice Hogan
James W. Maddock
Anatolyi I. Antonov
Mikhail S. Matskovsky

The authors of the preceding chapters have recognized the difficulty of making cross-cultural comparisons of families between two extremely complex, heterogeneous societies. They have referred to the current state of radical change in Soviet society and the uncertainty about its precise impact on families. "Economic ruin," "political chaos," and "societal collapse" are phrases frequently used to describe the cultural conditions that have emerged over the last decade, particularly in the past few years. Even now, things continue to worsen. Our coauthors have described the daily living conditions of Soviet families as extremely difficult, even chaotic. However, they view much of the difficulty as a necessary part of the transition from a rigid, authoritarian social structure that was fundamentally dishonest to an open and dynamic society characterized by greater regard for family and human rights and tolerance for a diversity of expression, not to mention the change from a centrally planned to a free-market economy.

Clearly, diverse opinions exist regarding the changes taking place in various regions of the former Soviet Union. The same is true of our efforts to understand Soviet families and to compare them with American families. In both societies, varying degrees of optimism and pessimism are expressed regarding the future of family life. We discuss some of these in this chapter; however, we first present a framework for thinking about families in their social context.

In order to avoid the "either–or" quality of the debate regarding the status of families—which leads, in turn, to predicting two very different alternatives for the future of the family—we take a dialectical stance[1] that views the family as the major unit of *transformation* in human experience, a structure within which humans both perceive and create their world. Furthermore, our perspective is ecological: We understand the family as an interface between the individual and society, creating a process of mutual adaptation. Individuals undergo personal development in the context of families, while families are major contributors to the sociogenetic evolution of a society. A family reflects the characteristics of its members, while at the same time contributing strongly to their personal identities. Similarly, the family is both producer and recipient of social change; thus, understanding families is important to understanding a society. However, family life cannot be fully comprehended without considering the cultural context within which family members conduct their lives.

One approach to considering the future of the family is to look at the possible, the probable, and the preferable. In what follows, we combine data analysis with knowledge about transition and continuities in the United States, the former Soviet society, and the new Russia. To this we add some normative forecasting—that is, our value-laden perspectives on a preferred future.

ALTERNATIVE FAMILY SCENARIOS

The relative optimism or pessimism of social commentators and futurists regarding Russian and other former Soviet families parallels the diversity of views on changes in American family life through the last half of the twentieth century.[2] In the United States, the term "family values" has become a political buzzword. Polarizing debates are common, with political conservatives talking about personal responsibility and moral behavior, while political liberals advocate economic support and workplace policies. In both societies, some now argue for a resurgence of "traditional values" to counteract what they view as the erosion of a particular form of family life. Others point to a broadened definition of "family" that includes a greater diversity of family forms, values, and life experiences. The underlying issues are the same: What is good for families, and what is a "good" family?

Differing perspectives set the stage for divergent predictions about the future of families. From one perspective, the family is failing as a social unit. From another, the family is undergoing radical reconstruction in line with other fundamental shifts in social structure. Various viewpoints emphasize various aspects of contemporary family life.

The Family in Decline

Antonov believes that the low birthrate and the high divorce rate are evidence of the clear decline of families as functional units in Soviet and post-Soviet society. Since one of the major functions of families is procreation, couples choosing not to replace the current generation are seriously defaulting on a social contract. This is much more than just an issue of the size of the Russian population relative to other ethnic groups. Rather, the declining birthrate is linked to a fundamental change in social values. Antonov believes that at least among Russians, the intrinsic value of children has lessened to such a degree that there is little desire to bear and nurture them as part of one's responsibility to future generations in the society.

Antonov discounts the argument that the declining birthrate is a direct result of economic chaos associated with the breakup of the Soviet Union. Although economic instability can be a factor—high unemployment rates, scarce housing, and long lines for limited food and consumer goods certainly make family life difficult—it does not explain why couples with higher income, education, and employment status have even fewer children than couples from the lower socioeconomic strata. Furthermore, birthrates have also declined over the past half century in much more economically prosperous countries, including the United States.

One serious difficulty in assessing the state of families in Russia and other former Soviet republics is the lack of reliable research data on even the most basic family issues. During the decades under Stalin, "social problems" were not identified, since they would have been incompatible with the ideals of socialism. Matskovsky has termed the "triple standard" in Soviet experience under Stalinist Communism: People said one thing, did another, and privately thought still a different way. Parents were unable to speak about social problems in the presence of their children without fear. As a result, important matters of values were characterized by white lies and silence between the generations. Family members could not help falling prey to stereotypes rather than honestly appraising issues. Many Soviet writers have noted the frustration, pessimism, and bitterness that have occurred within families, particularly alienating adolescents from their parents, the Communist Party, and the State.[3] According to Antonov, the personality formed by the Soviet system is characterized by apathy, lack of personal initiative, and a tendency to shift responsibility to others.

Antonov is hardly alone in his belief that the depersonalized bureaucracy has had a profoundly negative influence on Soviet family relationships. Under socialism, all men and women were expected to be employed by the state. Women who dedicated themselves to the family were seen as "sponges" on society. Since childrearing was viewed as the responsibility of the state, household work was thought to have little value; all meaningful activity took place outside of the home. Surely these social norms have a direct relationship to the low fertility rate and weak intrafamily commitment that currently exist, and particularly to the burden it places on women.

Antonov believes that the choice of most couples to have only one child testifies to the ineffectiveness of family life in a society that alienates its members from values that are critical to human existence. In fact, the emphasis on the impersonal collective good seems to come at the expense of families.[4] Here, children are often seen as a hinderance to self-fulfillment, rather than as a means to such fulfillment. Antonov identifies the emergence of "pseudofamilies"—that is, two-parent households with one parent permanently absent or with two parents who have no direct involvement in the rearing of their children. He believes that single-parent and pseudofamily households are replacing Russians' personal commitment to childbearing and childrearing.

Without the revival of the family as the principal mediator between individuals and society in post-Soviet society, Antonov postulates that many of the most important social problems will be impossible to resolve. He strongly advocates new priorities. He believes that more Soviet families should have several children and that the number of single-parent households should be minimized. The government should value family work for both women and men, and should strengthen families with policies that support family activities. Public health services, housing programs, cultural activities, and even the mass media should give special attention to families with children, according to Antonov. And most important of all, the bearing and rearing of children must again be viewed as the primary responsibility of families.

For decades, some American social critics predicted the "death" of the nuclear family. Recently, this extreme position has given way to a more moderate and less pessimistic discussion of family futures. Nevertheless, some American scholars believe that the family is in serious trouble, citing the statistics on marriage, divorce, child abuse and neglect, family stress, and birthrates, as well as the changed psychological nature of family relationships.

Writing about the decline of family life, David Popenoe agrees with Antonov that decreasing family size is evidence that people are less willing to invest their human and monetary resources in family life.[5] As additional evidence of family decline, he cites (1) increased individualism and less family cohesion, (2) the shift of important family functions to other social and governmental institutions, and (3) decreasing family stability. Although he does not believe that all changes in family life are negative—noting flexibility in women's roles and the quality of enduring companionate marriages as positive outcomes—Popenoe makes a strong case that social changes in the United States have had a real and profound negative effect on children, who represent the future of American society.

Other American social scientists support Popenoe's assertion of child neglect by American parents; however, they expand the argument to include a decline in public support for parenting and an increase in workplace demands made on parents.[6] Sylvia Hewlett states that compared to children in other countries in the advanced industrial world, American children are more likely to die before their first birthdays, to live in poverty, to be abandoned by their fathers, and to be killed before they reach adulthood. She notes serious resource deficits in American families, and criticizes federal and state governments for failing to invest enough public money in children and their parents. Hewlett concludes, "Our failure to invest either public resources or private time in the raising of children has left many families fragile and overburdened, unable to do a decent job in raising the next generation."[7]

Urie Bronfenbrenner, a Russian-American scholar with an international reputation in human development and cross-cultural research on children, maintains that poverty is the foremost factor interfering with positive parent–child relationships.[8] Expressing serious concern for the welfare of children in the United States, Bronfenbrenner also notes the "increasing instability, inconsistency, and hectic character of daily family life."[9] He cites work–family schedule conflicts, divorce and remarriage, geographic mobility, and competing activities and needs of family members as factors that disrupt contemporary family life. Recent research on work–family conflicts indicates that the demands of employment create the most family stress. Therefore, Bronfenbrenner and others propose that the primary contexts in which family members live—workplaces, schools, communities, and so on—need to be more interactive with families in order to establish mutual trust and accommodation, communication, and information exchange.

Social historian Barbara Whitehead argues that the American family has been weakened by "values that have been destructive of commitment, obligation, responsibility and sacrifice—and particularly destructive of the claims of children on adult attention and commitment."[10] She indicates that parents are not committed to putting children's needs before their own needs, that marriage is no longer a lifelong commitment, and that many men have defaulted on their obligations as husbands and fathers. Whitehead concludes that the principal source of family decline has been a cultural shift in values, and she calls for a culture-wide dialogue and broad social solutions.

Families in Transition

Matskovsky, is more optimistic than Antonov about post-Soviet family life. He perceives the changes in families as a radical reconstruction of social roles and of relationships between men and women. Since the data indicate that the majority of Soviet couples do have at least one child, he argues that the family's reproductive function is thereby fulfilled. Furthermore, the birth of a child is virtually always a planned act on the part of the mother or the couple, reflecting a conscious desire to have a child, according to Matskovsky. Childbearing continues to be a major motivation for marriage; he sees no significant trend toward childless liaisons or single parenthood.

Matskovsky believes that the desire of women for equality with men is probably the single most important factor leading to the Soviet single-child family, particularly in Russia. He hypothesizes that family stability is actually likely to *increase* in the future, as couples form more egalitarian marital relationships and husbands come to share equally the responsibility for child care and housework. Changes have already been occurring in patterns of household work and family decision making—patterns that deviate from traditional gender roles. Research data do, however, show a disparity between what many Soviet husbands and wives want in marital roles and in decision-making power. Given the resistance by men to increasing their responsibility for child care and household management, along with the growing unemployment rate for women, family stability may indeed be in question.

In Russia and a number of other former Soviet republics, personal happiness, sexual satisfaction, and continuing love throughout life together have gradually evolved as fundamental values in family relations, just as they have in the United States. Matskovsky argues that this represents great *progress*, rather than failure in the family as a social unit. At the same time, both post-Soviet and American societies must deal with the fact that many couples have rising standards for marital relationships that are based on some mythical model of a "perfect" marriage. Thus, they set themselves up for dissatisfaction, conflict, and eventual divorce. Recent Soviet research indicates that divorces today are more often initiated by women dissatisfied with the quality of their marriages, whereas in the past divorces were more likely to be linked to infertility, adultery and other institutional norms.

Certainly the very high divorce rate among young couples that results from impulsive marriages indicates the importance of better preparing teenagers for marriage through programs of family life education. According to Matskovsky, today's young people are forming their own ideas with less parental control; they are more strongly swayed by peers and by the media—and influenced by youths in other societies such as the United States, now that free exchange of information and ideas is permitted. He believes that changing patterns of premarital sexual behavior and personal choices such as childlessness represent primarily the growing freedom of Soviet life styles, rather than a decline of family values.

Loneliness is another factor influencing family formation and stability. From his review of the Soviet literature, Matskovsky concludes that loneliness is an acute problem in Soviet society, especially in the large cities. Recently, organizations have begun to be established by families and by youths to create a new community-based social order. For example, so-called "family clubs" have been formed, with programs for parents to share experiences in childrearing and to arrange cooperative child care. Housing construction cooperatives have also formed, not only to build residences (though these are desperately needed), but to create neighborhoods and to share leisure time. Matskovsky views these as attempts to stabilize family life amidst the chaotic changes of post-Soviet society.

Finally, Matskovsky asserts that the revival of religion will eventually strengthen Soviet families. Specifically, he believes that the religious renaissance now occurring is having a powerful effect on moral values that underlie family life. After decades of enforced silence, religious leaders are now speaking openly about spiritual matters and advocating empathy, care, and concern, thereby helping individuals to be both more self-aware and more sensitive to the needs of others. Religious leaders, who are frequently traditional males, will also need to address the issues of gender equality and of family planning. A strong bond between religion and family life can make an important contribution to family stability in Soviet society, though it may also create some challenging political issues, much as it has in the United States in recent years.

Many social scientists in the United States also believe that families are simply in transition, adapting to a rapidly changing social environment. Analyzing values, norms, and social organization, they are focusing on underlying processes of adaptation rather than on divorce statistics or fertility rates. Emerging gender roles, new patterns of sexual behavior, negotiation in family decision making, and changes in child care can be viewed as important positive transitions in American family structure.

Over a decade ago, family development specialist Joan Aldous labeled the transition from "role taking" to "role making" as a significant shift in family norms—a positive contributor to gender flexibility and marital equity.[11] More recently, family scholar Dennis Orthner has concluded that changing norms for close relationships, rather than fundamental changes in social values, are responsible for the emergence of many of today's most important family issues.[12] He notes that a cultural drift toward extreme individuality and autonomy does indeed threaten the well-being of children in American society. Other than this concern, Orthner's view of the future of the family is one of "cautious optimism."[13]

Even Popenoe, cited earlier for his concern about family decline, seems to be growing more optimistic. He cites the high 1990 United States birthrate and the growing emphasis on families and on marital stability, particularly by children of divorced parents. He suggests that these indicators may reflect a change in cultural values that seems to occur in thirty-year cycles as a new generation of Americans emerges into adulthood.[14]

Perhaps, then, the issues of contemporary family life simply represent the successful adaptation of families to a period of rapid change in American society. In this event, a period of relative stability may follow, as family members work to consolidate the changes made by integrating new relationship norms into existing moral values and fitting new styles of life into traditional family structures.

Additional Dimensions

The two family scenarios drawn by Antonov and Matskovsky provide alternative frameworks for the interpretation of demographic data on Soviet marriage, fertility, and divorce. An additional dimension is revealed in a recent survey of Russian men and women following the dissolution of the Soviet Union.

Preliminary data from a survey conducted by Olga Doudchenko, a coauthor of the chapter on family work roles (Chapter 6), and Anna Myti, a colleague at the Russian Academy of Sciences, indicate a gender difference in the level of anxiety about the future.[15] The survey of over 800 women and men, taken in May 1991 and again six months later, reveals that men's anxiety level seems to be declining while women's anxiety is increasing. Only 15% of the women questioned agreed with the statement "I am sure of my future," in contrast to 40% of the men. Conversely, 54% of the women indicated that they often felt anxious without any specific reason, while only 24% of the men reported this experience. About a third of the women and half of the men reported believing that they were well adjusted to contemporary life.

This relatively high inner anxiety of women is cause for concern. The researchers speculate that it is connected with the burden of responsibility women have for solving everyday family problems as living standards have steadily decreased. Whereas Matskovsky argues for more flexibility in employment, especially for women, Doudchenko and Myti believe that this will not address the problem sufficiently. They argue that women's increased anxiety is related to employment discrimination. The threat of job loss is substantially greater for women than for men. Russian news headlines observe that "Unemployment has a women's face." The researchers predict that men will become more concerned about sex discrimination in the workplace when they face supporting their families on only a single income.

Similarly, feminist and ethnic minority scholars in the United States have raised questions that challenge traditional European-American, male-dominated views of family life. For example, Barrie Thorne and other feminists have identified themes for rethinking the family, challenging the assumptions that there is one natural and legitimate family form and that men and women experience family life in the same ways.[16] Similarly, Peggye Dilworth-Anderson and Harriette Pipes McAdoo have noted that family relations among African-Americans and other cultural groups are frequently extended kin networks rather than nuclear family units.[17] They have called for fuller recognition of diverse family forms and multicultural differences in experience.

FAMILY POLICY IN THE NEW RUSSIA

Currently, the Russian Parliament is trying to give significant attention to family policy. A Parliamentary Committee on Women, Family, Motherhood, and Childhood was appointed on July 4, 1990, to construct policies aimed at resolving demographic problems and providing better protection of children.[18] One of the proposed changes would redefine "family" to include both legal marriages and *de facto* marriages (cohabitation), with or without children. Recent surveys have revealed that about 2 million more Russian women than men report being married. The proposed legislation would reflect this new reality. Homosexuality (the extent of which is largely unknown in post-Soviet society) is no longer illegal.

Members of the Parliamentary Committee have expressed grave concern about the current status of the Russian family, including the low birthrate. Their explanations for why couples are having fewer children cover the range of influences discussed above by Antonov and Matskovsky: poor living conditions, low family income, political instability, lack of proper marriage preparation, women's employment problems, a deep spiritual crisis due to the collapse of churches, and a lack of moral leadership. To date, the committee has proposed increased cash subsidies and privileges for families with children, in order to encourage couples to have more children; the goal is three children per family. One example of the privileges currently available is access by pregnant women to special shops to buy food—when food is available.

The Moscow City Council's Committee on Children and Family has also cited the declining fertility rate as one of that city's most pressing problems.[19] Here, the focus of discussion has been on the poor reproductive health of women as a result of too many abortions. Health officials note that many Russian wives wishing to become pregnant have infertility problems and a high incidence of illness during pregnancy. Family planning services and women's health clinics have just begun to appear in the metropolitan area.

The Moscow City Council has a broad agenda for improving family life. In 1991, legislation was passed to provide an extra subsidy to families with three or more children. The city already gives subsidies to single-parent families, families with handicapped children, orphans, and all school-age children. In February 1992, low-income families with children began receiving additional subsidies, the first example of a program incorporating an economic needs test.

The Union of Russian Women, the largest women's organization in Russia, is also concerned about the declining fertility rate.[20] However, the focus is on a different explanation for reduced family size—the impact of economic chaos on women. According to union officers, the burden of the transition to a market economy is falling on women. Up to 80% of the unemployed in Moscow are women. Child care is no longer provided, and women must stay home to care for children; at this stage, few couples can think of having more children. In addition, as suggested above, multiple abortions have left as many as one-third of Russian women infertile.

Antonov labels the current Russian family policy a "poverty policy." He is convinced that there cannot be any serious family policy until the economic situation improves and stabilizes. Within the past five years, the majority of Russian families have become very poor. In families with several children and/or elderly adults, the situation is critical, even with government subsidies. The government is still the major employer, and its minimal wages are barely enough to buy food. Therefore, all of the present measures to help families are simply necessary attempts to buffer poverty, rather than long-range efforts to plan for family well-being.

CONCLUSION

Clearly, predictions about the future of families in post-Soviet and American societies are extremely challenging because of the complexity of family life and the diversity of family forms. The pace and extent of change in both societies add further to the complexity of forecasting the future. Of course, there is continuity among past, present, and future, even with revolutionary change.

To some extent, humans can make choices and plan for the kinds of families they desire, guided by values and by principles that embody the collective wisdom of their experiences. Family members can creatively address the issues of family life that we have identified in common in our two societies—better ways to nurture children, healthier interdependence across the generations, more possibilities for trust and intimacy in marriage, and improved opportunities for both genders.

At the same time, the transformational processes of social systems, whether families or entire societies, introduce elements of randomness and uniqueness into the flow of history. The events of the past decade in Soviet and post-Soviet society are vivid evidence of the impact of the unexpected during times of transition. Furthermore, the dense circulation of information and images around the globe has aided the emergence of nationalism and cultural identity. As a result, multiple realities stand side by side, with equal claims to relevance and truth.[21] Thus, problem solving and planning in our two societies must be considered *ongoing processes* of coping with multiple stressors and balancing among a myriad of options, rather than straight-line efforts to find permanent solutions. We have choices, and we must make them wisely.

What are the principles that should guide our choices about families in the future? Here we can draw upon the reciprocal experiences of our two societies, bound together but kept apart for decades by the Cold War, so alike and yet so different. We propose five principles that should be considered essential in planning the future of families in both societies: (1) human rights, (2) gender equity, (3) economic security, (4) diversity of families, and (5) family policy.

1. *Human Rights.* The United Nations (UN) has referred to the family as the "smallest democracy at the heart of a society." In planning for the International Year of the Family in 1994, the UN has recommended that societies work to make values consistent with indi-

vidual rights of all family members, particularly the human rights of women and children.[22] Although we recognize the tension between individual rights and family well-being, we argue that both must be respected and accommodated.

2. *Gender equity.* The issue of gender has been addressed directly or indirectly in every chapter of this book. Most authors have suggested that it is a key issue in family life and in the larger society, linking marriage, childrearing, household work, and marketplace work. The equitable sharing of power, resources, and responsibilities between men and women is the cornerstone of a secure and stable family life, as well as an important contributor to the economic productivity of family units.

3. *Economic security.* Poverty has been identified as the single most important factor interfering with positive parent–child relationships.[23] It is often related to divorce and to the resulting increase in female-headed households. Our authors have noted that economic dislocation has such a powerful impact on family life that other aspects of family policy cannot be significantly addressed. That two large and politically powerful countries with contrasting economic systems should both be addressing poverty is a sad commentary on our failure to give sufficient attention to families in either society.

4. *Family diversity.* Families have long demonstrated a capacity to adapt to changing environments—from monarchies to democracies, from war to peace, from rural to urban settings, from poverty to affluence, and of course the reverse of these. Similarly, individual family members adapt to divorce, desertion, and the death of a spouse; they initiate new partnerships and structure new ways of relating. Even if there were an ideal family form valued by a particular society, variations on the ideal would always occur. The ability of social institutions to meet the changing needs of family members with changing resources and flexible support services is a crucial element of social stability.

5. *Family policy.* As we have indicated, a family is the primary interface between an individual and society; it is both a recipient and a producer of social change. Families are influenced by cultural evolution as well as revolution. Twentieth-century events in both Soviet and American societies have had an enormous impact upon the nature of family life, which has often not be sufficiently acknowledged by the governments involved. We believe that families are important enough to the welfare of society to deserve special attention. Future government policies, workplace practices, and community services ought to be carefully evaluated for their impact upon families and family members. Paying attention to creating a positive environment for families

will help ensure that families will create a better environment for their members—particularly for children, who are the architects of the next generation.

The agenda for future collaborative work between post-Soviet countries and the United States will include research on emerging issues, as well as a continuation of efforts to deal with the issues addressed in this book. Topics such as family violence (particularly wife battering, child abuse, and abuse of the elderly) and substance abuse (particularly alcoholism) are now being recognized as important problems in Russia. Let us hope that combining ideas and expertise on actual joint research projects—some of which are currently being undertaken by various of this book's authors—will both improve our understanding of families within each society and enable more meaningful cross-cultural comparisons.

Comparison of family life education and intervention programs is also important. The professions of marriage and family therapy and social work, which are developing rapidly in Russia, will provide useful insights into the resolution of family problems under particularly stressful social conditions. The dismal state of health care in Russia and other former Soviet republics is also of special concern to family professionals. In light of the crisis currently occurring in the privatized health care system of the United States, cooperative thinking and research might be helpful in bringing better health care to families in both societies.

Collaborative projects such as this book are likely to become more common in the future, as efforts are made on a global scale to gather data, assess alternative scenarios, and plan joint initiatives to solve mutual family problems. We believe that our efforts in compiling this book represent a step in the right direction, and we welcome the opportunity to work openly together on a common agenda for better family futures.

NOTES

1. The term "dialectical" can be problematic for both former Soviets and Americans, who may associate it only with Marxist philosophy and economics. Here, we use the term more generically to refer to the relationship between movement and form—that is, "trans-form-ation" that allows contradictory elements to be recognized and synthesized. See M. Baseeches, "Dialectical Schemata: A Framework for the Empirical Study of the Development of Dialectical Thinking," *Human Development, 23* (1980), 400–421.

2. D. Blankenhorn writes about "optimistic" and "pessimistic" schools of thought regarding families in the United States. Other authors in his recent edited book contribute chapters on the lack of investment in children, changes in family values and morality, and family law and individual rights. See D. Blankenhorn, S. Bayme, and J. Elshtain (eds.), *Rebuilding the Nest: A New Commitment to the American Family* (Milwaukee: Family Service of America, 1990).

3. For example, see articles on "The Soviet Family at a Time of Crisis," in *New Outlook: A Quarterly Publication of the American Committee on US–Soviet Relations*, 2(4) (Fall 1991), 10–61.

4. However, the emphasis on individualism so prominent in the United States can also be detrimental to family life, as many social critics have noted. Nevertheless, personal economic success for both men and women is now being touted by some Westerners as the answer to the post-Soviet malaise.

5. D. Popenoe, "Family Decline in America," in Blankenhorn et al. (eds.), *op. cit.*, 39–51.

6. See S. Hewlett, *When the Bough Breaks: The Cost of Neglecting Our Children* (New York: Basic Books, 1991). See also E. Zigler and E. Gilman, "An Agenda for the 1990s: Supporting Families," and U. Bronfenbrenner, "Discovering What Families Do," in Blankenhorn et al. (eds.), *op. cit.*, 237–250 and 27–38.

7. Hewlett, *op. cit.*, 15.

8. Bronfenbrenner, *op. cit.*

9. *Ibid.*, 35.

10. B. Whitehead, "Crossing the Cultural Divide: A New Familism?", *Family Affairs* (Institute for American Values), 5(1–2) (Summer 1992), 1–5.

11. J. Aldous, *Family Careers: Developmental Change in Families* (New York: Wiley, 1978).

12. D. Orthner, "The Family in Transition," in Blankenhorn et al. (eds.), *op. cit.*, 100–105.

13. *Ibid.*, 110.

14. D. Popenoe, one of fourteen respondents to the debate on a value shift to a "new familism," attributes this change to a generation shift: Children of the "baby boomers" are changing the culture. *Family Affairs* (Institute for American Values), 5(2) (Summer 1992), 11.

15. O. N. Doudchenko shared these research findings at a meeting in Moscow with one of us (Hogan) in March 1992. A research questionnaire probed perceptions about the future, using several different measures (inner anxiety, situational anxiety, problems, potential solutions). In addition, interviews were conducted with about 800 Muscovites (male–female ratio approximately 44:56) at two time periods, May and October 1991.

16. See, e.g., B. Thorne with M. Yalom (eds.), *Rethinking the Family: Some Feminist Questions* (New York: Longmans, 1982).

17. See P. Dilworth-Anderson and H. P. McAdoo, "The Study of Ethnic Minority Families: Implications for Practitioners and Policy Makers," *Family Relations*, 37 (1988), 265–267.

18. In March 1992, five Minnesotans were invited to Moscow to meet with the nine Supreme Soviet members of the Committee on Women, Family, Motherhood and Childhood. The delegation included one of us (Hogan) and Susan Hartman, along with Minneapolis Mayor Donald Fraser, Minneapolis City Council President Sharon Sayles-Belton, and University of Minnesota Regent Ann Wynia. Information was exchanged on family-related issues, including the conflicting political views that make passage of family policies very difficult in both countries. In March 1993, four members of the Supreme Soviet Committee came to Minnesota to continue the discussion about family policies.

19. The Minnesota delegation referred to in note 18 met with the Moscow City Council's Committee on Children and Families on March 16, 1992. This Committee was formed eleven years ago in an effort to develop policies and programs that would help stabilize family size. To date, the focus has been on providing special benefits to families with three or more children—for example, access to shopping for family food and children's needs without standing in lines to purchase goods.

20. On March 19, 1992, the Minnesota delegation discussed family issues with executive officers of the Union of Russian Women, focusing particularly on women's roles in the changing economic and political systems.

21. See K. Gergen, *The Saturated Self: Dilemmas of Identity in Contemporary Life* (New York: Basic Books, 1990).

22. United Nations Center for Social Development and Humanitarian Affairs, *1994 International Year of the Family* (Vienna: Author, 1991).

23. Bronfenbrenner, *op. cit.*, 35.

Index